T0330140

Microfoundations Reconsidered

Microfoundations Reconsidered

The Relationship of Micro and Macroeconomics in Historical Perspective

Edited by

Pedro Garcia Duarte

Department of Economics, University of São Paulo, Brazil

Gilberto Tadeu Lima

Department of Economics, University of São Paulo, Brazil

Edward Elgar

Cheltenham, UK • Northampton, MA, USA

© Pedro Garcia Duarte and Gilberto Tadeu Lima 2012

All rights reserved. No part of this publication may be reproduced, stored in a retrieval system or transmitted in any form or by any means, electronic, mechanical or photocopying, recording, or otherwise without the prior permission of the publisher.

Published by
Edward Elgar Publishing Limited
The Lypiatts
15 Lansdown Road
Cheltenham
Glos GL50 2JA
UK

Edward Elgar Publishing, Inc.
William Pratt House
9 Dewey Court
Northampton
Massachusetts 01060
USA

A catalogue record for this book
is available from the British Library

Library of Congress Control Number: 2012935325

Cover image:

"Meninos Nadando" ("Boys Swimming")
Candido Portinari, 1955
Tile panel
152 × 212 cm (panel)
15 × 15 cm (tiles)

Reproduction authorized by João Candido Portinari.
Image from the *Projeto Portinari* collection.

ISBN 978 1 78100 409 8 (cased)

Typeset by Columns Design XML Ltd, Reading
Printed and bound by MPG Books Group, UK

Contents

Contributors

Michel De Vroey, Université Catholique de Louvain, Belgium

Pedro Garcia Duarte, University of São Paulo, Brazil

D. Wade Hands, University of Puget Sound, USA

Kevin D. Hoover, Duke University, USA

Robert Leonard, Université du Québec à Montréal, Canada

Gilberto Tadeu Lima, University of São Paulo, Brazil

Philip E. Mirowski, University of Notre Dame, USA

Foreword

The 2008 financial crisis, that threatened the foundations of the world economy and precipitated severe economic contraction world-wide, was also a crisis for standard macroeconomic theory, which failed to anticipate the crisis, and then could not explain it when it happened. Mainstream macroeconomists, in fact, had generally shared Olivier Blanchard's mistaken verdict expressed at the beginning of the decade that "progress in macroeconomics" was "the success story of twentieth century economics" (Blanchard 2000: 1375). There were indeed dissenting voices, but they were mostly ignored and dismissed within the profession. Now it is time to revisit this dissent, much of which especially targeted the standard view that macroeconomics requires neoclassical microfoundations which assume that economic agents make rational choices and form rational expectations regarding the future.

Interestingly, whereas the Great Depression precipitated change in economics and led to the emergence of macroeconomics, the recent crisis was preceded over the previous several decades by considerable debate among microeconomists regarding the nature of rationality and behavior. This debate, however, clearly had little impact on most macroeconomists before the crisis, who were locked into traditional views about the nature of individual behavior and its relation to the macroeconomy. But this debate is now beginning to find a place in macroeconomics with increasing attention being given to crisis phenomena, doubts about rational expectations and the efficient markets hypothesis, information cascades, aggregation problems, herding behavior, and complex systems.

This volume, written by some of the most accomplished historians of macroeconomics today, provides readers with a deeper understanding of many of the issues surrounding the relationship between macroeconomics and microfoundations. This historical perspective is very important. Not only was dissent from mainstream macroeconomics ignored over the past decade, but the historical record regarding earlier thinking on the subject was mis-stated and reconstructed in such a way as to represent the standard view as "the success story of twentieth century economics." The 2008 crisis thus had one positive: it has reminded economists of the need to reflect upon their unexamined (and often suppressed) assumptions. Thus this volume is a welcome addition to the macroeconomic research literature. Readers can expect not only to learn about where macroeconomics has been, but also where it might go in the future.

John B. Davis
Marquette University and University of Amsterdam, The Netherlands

REFERENCES

Blanchard, O. (2000). What Do We Know About Macroeconomics that Fisher and Wicksell Did Not? *Quarterly Journal of Economics*, 115: 1375–409.

Acknowledgements

This book results from a series of efforts to which many people contributed. After a conversation in 2008, we decided to organize an international symposium on the history of recent economics at the University of São Paulo (FEA-USP), Brazil, aiming to bring together renowned international and local scholars in this field. We then agreed that having as a theme the relationship of micro and macroeconomics would make way for a fruitful historical discussion among not only the invited speakers and discussants but also with the audience at large.

We were honored to have as invited speakers Robert J. Gordon (Northwestern University), Kevin D. Hoover (Duke University), Robert Leonard (Université du Québec à Montréal), D. Wade Hands (University of Puget Sound), Philip Mirowski (University of Notre Dame), and Michel De Vroey (Université Catholique de Louvain), in addition to Pedro Garcia Duarte (FEA-USP). As discussants we were very pleased to have Ana Maria Bianchi (FEA-USP), David Dequech (Unicamp), Eleutério da Silva Prado (FEA-USP), Fabio Barbieri (Department of Economics at Ribeirão Preto, FEARP-USP), Franklin Serrano (Federal University of Rio de Janeiro, UFRJ), Gilberto Tadeu Lima (FEA-USP), José Raymundo Chiappin (FEA-USP), Mauro Boianovsky (University of Brasília, UnB), Raul Cristóvão dos Santos (FEA-USP), and Roberta Muramatsu (Mackenzie University and Insper). We were also delighted to have Professor João Sayad (FEA-USP) giving the opening remarks.

Soon after we started organizing the symposium, that took place on August 3–5 2009, we received crucial support from Professor Antonio Delfim Netto (Emeritus Professor, Department of Economics, FEA-USP). Professor Delfim was not only a great enthusiast of the symposium but also played a pivotal role in helping us obtain financial support complementary to that obtained from research financing agencies: we are very grateful to FAPESP (São Paulo Research Foundation), Banco Bradesco and FIPE (Foundation of Economic Research) for financial support to the symposium. We acknowledge the support given by the Department of Economics and by the School of Economics, Business and Accounting at the University of São Paulo (FEA-USP), without which we would not have been able to organize the symposium. We also thank Andre Bueno Rezende de Castro for assisting us in the organization of the symposium.

After the symposium, both at a follow-up session held at the 2010 Annual Meeting of the Allied Social Science Associations (ASSA) – chaired by John B. Davis and with Perry Mehrling as overall discussant – in Atlanta, USA, and during the preparation of this book, we had the good fortune to receive the support, criticisms and suggestions of Kevin Hoover, Michel De Vroey, Perry Mehrling (Barnard College, Columbia University) and Craufurd Goodwin (Duke University), as well two anonymous readers. We thank John Davis for writing the Foreword. We are also very grateful to "Projeto Portinari" and to João Candido Portinari for authorizing us to use the beautiful artwork "Boys Swimming" (1955) by Candido Portinari both on the poster for the symposium and on the cover of this book.

We are very thankful to the authors and to all of the other people that in their way have contributed to the publishing of this book. Here we would very much like to express our gratitude to Edward Elgar for the interest in this project and for the highly professional support it gave us throughout the process: we are especially grateful to Tara Gorvine, Alexandra Mandzak, Suzanne Giles, and Nicolas Wilson for all their editorial help.

Pedro Garcia Duarte
Gilberto Tadeu Lima
São Paulo, February 2012

Introduction: Privileging micro over macro? A history of conflicting positions

Pedro Garcia Duarte and Gilberto Tadeu Lima[1]

1. THE STANDARD NARRATIVE

Mainstream macroeconomists agree that we live in the age of microfoundations. The worldwide financial crisis of 2008 to the present may have emboldened critics of this microfoundational orthodoxy, but it remains the dominant view that macroeconomic models must go beyond supply and demand functions to "the level of objective functions, constraint sets, and market-clearing conditions" (Sargent 1982: 383). Only by doing this, the argument goes, can we truly understand "the way in which optimizing agents make their decision rules", which in turn "depend on the dynamic environment in general, and the government policy rules in particular" (Sargent 1982: 383). The goal of the microfoundations project, as articulated in the 1980s, was to reincorporate "aggregative problems such as inflation and the business cycle within the general framework of 'microeconomic' theory" (Lucas 1987: 107). Microeconomics on this view is prior to macroeconomics, because "only when macroeconomic aggregates are explicable as consequences of well-formulated optimization problems for individuals ... will macroeconomic reasoning be secure" (Hoover 1988: 87; see also Backhouse 1995: ch. 8). The ultimate aim is the "euthanasia of macroeconomics" (Hoover 1988: 87; 2010: 331). As Robert Lucas puts it, if the microfoundations project succeeds, "the term 'macroeconomic' will simply disappear from use and the modifier 'micro' will become superfluous. We will simply speak ... of economic theory ..." (Lucas 1987: 107–108).

The priority of microeconomics appeared to the proponents of microfoundations as the inevitable consequence of the very notion of economics understood, as Lionel Robbins (1932) famously put it, as the study of choice under constraint.[2] It is probably no coincidence that microfoundations began to gain their greatest traction only in the 1970s since, as Backhouse and Medema (2009) have argued, Robbins' definition finally conquered mainstream economics only at about that time.

The attitudes that were reflected in one side of the debate on microfoundations in the 1980s have become in the new millennium the common wisdom of macroeconomists. Michael Woodford's *Interest and Prices* (2003) is emblematic of the new consensus between new Keynesians and new classicals about macroeconomics needing microfoundations:

> I consider the development of a model of the monetary transmission mechanism with clear foundations in individual optimization to be important for two reasons: It allows us to evaluate alternative monetary policies in a way that avoids the flaw in policy evaluation exercises using traditional Keynesian macroeconometric models stressed by Lucas (1976); and the outcomes resulting from alternative policies can be evaluated in terms of the preferences of private individuals that are reflected in the structural relations of one's model. ... My preference for this form of structural relations is precisely that they are ones that should remain invariant (insofar as the proposed theory is correct) under changes in policy that alter the stochastic laws of motion of the endogenous variables. ...
>
>   A second advantage of proceeding from explicit microeconomic foundations is that in this case, the welfare of private agents ... provides a natural objective in terms of which alternative policies should be evaluated. (Woodford 2003: 11–12)[3]

The standard narrative of the rise of microfoundations locates their origins in the work of Lucas and his new classical friends and followers in the 1970s (see Hoover, Chapter 1).[4] Lucas and Rapping (1969) attempted to provide microeconomic underpinnings for the labor market in an otherwise Keynesian (IS-LM) model. This first attempt was "classical" in the sense of relying on a market-clearing framework. It was "new" in its emphasis on the importance of intertemporal choice in labor markets. However, for the lack of a more plausible hypothesis, they relied on adaptive expectations in their labor-market model, which did not please Lucas because agents could make systematic mistakes. In subsequent work, Lucas (1972a,b, 1973) introduced rational expectations, which he regarded as the natural consequence of the attempt to provide a general-equilibrium account of the macroeconomy. The notion of rational expectations as model-consistent, equilibrium, expectations has a general-equilibrium character. Sargent (1973) and Sargent and Wallace (1975) independently introduced rational expectations into an IS-LM model.

The rational expectations hypothesis seemed to require a general-equilibrium approach. The IS-LM model could be seen as an *aggregate* general-equilibrium model; but it was not, in itself microfoundational: its equations were not derived from the optimization problems of individual agents. Although Lucas and Rapping had explored models based on optimization, it was only with Lucas's (1976) famous critique of econometric policy evaluation that rational expectations came to be seen to require models based on the optimization problems of individuals (models based on "first principles") and that microfoundations began to seem to be compulsory for macroeconomics. The target of Lucas's critique was the large-scale macroeconometric models that had emerged through the work of Lawrence Klein, among others, out of the work of Tinbergen in the 1930s and the Cowles Commission's econometric program of the 1940s and 1950s (a program discussed by Philip Mirowski, Chapter 4). The essence of the critique was that rational agents solved their optimization problems with knowledge of the prevailing policy regime. If an alternative policy were instituted, rational agents would have to solve a different optimization problem and the relationships among aggregate data, which are the economy-wide consequences of the solution of individual optimization problems, would change in response. It was not, therefore, acceptable to treat the estimated aggregate econometric relationships of the large-scale macroeconometric models as invariant under alternative policies, thus calling into question their use for evaluating macroeconomic policy.[5]

The Lucas critique provided an intellectual basis for the requirement that macroeconomic models possess precise microfoundations of a specific format; while the market-clearing assumptions preferred by the new classicals in conjunction with the rational-expectations hypothesis provided grounds for a vigorous rejection of the policy activism associated with Keynesian economics. As Kevin Hoover (Chapter 1) and Michel De Vroey (Chapter 5) discuss, Keynes was blamed for having "freed a generation of economists from the discipline imposed by equilibrium theory," a freedom that "was rapidly and fruitfully exploited by macroeconometricians" (Lucas 1977: 12) in their "nascent program of aggregative econometric modeling" (Hoover, Chapter 1, p. 19).

Lucas and his followers argued that macroeconomics could be secured against the Lucas critique only when it was grounded in adequate microfoundations, a belief that remains strongly held until today (as evidenced by the earlier quotation of Woodford 2003). The standard narrative sees Lucas as having inaugurated a new microfoundational era in macroeconomics and in policymaking. His work is seen to have naturally developed into the real business cycle models of Kydland and Prescott and their students and followers (for example, Kydland and Prescott 1982). Economists with a Keynesian orientation rejected market clearing as an acceptable basis for macroeconomics and, equally, insisted on the possibility of monetary and fiscal policies improving macroeconomic outcomes. Those who nonetheless accepted the Lucas critique and the microfoundational imperative that it implied were transformed into "new Keynesians". As a further development, the so-called dynamic stochastic general-equilibrium (DSGE) models, which were structurally related to real business cycle models, but flexible enough to incorporate Keynesian concerns, became the foundation for a "new neoclassical synthesis" (see Duarte, Chapter 6). While debates continue over the best model of the economy and its policy implications, the mainstream consensus among new Keynesians, as well as new classicals (and RBC theorists), uniformly embraces Lucas's program of microfoundations for macroeconomics.

What should we think of the standard narrative? The operating premise in assembling the present volume was that the internal narrative of mainstream macroeconomics is likely to be unreliable, its principal function being to buttress a particular, historically contingent methodological argument. Our purpose in assembling the present volume is to step back and to re-examine the history of the relationship of microeconomics and macroeconomics without presupposing the truth of the standard narrative. We begin with the emergence of micro and macroeconomics as self-consciously distinct fields within economics in the early 1930s. The authors in this collection seek to get behind and beyond the potted history of the development of the fields that is often told and written by practicing economists. From different perspectives and entry points, they challenge the association of microfoundations with Lucas and rational expectations, and offer both a more complete and deeper reading of the very relationship between micro and macroeconomics. The chapters grew out of papers presented to the First International Symposium on the History of Economic Thought sponsored by the Economics Department of the University of São Paulo (USP), São Paulo, Brazil, on 3–5 August 2009. Its theme was "The Integration of Micro and Macroeconomics from a Historical Perspective."[6]

2. BEYOND THE STANDARD NARRATIVE

Far from a new concern of the 1970s, microfoundations – or, at the least, the question of the relationship of microeconomics to macroeconomics – was actively discussed from nearly the moment that the distinction between micro and macroeconomics emerged in the 1930s. What was the right scale of analysis? Should the focus be on individual behaviour or on macroeconomic (aggregate) relationships? What kind of models can we use to analyse problems at each level? Are macroeconomic relationships consistent with microeconomic behavior? For example, what is the relationship of aggregate consumption and the individual's consumption decision? How does an aggregate money demand function relate to an individual's decision over the division of his financial wealth between money and interest-bearing assets? Can fluctuations of inventories at the level of the firm explain fluctuations of overall economic activity? Can we aggregate individual decisions into a demand or supply function for output as a whole? How? And what properties do aggregate functions inherit from the individuals behind them? Putting these questions in a broader frame:

> One crucial issue in the microfoundations literature is the extent to which aggregate economic variables and/or relationships exhibit features that are similar to the features of individual variables and/or relationships, and in particular whether certain features are emergent properties at the macro level that do not have a natural counterpart at the individual level. (Maarten C.W. Janssen 2008)

Such foundational issues concerning the relationship between micro and macroeconomics were bound to shape the economics produced since the 1930s. Against the standard narrative stands the fact that the term microfoundations was coined in the 1950s, well before Lucas's first forays into macroeconomics challenged the mainstream (see Hoover, Chapter 1). Microfoundations was an integral part of the discussions within general equilibrium theory, as well as a central concern of critical alternatives to Walrasian general equilibrium theory (see Weintraub 1979, ch. 7, and Harcourt 1977). Microfoundations was already an established concern when Phelps convened the conference that led to the first book to bear the title "microeconomic foundations" (Phelps 1970). Although Lucas and Rapping (1970) participated in that conference and it ultimately proved to be a key event in the establishment of the representative-agent approach to microfoundations, the approach to microfoundations was by no means the approach of the standard narrative (see Hoover, Chapter 1). Phelps characterized the volume as a "new kind of microeconomics of production, labor supply, wage and price decisions" intended "to found a theory of aggregate supply, in that it sticks doggedly to the neoclassical postulates of lifetime expected utility maximization and net worth maximization, [while] it makes no appeal to faulty perceptions and it does not fundamentally require that price-setters economize on their decision-making time." The goal was to illuminate "some old problem areas in Keynesian economics" (Phelps 1970: 3).[7]

In their own contribution to the volume, Phelps and Winter tried to go beyond Walrasian, perfectly competitive, general equilibrium theory. While they recognized that "the agenda of unfinished business is enormous" (Phelps and Winter 1970: 336), they concluded that "a landing on the non-Walrasian continent has been made. Whatever further exploration may reveal, it has been a mind-expanding trip..." (Phelps and Winter 1970: 337).

Nor were the concerns with microfoundations unique to the participants in Phelps's conference. The problem of the consistency of aggregate outcomes with individual optimization behavior also animated the so-called general disequilibrium analysis associated with the works of Don Patinkin ([1956] 1965), Robert Clower (1965, 1967), Axel Leijonhufvud (1968), Robert Barro and Herschel Grossman (1971, 1976), Edmond Malinvaud (1977), and others.

Although many economists before the 1960s understood microeconomics and macroeconomics as part of a division of labor in which separate questions were addressed with distinct tools and models, other economists from the very beginnings of the micro/macro distinction in the 1930s and, especially, in the period of the "neoclassical synthesis" starting in the mid-1950s, tried to link those fields through general equilibrium models (Weintraub 1974: 49; Leijonhufvud 1992: 28; Laidler 2008: 1–3).[8] The basic idea was that one could start with individual behaviors and somehow aggregate them up to form aggregate relationships. These efforts faced major challenges: How could expectations be integrated into the models? Was there room for money? For unemployment? The technical problems were daunting, but resolving them would be essential if general equilibrium models were to be made practically useful to address the traditional concerns of macroeconomics – for example, the relationship of inflation and involuntary unemployment.[9]

E. Roy Weintraub nicely summarized the general equilibrium theory of the neoclassical synthesis:

> For many years the division between microeconomics and macroeconomics has been detailed and condemned by economists, while the link between the two, general equilibrium theory, has suffered from a curious form of neglect. Although it has been well understood that macroeconomic structures could be "aggregated up" from general systems models, this insight remained so unworldly; concern for axiomatisation of production relations in a timeless barter world, while not uninteresting, cannot be the hallmark of a worldview flexible enough to cope with problems of inflation or involuntary unemployment.
>
> Yet it is to the credit of various general equilibrium theorists that such important concerns were never so far from their analytic work that they ignored completely the macro implications of their models. ... If it is true, as many observe, that time and money are essential characteristics of actual economic systems, general equilibrium theory cannot be faulted for its inattention to these details, though its meager and sometimes confusing conclusions can be derided. (Weintraub 1974: 49)

The neoclassical synthesis brought with it a new interpretation of the history of macroeconomics. Keynes's *General Theory* and Keynesian economics were reduced to a special case of the general equilibrium theory, one that was "hardly worth even a footnote" (Weintraub 1974: 54). The most important macroeconomic issues were not seen as fundamental. While Patinkin ([1956] 1965), for instance, offered an integration of money into the general equilibrium model, such outcomes as involuntary unemployment could be explained only through *deviations* from normal functioning of market mechanisms – for example, either through wage rigidity in the labor market or the irrationality of workers who are off their supply curves.

Of course, the reduction of macroeconomics to a secondary role was not acceptable to all. Keynesian economists "have clearly understood why the neoclassical prism distorts the Keynesian vision" (Weintraub 1974: 54) and some, like Robert Clower and Frank Hahn among others, tried to build general equilibrium models in which Keynes was not a mere footnote (see Weintraub 1974: 54–6).[10] Hoover (Chapter 1) argues that Barro and Grossman (1971, 1976) and Malinvaud (1977) "popularized the non-Walrasian models as aggregative, general disequilibrium models with representative agents" (p. 38), but this general disequilibrium theory is not linked closely to the microfoundations as understood by the standard narrative. Disequilibrium models provide but one example of how market clearing, representative-agent microfoundations eclipsed alternative approaches. Several economists represented in the Phelps volume approached the microfoundations of aggregate supply not through the representative-agent model, but through search models. Phelps (1970: 6) proposed to "picture the economy as a group of islands between which information flows are costly": the "island model," as it came to be known later, is one in which an individual producer cannot distinguish perfectly whether a signal of a higher price for his good indicates an increase in a relative price, which would stimulate him to produce more, or an increase in the general price level, which would leave his supply decision unaltered.[11]

As Hoover (Chapter 1) shows, the great boom in explicit discussions of microfoundations is traceable to the early 1970s when a variety of competing approaches were in play. The Phelps volume was a key contribution. And it was reinforced by Weintraub's survey article in the *Journal of Economic Literature* (1977), subsequently developed into a book (1979), as well as by Geoffrey C. Harcourt's (1977) edited conference volume. Although Weintraub's article and book and Harcourt's edited volume focus on aspects of microfoundations different from those emphasized by Phelps,

the two names most closely associated with microfoundations in the journals are Phelps and Lucas, with Lucas's importance growing relatively over
time (Hoover, Chapter 1, Table 1).

Although microfoundations had been a concern of macroeconomics
from the early 1930s, even before the term "microfoundations" became
current and even though competing approaches were on the table in the
1970s, the various threads of the microfoundations literature subsequently
drifted apart and lost contact with each other.

Lucas's thread, as already mentioned, advocated that the optimizing
behavior of individual agents determined the aggregate outcome. But the
task was by no means trivial. The theorems of Hugo Sonnenschein, Rolf
Mantel and Gerard Debreu in the early 1970s established that the restrictions that generate well-behaved individual demand functions do not
constrain aggregate demand functions to exhibit the same properties (see
Wade Hands, Chapter 3, and Rizvi 1994). The new classicals sidestepped
the problem of aggregation either by imagining an economy composed of
identical individuals or by assuming that there is one individual who
represents the whole economy, so that the solution to the optimization
problem of this *representative agent* gives the aggregate relationships in that
economy. In fact, they adopted the representative-agent model from the
optimal-growth literature of the 1960s.

Using such models, Lucas and others developed the characteristic conclusions of the new classical school, such as the ineffectiveness of monetary
policy with respect to the real economy (see Hoover 1988). Policy ineffectiveness was widely regarded by Keynesians as a politically conservative
conclusion. Initially, it was interpreted as a direct consequence of the
rational-expectations hypothesis, which was then regarded as politically
suspect. Later, economists came to see that the assumptions of flexible
prices and perfect competition were the critical factors in the policy
ineffectiveness proposition. Once a wedge had been driven between policy
ineffectiveness and the assumption of rational expectations, the rational-
expectations hypothesis was accepted by a wider spectrum of macroeconomists (see Duarte, Chapter 6). New Keynesians found that rational
expectations did not rule out an important role for the government in
stabilizing the economy.

The use of the representative agent was rarely, if at all, explicitly justified
and despite the efforts by some macroeconomists to introduce heterogeneous agents into their models, it became the benchmark model that provides
the framework for most mainstream business-cycle models of the present
day. What is important to the theme of this volume is that the
representative-agent framework proposes a particular way of relating
microeconomics to macroeconomics – and it is neither the only way nor the

first way proposed. It is what Hoover (Chapter 1) calls "eliminative micro-foundations" – that is, microfoundations which ultimately aim to eliminate macroeconomics in favor of microeconomics rather than to explain the relationship of microeconomics and macroeconomics, while acknowledging their independent utility. The representative agent begs the question of aggregation, simply ignoring the difficulties highlighted in the analyses of Sonnenschein, Mantel and Debreu discussed above. Leijonhufvud (1992: 28) captures well the eliminativist ambitions of the representative-agent approach:

> Those of us who came out of graduate programmes in the early 1960s had been taught a micro and a macro theory that could not have applied to the same world at the same time. So this problem was of intense concern to many of us. Our label for it was "microfoundations of macroeconomics". Quite a lot was written about it at one time (cf. Weintraub 1979).
>
> Robert Lucas resolved this tension between micro and macro by declaring that the problem did not really exist. The appearance of a problem was due simply to the fact that macroeconomics had not been done right. The microfoundations problem would evaporate once we decided to do macro theory in strict obedience to micro-theoretical modelling principles.

The representative-agent approach was adopted not only by new classicals, such as Lucas, and their natural successors, such as the real-business cycle theorists, including Edward Prescott and Finn Kydland, but also by new Keynesians such as N. Gregory Mankiw, David Romer, and Olivier Blanchard. Although these two groups differed over many points of economic substance (such as the source of business cycles and the role of government over them), they both responded similarly to the Lucas critique: macroeconomics requires sound microfoundations; sound microfoundations require general equilibrium models in which optimizing agents have rational expectations.[12] The methodological consensus (the "new neo-classical synthesis") of the late 1990s replaced the sharp substantive debates of the 1970s and 1980s (see Duarte, Chapter 6). Most new neoclassical models employ the representative agent. Mainstream macroeconomics is now defined not only by microfoundations, but by a particular type of microfoundations (Hoover, Chapter 1).

James Tobin had already noted the hegemony of microfoundations in the macroeconomics of the mid-1980s:

> [with] [t]his [microfoundations] counter-revolution [that] has swept the profession until now it is scarcely an exaggeration to say that no paper that does not employ the "microfoundations" methodology can get published in a major professional journal, that no research proposal that is suspect of violating its precepts can survive peer review, that no newly minted Ph.D. who can't show

that his hypothesized behavioral relations are properly derived can get a good academic job. (Tobin 1986: 350)

But not any microfoundations would do. And representative-agent micro-foundations increasingly dominated other approaches, largely ignoring problems of coordination, heterogeneity among individuals, and financial imperfections. Yet it is these features that have been targeted (implicitly or explicitly) by critics of modern macroeconomics during the financial and economic crisis that started in 2007.[13] An open question, therefore, is whether a methodological turn undermined the ability of macroeconomics to respond to pressing policy issues.

The hegemonic claims of microfoundations are most often justified with reference to the sort of problems highlighted by the Lucas critique. But what justifies the hegemony of the representative agent? Mainstream mac-roeconomists are rarely explicit on this question; but, implicitly, the argu-ment seems to be that the assumption of a representative, optimizing, agent is mainly technical – both a compromise between the ambitions and the computational capacities of the macroeconomist and a convenient way to introduce a welfare measure for the evaluation of economic policy.[14] The implicit argument is what Hoover refers to as "eschatological justification": "the representative-agent model is but the starting point for a series of fuller and richer models that eventually will provide the basis for an adequate macromodel, and that, therefore, the current generation of models is entitled to credence" (Hoover 2006: 146, which is a comment on Woodford 2003). Mainstream macroeconomists frequently take a defensive attitude towards their modeling choices and tend not to discuss in detail the limitations they imply. Important exceptions include Ricardo Caballero (1992, 2010) and Solow (2008). Although V.V. Chari (2010: 3) tried to defend mainstream macroeconomics against the charge that it is all about representative agents by stating that "any claim that modern macro is dominated by representative agent models is wrong," the existing literature of heterogeneous-agent models has hardly been integrated into the kind of models that mainstream macroeconomists have tried to bring to policy-making (Duarte, Chapter 6).[15] What is more, Chari's conception of what constitutes the representative-agent assumption is limited. A few types of agents, each representing some larger class of heterogeneous agents, raise issues hardly different from those raised by a single representative agent.

Unlike mainstream macroeconomists, heterodox economists, as well as methodologists and philosophers have demonstrated a deep interest both in the particular limitations of the representative agent and in the broader issues of microfoundations and the relationship between micro and macro-economics.[16] Historians of economics, however, have not delved deeply into these issues, the main exceptions being Weintraub's (1979) Lakatosian analysis and David Laidler's (2008) reading of the development of macro-economics and the neoclassical synthesis through the works of Axel Leijonhufvud. The present volume thus tills relatively fallow ground. It brings together a renowned group of historians who have previously worked on diverse but related problems to attempt to shed historical light on how economists dealt with foundational questions, roughly since the 1930s, and how over time they came to understand the relationship of micro and macroeconomics after it was clearly articulated by Ragnar Frisch.

Microfoundations à la Lucas provides one answer to the question of the relation of micro to macroeconomics, one that assigns priority to the micro over the macro. The priority of microeconomics was already implicit in the criticisms that Wassily Leontief (1936) directed to Keynes's *General Theory*, reading it against a general equilibrium model. But this is far from being the only option when addressing the relationship: for Frisch, writing in the 1930s, macroeconomics (or macrodynamics, as he more commonly refers to it) takes priority over microeconomics because the microeconomics "is an analysis by which we try to explain in some detail the behaviour of a certain section of the huge economic mechanism, *taking for granted that certain general parameters are given*" (Frisch 1933: 172, emphasis added). The macroeconomic environment is a requirement for microeconomic analysis, and it is here represented by the fixity of background parameters. Further-more, Frisch built a simplified macroeconomic model that ignored the many details of the entire economy due to the limitations of data and analytical capacity (Hoover, Chapter 1). His view was that interdependence among "sections of the [economic] system" (1933: 173) is what distinguishes macro-dynamics from microdynamics, not the scaled up relationships that result from aggregating individual decisions in a Walrasian general-equilibrium model.

The central issues in understanding the relationship between micro and macroeconomics are thus the direction of influence, the independence or coexistence of the two fields, and whether one field effectively eliminates or dominates the other.

The current volume then addresses a host of related historical questions:

- First, how do we identify and understand historically alternative microfoundational programs? This is the main question addressed by Hoover (Chapter 1) and is central to rejecting the standard narrative that treats microfoundations as a creature of the Lucas critique and the new classical macroeconomics in the 1970s.
- Second, how does the variety of approaches to microeconomics shape microfoundations? According to Robert Leonard (Chapter 2),

Oskar Morgenstern, for example, resisted Walrasian general equilibrium analysis. From his Austrian upbringing, through his Princeton period, to collaboration with von Neumann, Morgenstern saw the central issue as how to treat time and expectations in economics. Morgenstern rejected the view of many economists that general equilibrium theory was a middle ground between the micro and macroeconomics.

- Third, can general equilibrium be seen legitimately as emerging at the boundary between the micro and macroeconomics divide? Wade Hands (Chapter 3) argues that historically it has been a two-way street, a co-evolution that resulted in the emergence of both a particular kind of Keynesian economics that drew on insights from general equilibrium theory and a kind of general equilibrium theory that stabilized in response to the macroeconomics of the 1950s and 1960s.

- Fourth, how does the problem of microfoundations relate to contemporaneous developments in other fields of economics? Econometrics, for example, was founded as a distinct discipline at precisely the same time – and to a large extent by the same people – as micro and macroeconomics. And developments in econometrics were central to the evolution of microfoundations. In particular, the dominance of the Lucas program is intimately related to his econometric criticism of Keynesian macroeconometric models. Philip Mirowski (Chapter 4) argues that Keynes's economics had to be divested of much of his content to be expressed, in the US, in a general-equilibrium, quantitative model with microfoundations usable for policy analysis. He focuses on the reaction to Keynes in the citadel of postwar Walrasian economics in the US, namely, the Cowles Commission, which was, at the same time, the key player in the foundation of modern econometrics. (Aspects of this story are also discussed by Hoover, Chapter 1, and De Vroey, Chapter 5.) Mirowski concludes that, unlike the other pro-Keynesian schools in America, such as Paul Samuelson's Massachusetts Institute of Technology (MIT), the Cowles Commission during its Chicago incarnation (1943–54) was lukewarm towards Keynes. Mirowksi argues, therefore, that there were fewer genuine Keynesians among postwar neoclassical American economists than is usually believed.

- Fifth, what light does the history of microfoundations shed on current macroecononomic practice? De Vroey (Chapter 5) addresses the literature on real-business-cycle models, while Duarte (Chapter 6) examines the new neoclassical synthesis. The challenge in both cases is to re-examine the standard narrative of microfoundations, and especially how that relates to the role of macroeconomics in the recent worldwide financial crisis, from a more historical perspective. De Vroey enlarges on the transformation of the new classical macroeconomics of the 1970s into the real-business-cycle modeling program of the 1980s and 1990s. Economic policy emerges as a central theme in both chapters. De Vroey probes the responses of the real-business-cycle school to the Lucas critique and their construction of microfoundations that effectively support earlier policy-ineffectiveness propositions. Duarte, in contrast, argues that new neoclassical synthesis models, which grew out of similar roots, nonetheless revived macroecononomic policy analysis.

Despite the fact that the need for macroeconomic models to have microfoundations has now become unassailable dogma among mainstream macroeconomists, those same economists have very rarely engaged in explicit reflection on the relationship between micro and macroeconomics, and the limitations inherent to the ways they proposed to integrate these fields. Many of the shortcomings of macroeconomic modeling that have been raised by critics in relationship to the recent financial crisis – the lack of focus on heterogeneity and coordination problems, the inadequacy of the standard representation of the financial system, the failure to address the possibility of systemic market failure – are related, in part, to the particular ways in which mainstream macroeconomics has attempted to provide microfoundations. The aim of the present volume is to provide a historical perspective on how the central dogma of current macroeconomics came to be, and to explore how the essential questions about the relationship between micro and macroeconomics were first posed and resolved: Which possibilities were once open? Which avenues were closed and why? Why did current mainstream views come to dominate? While it is not the purpose of historians to say what should be done next, it is our hope that a rich understanding of historical context may clarify pressing issues for the current generation of macroeconomists. We recognize, however, that this story is far richer than can be addressed in a single volume. We hope that our fellow historians will regard it as an introduction, an invitation to further exploration of some of the most important foundational questions in modern economics.

NOTES

1. In writing this introduction we greatly benefited from many conversations we had with Kevin Hoover, Michel De Vroey and Perry Mehrling. We are grateful to them for this, without implying that they agree with the final outcome. Hoover was not only very supportive and willing to contribute, but also made several suggestions to improve the

structure and fluency of the text for which he deserves our very special gratitude. We also gratefully acknowledge research funding provided by the Brazilian National Council of Scientific and Technological Development (CNPq).

2. Robbins (1932, 15) defined economics as "the science which studies human behavior as a relationship between ends and scarce means which have alternative uses". He emphasized that "when time and the means for achieving ends are limited *and* capable of alternative application, then behavior necessarily assumes the form of choice" (13), which is then "the unity subject of Economic Science" (15).

3. John B. Taylor (1989, S170) had made earlier a similar point (though with less emphasis on explicit microfoundations): "One of the purposes of developing quantitative rational expectations models is that they can deal with the Lucas critique which says that the equations of traditional non-rational expectations models might change if the policy rule changed."

4. References to chapters in the present volume are identified by number without dates.

5. Lucas and Sargent (1979, 55) emphasized the role of rational expectations in their criticism to the Keynesian macroeconometric models: "The casual treatment of expectations is not a peripheral problem in these models, for the role of expectations is pervasive in the models and exerts a massive influence on their dynamic properties (a point Keynes himself insisted on). The failure of existing models to derive restrictions on expectations from any first principles grounded in economic theory is a symptom of a somewhat deeper and more general failure to derive behavioral relationships from any consistently posed dynamic optimization problems."

6. The full program of this symposium as well as the videos of all sessions are available online at: http://www.usp.br/feaecon/ishet/index.htm. A subset of these papers (Hoover, Hands, Mirowski, and Duarte) was then presented at the 2010 Annual Meeting of the Allied Social Science Associations (ASSA) in Atlanta and benefited from the comments by Perry Mehrling.

7. Hoover (Chapter 1) states that the publication of the Phelps (1970) book "was the watershed event in the establishment of the representative-agent microfoundational program" (p. 46).

8. There are diverse meanings that economists attribute to the term "neoclassical synthesis." Here, as in Weintraub (1974, 52), it means "the marriage of modern monetary theory to the 'classical' (meaning Walrasian) general equilibrium (or value) theory".

9. The struggle to find room for money in general equilibrium led Frank Hahn to state in the late 1960s that "Economic Theory still lacks a 'Monetary Debreu'" (Hahn 1969, 172) – a situation that he still regarded as unsatisfactory in the early 1980s (Hahn 1982, 1). In the 2010 ASSA meeting at which preliminary versions of some of the papers in this volume were presented, Perry Mehrling argued that before the emergence of macroeconomics it was in monetary economics that the overall price level and its relation to business fluctuations were analysed (relative prices and real allocations were part of value or price theory). Although "monetary economics is the historical origin of macroeconomics, ... monetary economics has no obvious connection to microeconomics". Hicks (1935, [1939] 1946) began the effort of bridging the gap between monetary (macro) and microeconomics by recasting money in the same supply-and-demand framework that he applied to the general equilibrium of the real economy, which eventually led to the absence of money in the Arrow-Debreu version of the Walrasian general equilibrium model (for reasons demonstrated by Hahn). Mehrling then suggests that "in a larger context, the project to find *micro* foundations for macro was part of a longer process of knocking macro off of its original *monetary* foundations."

10. This volume does not address another strand in the literature. Post-Keynesian economists, in particular, rejected the idea that individualistic general-equilibrium models were compatible with macroeconomics (Weintraub 1979, ch. 1). Some argued for an alternative microeconomics that could provide underpinnings compatible with the central concerns of Keynes's theory: uncertainty and expectations. It was impossible to resolve

the micro/macro split "without abandoning either general equilibrium theory or Post-Keynesian economics" (Weintraub 1979, 13). See Janssen (2008) for a brief summary of and a few references to non-mainstream approaches to microfoundations of macroeconomics.

11. Phelps (1970, 6–10) talked about workers in different islands facing such a decline in the demand for labor that they cannot know if it is due to an overall decrease of aggregate demand or not. He interprets several papers in his volume as following this island story (and his own contribution with Winter follows this non-Walrasian general equilibrium model). Lucas (1972a, 104) takes Phelps as the forerunner of his approach and is considered to be the creator of a formal "island model". However, he does not use such a metaphor in this paper.

12. Drazen (1980, 293) had emphasized earlier the need to explain macroeconomic phenomena in a general-equilibrium model based on choice theoretical behavior: "Explanations of macroeconomic phenomena will be complete only when such explanations are consistent with microeconomic choice theoretic behavior and can be phrased in the language of general equilibrium theory."

13. See Colander, Howitt, Kirman, Leijonhufvud and Mehrling (2008), Duarte (2011) and references therein for criticisms of modern macroeconomics during the current recession.

14. See Woodford (2003, 11–12), quoted above, on the use of the representative agent to provide a welfare measure. Robert Solow (2000, 152) warned against this practice.

15. Examples of these representative models aimed to policymaking include Christiano, Eichenbaum and Evans (2005) and Smets and Wouters (2007).

16. An incomplete selection includes: Nelson (1984), Janssen (1991, 1993, 2008), Kirman (1992, 2006), Leijonhufvud (1993), Rizvi (1994), the several authors who contributed to the volume edited by Colander (1996), Hartley (1997), Forni and Lippi (1998), Horwitz (2000), van den Bergh and Gowdy (2003), Colander, Howitt, Kirman, Leijonhufvud, and Mehrling (2008), and Hoover (2009, 2010).

REFERENCES

Backhouse, Roger E. (1995). *Interpreting Macroeconomics: Explorations in the History of Macroeconomic Thought.* London: Routledge.

Backhouse, Roger E., and Steve G. Medema (2009). Defining Economics: The Long Road to Acceptance of the Robbins Definition. *Economica,* 76 (Supplement):805–20.

Barro, Robert J., and Herschel I. Grossman (1971). A General Disequilibrium Model of Income and Employment. *American Economic Review,* 61 (1):82–93.

Barro, Robert J., and Herschel I. Grossman (1976). *Money, Employment and Inflation.* Cambridge: Cambridge University Press.

Caballero, Ricardo J. (1992). A Fallacy of Composition. *American Economic Review,* 82 (5):1279–92.

Caballero, Ricardo J. (2010). Macroeconomics After the Crisis: Time to Deal with the Pretense-of-knowledge Syndrome. *NBER working paper,* no. 16429.

Chari, V.V. (2010). *Testimony before the Committee on Science and Technology.* Subcommittee on Investigations and Oversight, U.S. House of Representatives, July 20. Washington, D.C. (available at: http://science.house.gov/publications/hearings_markups_details.aspx?NewsID=2916, accessed on Oct. 13, 2010).

Christiano, Lawrence J., Martin Eichenbaum, and Charles L. Evans (2005). Nominal Rigidities and the Dynamic Effects of a Shock to Monetary Policy. *Journal of Political Economy,* 113 (1):1–45.

Clower, Robert W. (1965). The Keynesian Counterrevolution: A Theoretical Appraisal. In *The Theory of Interest Rates*. Edited by F.H. Hahn, and F.P.R. Brechling. London: Macmillan.

Clower, Robert W. (1967). A Reconsideration of the Microfoundations for Monetary Theory. *Western Economic Journal*, 6 (1):1–8.

Colander, David (ed.) (1996). *Beyond Microfoundations: Post Walrasian Macroeconomics*. Cambridge: Cambridge University Press.

Colander, David, Peter Howitt, Alan Kirman, Axel Leijonhufvud, and Perry Mehrling (2008). Beyond DSGE Models: Toward an Empirically Based Macroeconomics. *American Economic Review, papers and proceedings*, 98 (2):236–40.

Drazen, Allan (1980). Recent Developments in Macroeconomic Disequilibrium Theory. *Econometrica*, 48 (2):283–306.

Duarte, Pedro Garcia (2011). Recent Developments in Macroeconomics: The DSGE Approach to Business Cycles in Perspective. In *The Elgar Companion to Recent Economic Methodology*. Edited by John B. Davis, and D. Wade Hands. Cheltenham, UK: Edward Elgar, pp. 375–403.

Forni, Mario, and Marco Lippi (1998). *Aggregation and the Microfoundations of Dynamic Macroeconomics*. Oxford: Oxford University Press.

Frisch, Ragnar (1933). Propagation Problems and Impulse Problems in Dynamic Economics. In *Economic Essays in Honor of Gustav Cassel*. London: George Allen and Unwin.

Hahn, Frank (1969). On Money and Growth. *Journal of Money, Credit and Banking*, 1 (2):172–87.

Hahn, Frank (1982). *Money and Inflation*. Oxford: Basil Blackwell.

Harcourt, Geoffrey C. (ed.) (1977). *The Microeconomic Foundations of Macroeconomics*. Boulder: Westview Press.

Hartley, James E. (1997). *The Representative Agent in Macroeconomics*. London: Routledge.

Hicks, John R. (1935). A Suggestion for Simplifying the Theory of Money. *Economica*, 2 (5):1–19.

Hicks, John R. ([1939] 1946). *Value and Capital: An Inquiry Into Some Fundamental Principles of Economic Theory*. 2nd edn. Oxford: Clarendon Press.

Hoover, Kevin D. (1988). *The New Classical Macroeconomics: A Sceptical Inquiry*. Oxford: Basil Blackwell.

Hoover, Kevin D. (2006). A Neowicksellian in a New Classical World: The Methodology of Michael Woodford's Interest and Prices. *Journal of the History of Economic Thought*, 28 (2):143–9.

Hoover, Kevin D. (2009). Microfoundations and the Ontology of Macroeconomics. In *Oxford Handbook of the Philosophy of Economic Science*. Edited by Harold Kincaid, and Donald Ross. Oxford: Oxford University Press.

Hoover, Kevin D. (2010). Idealizing Reduction: The Microfoundations of Macroeconomics. *Erkenntnis*, 73 (3):329–47 .

Horwitz, Steven (2000). *Microfoundations and Macroeconomics: An Austrian Perspective*. London: Routledge.

Janssen, Maarten C.W. (1991). What is this Thing called Microfoundations? *History of Political Economy*, 23 (4):687–712.

Janssen, Maarten C.W. (1993). *Microfoundations: A Critical Inquiry*. London: Routledge.

Janssen, Maarten C.W. (2008). Microfoundations. In *The New Palgrave Dictionary of Economics*. 2nd edn. Edited by Steven N. Durlauf, and Lawrence E. Blume.

Palgrave Macmillan (available as *The New Palgrave Dictionary of Economics Online*. Palgrave Macmillan. Accessed 12 March 2012: http://www.dictionaryofeconomics.com/article?id=pde2008_M000380).

Kirman, Alan P. (1992). Whom or What Does the Representative Individual Represent? *Journal of Economic Perspectives*, 6 (2):117–36.

Kirman, Alan P. (2006). Demand Theory and General Equilibrium: From Explanation to Introspection, a Journey down the Wrong Road. *History of Political Economy*, 38 (Annual Supplement):246–80.

Kydland, Finn E., and Edward C. Prescott (1982). Time to Build and Aggregate Fluctuations. *Econometrica*, 50 (6):1345–70.

Laidler, David (2008). Axel Leijonhufvud and the Quest for Micro-Foundations: Some Reflections. In Roger E.A. Farmer (ed.), *Macroeconomics in the Small and the Large: Essays on Microfoundations, Macroeconomic Applications and Economic History in Honor of Axel Leijonhufvud*. Cheltenham, UK: Edward Elgar.

Leijonhufvud, Axel (1968). *On Keynesian Economics and the Economics of Keynes: a Study in Monetary Theory*. New York: Oxford University Press.

Leijonhufvud, Axel (1992). Keynesian Economics: Past Confusions, Future Prospects. In *Macroeconomics – a Survey of Research Strategies*. Edited by Alessandro Vercelli, and Nicola Dimitri. Oxford: Oxford University Press.

Leijonhufvud, Axel (1993). Towards a Not-Too-Rational Macroeconomics. *Southern Economic Journal*, 60 (1):1–13.

Leontief, Wassily W. (1936). The Fundamental Assumption of Mr Keynes' Monetary Theory of Unemployment. *Quarterly Journal of Economics*, 51 (1):192–7.

Lucas, Robert E., Jr. (1972a). Expectations and the Neutrality of Money. *Journal of Economic Theory*, 4 (2):103–24.

Lucas, Robert E., Jr. (1972b). Econometric Testing of the Natural Rate Hypothesis. Reprinted in *Studies in Business-Cycle Theory*. Oxford: Blackwell, 1981.

Lucas, Robert E., Jr. (1973). Some International Evidence on Output-Inflation Tradeoffs. *American Economic Review*, 63 (3):326–34.

Lucas, Robert E., Jr. (1976). Econometric Policy Evaluation: A Critique. *Carnegie-Rochester Conference Series on Public Policy*, 1:19–46.

Lucas, Robert E., Jr. (1977). Understanding Business Cycles. *Carnegie-Rochester Conference Series on Public Policy*, 5:7–29.

Lucas, Robert E., Jr. (1987). *Models of Business Cycles*. Oxford: Blackwell.

Lucas, Robert E., Jr., and Leonard A. Rapping (1969). Real Wages, Employment, and Inflation. *Journal of Political Economy*, 77 (5):721–54.

Lucas, Robert E., Jr., and Leonard A. Rapping (1970). Real Wages, Employment, and Inflation. In Edmund S. Phelps (ed.) (1970), pp. 257–308.

Lucas, Robert E., Jr., and Thomas Sargent (1979). After Keynesian Macroeconomics. *The Federal Reserve Bank of Minneapolis Quarterly Review*, 3 (2):49–72

Malinvaud, Edmond (1977). *The Theory of Unemployment Reconsidered*. Oxford: Basil Blackwell.

Nelson, Alan (1984). Some Issues Surrounding the Reduction of Macroeconomics to Microeconomics. *Philosophy of Science*, 51 (4):573–94.

Patinkin, Don ([1956] 1965). *Money, Interest and Prices*. 2nd edn. New York: Harper and Row.

Phelps, Edmund S. (ed.) (1970). *Microeconomic Foundations of Employment and Inflation Theory*. New York: Norton.

Phelps, Edmund S., and Sidney G. Winter (1970). Optimal Price Policy under Atomistic Competition. In Edmund S. Phelps (ed.) (1970), pp. 309–37.

Rizvi, S. Abu T. (1994). The Microfoundations Project in General Equilibrium Theory. *Cambridge Journal of Economics*, 18 (4):357–77.

Robbins, Lionel (1932). *An Essay on the Nature and Significance of Economic Science*. London: Macmillan.

Sargent, Thomas J. (1973). Rational Expectations, the Real Rate of Interest, and the Natural Rate of Unemployment. *Brookings Papers on Economic Activity*, 1973 (2):429–72.

Sargent, Thomas J. (1982). Beyond Demand and Supply Curves in Macroeconomics. *American Economic Review*, 72 (2):382–9.

Sargent, Thomas J., and Neil Wallace (1975). Rational Expectations, the Optimal Monetary Instrument, and the Optimal Money Supply Rule. *Journal of Political Economy*, 83 (2):241–54.

Smets, Frank, and Raf Wouters (2007). Shocks and Frictions in US Business Cycles: A Bayesian DSGE Approach. *American Economic Review,* 97 (3):586–606.

Solow, Robert M. (2000). Toward a Macroeconomics of the Medium Run. *Journal of Economic Perspectives*, 14 (1):151–8.

Solow, Robert M. (2008). The State of Macroeconomics. *Journal of Economic Perspectives,* 22 (1):243–6.

Taylor, John B. (1989). Monetary Policy and the Stability of Macroeconomic Relationships. *Journal of Applied Econometrics*, 4 (Supplement):S161–S178.

Tobin, James (1986). The Future of Keynesian Economics. *Eastern Economic Journal*, 12 (4):347–56.

van den Bergh, Jeroen C., and John M. Gowdy (2003). The Microfoundations of Macroeconomics: An Evolutionary Perspective. *Cambridge Journal of Economics,* 27 (1):65–84.

Weintraub, E. Roy (1974). *General Equilibrium Theory*. London: Macmillan.

Weintraub, E. Roy (1977). The Microfoundations of Macroeconomics: A Critical Survey. *Journal of Economic Literature*, 15 (1):1–23.

Weintraub, E. Roy (1979). *Microfoundations – The Compatibility of Microeconomics and Macroeconomics*. Cambridge: Cambridge University Press.

Woodford, Michael (2003). *Interest and Prices: Foundations of a Theory of Monetary Policy*. Princeton: Princeton University Press.

1. Microfoundational programs

Kevin D. Hoover[1]

1. THREE PROGRAMS

At least since the early 1980s with the ascent of the new classical macro-economics, only macroeconomic models with explicit microfoundations have been regarded as fully acceptable.[2] Typical graduate textbooks – and, increasingly, undergraduate textbooks – open with dynamic optimization problems that are meant to connect the ordinary microeconomics of the consumer and firm to the behavior of aggregate data and to classic macroeconomic concerns such as the business cycle, growth, inflation, and interest rates (see *inter alia* Romer 1996, Blanchard and Fischer 1989, Barro 1984). How did microfoundations become the *sine qua non* of sound macroeconomics? There are many ways to tell this story – and, indeed, it has been told before. Here I will tell it from the perspective of the currently dominant practice. This is an exercise in economy rather than in Whig history. The story features neither triumph nor inevitable progress; rather it seeks to know why current practice is the way it is; and, as a result, it omits or minimizes alternative paths, including heterodox programs, such as post-Keynesian macroeconomics, and heterodox criticisms, such as those lodged by the Austrian school, as well as mainly pointing to certain aspects that are already well discussed elsewhere.[3]

Lucas's well-known article "Understanding Business Cycles" (1977) exemplified a widely accepted understanding of the emergence of modern microfoundations. In Lucas's telling, modern macroeconomics began with John Maynard Keynes's *General Theory of Employment, Interest, and Money* (1936). Keynes, according to Lucas, rejects a dynamic analysis of business cycles in favor of a static account of output determination (pp. 215–16); he rejects equilibrium theory (p. 219); and individual optimi-zation – at least in the labor market (p. 220). Keynes's theoretical strategy gives a boost to the nascent program of aggregative econometric modeling:

> The decision on the part of the most prestigious theorist of his day freed a generation of economists from the discipline imposed by equilibrium

theory, and ... this freedom was rapidly and fruitfully exploited by macro-econometricians. (p. 220)

Lucas is, of course, aware that many Keynesian economists did consider the microeconomic bases for various components of the Keynesian model – the consumption function, the money-demand function, the investment function, the Phillips curve, and, in Lucas's own work with Rapping, the labor-supply function – but these exercises fell short of incorporating the discipline of the optimization problem into the general-equilibrium framework (Lucas 1981: 2–3; Lucas 2004: 20–21; Lucas and Rapping 1969, 1970). The microeconomics of the various functions mainly served to suggest a list of regressors to "explain" their target variables. The regressions themselves were, in effect, merely rules of thumb – decisions rules for particular stable environments. Lucas (1977: 220–21) did not deny that macroeconometric models constructed in this manner could well mimic the behavior of the actual economy, but appealing to the main theme of his famous article "Econometric Policy Evaluation: A Critique" (1976), he argued that the regressions would not isolate the invariants in the economy and that conditional forecasting (policy analysis) requires such invariants.

Lucas (1980a: 286; 1987: 108) was willing to excuse the theoretical choices of Keynesian economists as the product of the exigencies of the Great Depression and the absence of appropriate tools. But economists after the development of the Arrow-Debreu contingent-claims framework can no longer be excused. New classical microfoundations begins with the optimization problems of individual agents. These are incorporated into a dynamic general-equilibrium model based in the contingent-claims framework. Dynamics in an uncertain world requires the formation of expectations. Rather than taking expectations to be exogenously-given or based on arbitrary rules of thumb, the rational-expectations hypothesis assumes that self-interested agents will somehow find expectations that are consistent with a true model of the economic process. They may make expectational errors, but they will not make systematic errors. The rational-expectations hypothesis, because it incorporates – implicitly, at least – the whole model of the economy, imposes consistency restrictions across the various equations. No part of the system is independent from the other parts.

In Lucas's account, modern microfoundations begins with the new classical revolution of the 1970s, the opening shot of which was the introduction of rational expectations into otherwise standard macromodels (for example, Lucas 1972b; Sargent and Wallace 1975, 1976). While many economists find the perfectly competitive general-equilibrium model too perfect and seek to capture some features with a Keynesian flavor by introducing realistic barriers to smoothly-functioning markets, even these new Keynesians accept the main lines of Lucas's story and support a nearly identical view of the nature and necessity of microfoundations (see, for example, Blanchard 2000). Call this common view the *mainstream narrative.*[4]

There is – as there usually is in Whig histories – some truth to this story. But in telling a story of linear progress, the mainstream narrative misses a more complicated and more interesting story, and misrepresents key elements. The microfoundations of macroeconomics was a problem long before the new classical revolution and long before the term "microfoundations" was current. Indeed, Keynes himself had a distinct approach to microfoundations. As I reconstruct the development of microfoundations, it comprises a prehistory and three distinct microfoundational programs. One program, which I associate with Lawrence Klein, was mainly concerned with accessible data. The data was aggregate, and Klein wanted to know that its behavior was compatible with the economic behavior of individuals. Call this the *aggregation program.* A second program was theoretical. Taking macroeconomics to describe (theoretically or econometrically) robust features of the economy, it asked whether a fully disaggregated, general-equilibrium model could generate those features as a characteristic of the normal operation of the system. Call this the *general-equilibrium program.*

The aggregation and general-equilibrium programs seek *non-eliminative* microfoundations. If they were perfectly successful, we would nonetheless continue to use macroeconomics. In contrast, Lucas advocates *eliminative* microfoundations:

> If these developments succeed, the term "macroeconomics" will simply disappear from use, and the modifer "micro" will become superfluous. We will simply speak, as did Smith, Ricardo, Marshall, and Walras, of *economic* theory. (Lucas 1987: 107–108)[5]

For reasons that will become clearer presently, we shall call the currently dominant, eliminative microfoundations the *representative-agent program.*[6] I do not wish to argue that the three programs are entirely separate. There are many connections among them. Yet, a key thesis in this account is that the representative-agent program provides a plausible account of microfoundations only by systematically ignoring important elements of the prehistory and other microfoundational programs.

2. A BIBLIOGRAPHIC MAP OF THE MICROFOUNDATIONS LITERATURE

The notion of a microfoundations for macroeconomics presupposes notions of both microeconomics and macroeconomics. Macroeconomic issues – for example, the relationship between money and the aggregate price level – are ancient and no less venerable than microeconomic issues. While he did not use the modern terminology, when Keynes distinguished between

> the theory of the individual industry or firm and of the rewards and the distribution between different uses of a *given* quantity of resources on the one hand, and the theory of output and employment *as a whole* on the other hand (Keynes 1936: 293)

he drew a recognizable micro/macro distinction. The introduction of the terms "microeconomics" and "macroeconomics" nonetheless made the distinction more palpable and easier to keep straight. These terms seemed to have been coined by Ragnar Frisch.

It is well known that Frisch (1933: 172) distinguished between *microdynamics* and *macrodynamics*, employing these terms in essentially the same sense as we now use "microeconomics" and "macroeconomics." The earliest usages of the modern terms to be found in JSTOR are due to Tinbergen (1936: 177) writing in *macroéconomique* in French, and to Fleming (1938: 333) writing the English term as "macro-economic."[7] It is likely that Tinbergen and Fleming were using terminology that was already in use in oral exchanges, very likely in the early meetings of the Econometric Society (see Louçã 2007: 35, 190ff). Frisch is probably the ultimate source.[8] In a set of widely circulated, mimeographed lectures, Frisch (1933/34) uses the Norwegian adjectives *mikroøkonomiske* and *macroøkonomiske* in senses synonymous with "microdynamic" and "macrodynamic."[9]

While the micro/macro distinction gained currency over time, usage developed surprisingly slowly. Figure 1.1 (p. 24) plots the articles in JSTOR that use some terms in the microeconomics or macroeconomics family as a proportion of all articles published in 97 economics journals.[10] There are few uses before the end of World War II. Growth in the use of "microeconomics" is fairly steady, finally stabilizing around 10 percent only in the 1990s. "Macroeconomics" shows a similar pattern, although its growth is faster and stablizes at something over 20 percent a few years later. I conjecture that the much higher usage of "macroeconomics" is essentially the result of microeconomics being regarded by many (as perhaps implied in Lucas's pleas for eliminative microfoundations cited above) to be what economics *really* is. There are many fields regarded as microeconomic; but given that these fields have independent names (industrial organization, consumer theory, labor economics, etc.) one need mention microeconomics mainly when one needs to draw a contrast with macroeconomics. But "macroeconomics" is the name of a field with few subdivisions that do not also employ its name – adjectivally, at least.

While the issue of the relationship of macroeconomics to micro-economics is simultaneous with the introduction of the terminology, given the slow diffusion of these terms, it is hardly surprising that "micro-foundations" first appears more than 20 years later. The earliest use recorded in the JSTOR archive is due to Sidney Weintraub (1956: 854), where he refers to "microeconomic foundations." A year later he titles an article "The Micro-Foundations of Aggregate Demand and Supply," and refers to "micro-economic foundations" in the text (Weintraub 1957: 455).

The diffusion of microfoundations is displayed in Figure 1.2 (p. 25), which plots the number of articles among 97 economics journals in the JSTOR archive that use a family of microfoundation terms as a proportion of all economics articles and as a proportion of all macroeconomics articles.[11] The apparent boom in microfoundations at the end of the 1950s (viewed against macroeconomics articles) is an artifact of small numbers. There are relatively few macroeconomics articles, and almost all of the micro-foundational articles are simply citations of Weintraub's 1957 article and do not discuss microfoundations *per se*. The real boom appears in the early 1970s. It coincides with the first book to carry "microfoundations" in its title, *Microeconomic Foundations of Employment and Inflation Theory* (Phelps 1970a). E. Roy Weintraub's survey article (1977) and Lakatosian history (1979) no doubt reinforced the boom, increasing self-consciousness about microfoundations among macroeconomists.

Depending on the base of comparison, the data look somewhat different: steady when viewed against all articles, and declining until the 1990s when viewed against macroeconomics articles. I conjecture that the difference in the behavior of these data after about 1976 reflects the naturalization of the microfoundational world view. Increasingly macroeconomists abide by the strictures of the mainstream microfoundational program without feeling the necessity to discuss microfoundations explicitly. Hence, the subclass of macroeconomics articles explicitly addressing microfoundations has fallen as a share of *all macroeconomics articles*. This could be consistent with articles concerning microfoundations maintaining a nearly constant share of *all economics articles*, provided that macroeconomics articles grow at a faster rate than all articles, which Figure 1.1 shows that they do.

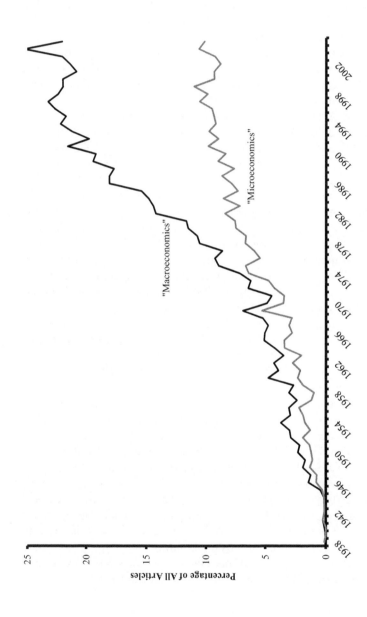

Notes: Entries are the ratio of the number of articles in 97 JSTOR economics journals for each year 1938–2006 using either a term in the microeconomics family or a term in the macroeconomics family to the total number of articles. See main text, note 6 for definitions of these families.

Figure 1.1 The Diffusion of "Microeconomics" and "Macroeconomics"

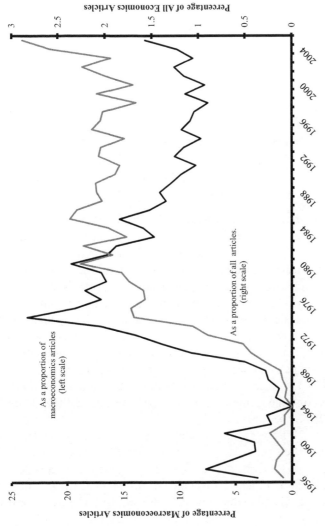

Notes: Entries are the ratio of the number of articles in 97 JSTOR economics journals for each year 1956–2006 using a term in the microfoundational family to either all articles or to all articles using a term in the macroeconomics family. See main text, notes 6 and 7 for definitions of these families.

Figure 1.2   The Diffusion of Microfoundations

Table 1.1   Microfoundations and Individual Economists

	Barro and Grossman	Clower	Lucas	Phelps	Weintraub
Barro and Grossman	214	82	113	101	14
Clower	82	267	103	62	38
Lucas	113	103	652	303	33
Phelps	101	62	303	653	30
Weintraub	14	38	33	30	142

Notes: Entries are the number of articles in 97 JSTOR economics journals 1956–2009 that include terms from the microfoundational family (see main text note 7 for a definition) and each of the economists' names. Entries along the main diagonal are total occurrences; entries in off-diagonal cells are the co-occurences of corresponding pair. While the probability of assignment of an economist with the same surname as the target seems low, there is no effort to distinguish Sidney from E. Roy Weintraub.

To get a further handle on the filiation of microfoundational ideas, Table 1.1 displays the number of articles that use terms in the microfoundational family and various economists, some of whom are mentioned in the mainstream narrative in section 1 and others of whom will be introduced in due course. Total occurrences of single authors appears on the main diagonal; while co-occurrences appear in the off-diagonal cells. For the moment, the most significant points are the dominance individually, and in terms of co-occurrences, of Robert Lucas and Edmund Phelps. Lucas not only contributed to *Microeconomic Foundations*, which Phelps edited, he also credits Phelps's "island model" with providing the key to his own appreciation of the microfoundations of the labor market, extended to a wider macroeconomic framework in his "Expectations and the Neutrality of Money" (1972a; see also 1981: 7).

As well as tracking people, we can also track concepts. Table 1.2 shows the number of articles that use terms in the microfoundational family plus another term – or (sometimes) two – linked to pertinent concepts. Most of the concepts listed in Table 1.2 are evident from the mainstream narrative; others will be considered in due course. Consistent with Figure 1.2, most of the discussion of microfoundations occurs in the later period, although the patterns are qualitatively similar before and after 1970. The largest entries after 1970 refer to "expectations," "Keynes or Keynesians," "labor," and,

Table 1.2   Microfoundations and Key Concepts

Search Terms	Through 1969	1970 and after
Expectations	1	1,344
Expectations and Labor	12	850
Rational Expectations	0	718
General Equilibrium	1	810
Keynes or Keynesian	16	1,048
Labor	19	1,330
Labor and Expectations	12	850
Lucas-Critique Family[1]	0	77
Phillips Curve	7	579
Representative Agent Family[2]	1	380
Representative Agent	0	153
Representative Consumer	1	107
Representative Firm	0	151
Representative Household	0	69

Notes: Entries are the number of articles in 97 JSTOR economics journals 1956–2009 that include terms from the microfoundational family (see main text note 7 for a definition) and each of the search terms.

[1]   *Lucas-critique family* = "Lucas critique" or "noninvariance" or "non invariance."
[2]   *Representative agent family* = any of the terms listed separately as subcategories.

substantially fewer, to "general equilibrium." These patterns reflect the close connection of microfoundations to the new classical macroeconomics and the "rational-expectations revolution." They are consistent with the mainstream narrative in which the application of rational expectations to labor markets in the context of the Phillips curve (which is itself mentioned in 579 articles) was the opening gambit. Since the importance of the Lucas critique is a key element in the mainstream narrative, one surprise is the strikingly small number of articles mentioning terms in the Lucas-critique family in connection with microfoundations. Nor does this reflect a paucity of references to the Lucas critique itself. Terms in the Lucas critique family are, in fact, mentioned in 506 articles after 1970 irrespective of whether the microfoundations family is itself mentioned.

It might be objected that the linguistic evidence offered here adds little to the real history of macroeconomics or microfoundations because it does not address the substance of the economics. Of course, I agree that one need not use the term "macroeconomics" to do macroeconomics, and many economists both earlier than, and contemporary with, Frisch addressed macroeconomic problems without the terminology. Keynes, as we have already seen, fits this pattern. Similarly, the issue of the microfoundations of macroeconomics can be addressed without using the term "micro-foundations" – as indeed it was by the earliest protagonists in two of the three programs discussed below. Language, however, is not epiphenomenal. While the term "microfoundations" is dispensable, perhaps, without some terminology drawing a conceptual distinction between micro-economics and macroeconomics, the problem of microfoundations – even for those who did not use the name – could not be articulated; and it is doubtful that any coherent programs addressing microfoundations could have evolved.

3. THE PREHISTORY OF MICROFOUNDATIONS

While the term "microfoundations" did not achieve currency until well after the distinction between microeconomics and macroeconomics had become a key organizing element in the structure of the discipline, the relationship of macroeconomics to microeconomics was an issue from the beginning. Two of the three microfoundational programs that I will identify antedate "microfoundations." And there is a history of microfoundations that ante-dates any coherent programs. I call this a "prehistory," because its players clearly understood that the issue of the relationship of macroeconomics to microeconomics was important, and they contributed elements on which the later systematic microfoundational programs built, but they did not themselves turn the relationship of macroeconomics to microeconomics into a systematic program of inquiry pursued for its own sake. We single out Frisch, Keynes, and Hicks as playing particularly important roles in this prehistory.

3.1 Frisch

We begin with Frisch – and not merely because of his coinage of the terms "microeconomics" and "macroeconomics." In drawing the distinction between them, Frisch was among the first explicitly to pose the problem of their relationship. This would perhaps not have mattered had Frisch not also been overwhelmingly important in the intellectual development of macroeconomics, econometrics, and central institutions of mid-20th-century economics – a driving force behind the Econometric Society and the founding editor of *Econometrica* (Bjerkholt 1998, Louçã 2007).

In his article "Propagation and Impulse Problems," Frisch wrote:

> micro-dynamic analysis is an analysis by which we try to explain in some detail the behaviour of a certain section of the huge economic mechanism, taking for granted that certain general parameters are given... The essence of this type of analysis is to show the details of the evolution of a given specific market, the behaviour of a given type of consumers, and so on.
>
> ...
>
> ... macrodynamic analysis, on the other hand, tries to give an account of the fluctuations of the whole economic system taken in its entirety. Obviously in this case it is impossible to carry through the analysis in great detail. Of course, it is always possible to give even a macro-dynamic analysis in detail if we confine ourselves to a purely formal theory... Such a theory, however, would only have a rather limited interest. In such a theory, it would be hardly possible to study such fundamental problems as the *exact time shape* of the solutions, the question of whether one group of phenomena is lagging behind or leading before another group, the question of whether one part of the system will oscillate with higher amplitudes than another part, and so on. But these latter problems are just the essential problems in business cycle analysis. In order to attack these problems on a macro-dynamic basis so as to explain the movement of the system taken in its entirety, we must deliberately disregard a considerable amount of the details of the picture. We may perhaps start by throwing all kinds of production into one variable, all consumption into another, and so on, imagining that the notions "production," "consumption," and so on, can be measured by some sort of total indices. (Frisch 1933: 172–3)

As with Keynes's analysis in the *General Theory*, which was being developed at the same time, the fundamental distinction that Frisch draws is between the operation of parts in isolation and the characteristics of "the whole economic system taken in its entirety." Macroeconomics is not identified as the economics of aggregates. It is pragmatic, not conceptual considerations that warrant the use of aggregates ("some sort of total indices"). We must sacrifice details and stick to the bird's-eye view because detailed models would not be tractable and detailed data would not be available.

Despite appearing in a volume in honor of Gustav Cassel, Frisch's article does not advocate a general-equilibrium approach in the sense of a model that stresses mutual dependence above all else. Dynamics – change rather than coordination – are his main concern.[12] This is not to say that interdependence is ignored; for, indeed, it is precisely that interdependence, rather than the bird's-eye view of aggregation, that distinguishes macrodynamics from microdynamics. Frisch fleshes interdependence out, not as individual actors in an economy-wide auction as in Walras's vision of general equilibrium, but as a "circulation in and out of certain sections of the system," or, as he puts it, using the Physiocrats term, as "*Le Tableau Économique*" (Frisch 1933: 173–5).

Frisch does not address the issue of microfoundations except to the degree that the relationship of macroeconomics to microeconomics is implicit in his definitions. We can see, nonetheless, that his vision is not one of the micro as more fundamental than the macro or the macro as simply a dispensable representation of the micro. Yes, the micro, the "sections" of "the economic system taken in its entirety" are constitutive; but the dynamics of the micro, where dynamics are the desiderata of Frisch's economics, are themselves the special case "taking for granted that certain general parameters are given." Any association of macroeconomics with aggregates is merely a byproduct of the limitations of our analytical capacity and of the data.

3.2 Keynes

Keynes did not adopt Frisch's coinages – "macroeconomics" or "macrodynamics." Yet in drawing a distinction between the theory of the individuals, firms, or industries, taking resources as given, and a theory of the determination of "output as a whole" – a phrase that recurs frequently throughout the *General Theory* – Keynes makes the same distinction as Frisch (Keynes 1936: 26, 27, 40, 43, 281, 285, 294, 322). And Keynes shares Frisch's concern for dynamic economics. In his *Treatise on Money* ([1930] 1983: 120), Keynes introduced the idea of a monetary economy explicitly as part of a dynamic analysis, and he carries the idea into the *General Theory*, in which money and expectations about the future play a key part in real outcomes. Despite his modern reputation, promoted in large measure by the mainstream narrative, Keynes is generally explicit about microeconomics and its connection to the theory of output as a whole. Where Frisch had sacrificed microeconomic detail for explicit dynamics, Keynes draws macrodynamics somewhat impressionistically, while providing a wealth of microeconomic detail.

It is an underappreciated element of Keynes's approach in the *General Theory* that it respects the heterogeneity of individual agents to a degree rarely found in macroeconomics. In place of Frisch's *Tableau Économique*, Keynes introduces a set of accounting conventions, closely analogous to modern national accounts, which were first developed at roughly the same time by Colin Clark, Simon Kuznets, and Richard Stone.[13] Since the accounts are measured in monetary terms, the incomes, expenditures, and products of disparate workers, consumers, and firms can be added up unproblematically in a common unit. Naturally, behavioral relationships must in some sense be formulated in "real," rather than monetary, terms. Despite – or, perhaps, because of – a deep knowledge of index numbers, Keynes does not appeal to a price index as a deflator, but re-expresses monetary quantities in wage units (the ratio of the monetary quantity to the typical wage rate for manual workers), in effect adopting a relative social standard for real value rather than deflating by the price of a basket of disparate goods with somewhat arbitrary weights (Keynes [1909] 1983; [1930] 1983, book II).[14] (Keynes's measure of value is not far from Smith's or Malthus's "labor-commanded" standard of value.)

Whereas in practical cases Frisch adopts the coarser-grained bird's-eye view when discussing behavioral relationships, Keynes nearly always refers to individual actors and declines to bury their behavior in aggregates. In most cases, he accounts for individual behavior using the usual Marshallian tools of utility or profit maximization. Keynes's account of the investment decision of an individual firm is, as he acknowledges, Fisher's intertemporal analysis (Keynes 1936: ch. 11, esp. p. 140). Fisher's "internal rate of return" is Keynes's "marginal efficiency of capital" – namely, that rate of discount that makes the expected future profit stream of an investment equal to its supply price. The decision to invest, then, is a matter of comparing the marginal efficiency of capital to the available alternative investments and financial asset returns.

What is distinctively Keynesian, however, is that the marginal efficiency of capital of the economy as a whole is not constructed by aggregating the investment opportunities of disparate firms to construct an investment schedule in which the aggregate of those projects that are just barely profitable at the market rate of interest define the margin – a construction wrongly attributed to Keynes in some early macroeconomics textbooks. Instead, for Keynes "[t]he greatest of these marginal efficiencies [of individual projects] can be regarded as the marginal efficiency of capital in general" (Keynes 1936: 135–6; cf. LeRoy 1983). Here the investment project of a *particular* firm is the marginal efficiency of capital for the economy as a whole.

Unlike the textbooks, Keynes is not describing a static equilibrium, but supplying a causal account of the forces that drive the economy. Implicitly, Keynes is identifying the causes of economic dynamics – a concern that had been more explicit in the *Treatise* (Keynes [1930] 1983: 120; see also Hoover 2006).[15] An individual firm's marginal efficiency of capital can be identified with that of the economy because the individual firm is embedded in a financial system that connects heterogeneous firms through the common denominator of money.

The case of liquidity preference is similar. An individual must decide whether to hold money (clearly, short, interest-bearing bills on Keynes's definitions) or (long) bonds. If one expects market interest rates to fall, then it is profitable to go long, and vice versa. The interesting point in this context is that Keynes does not construct an economy-wide liquidity-preference schedule by assuming that each individual has a well-defined, stable demand-for-money function and adding them up at each conjectured interest rate. Rather, he envisages ranking individuals according to their subjective normal rate of interest – that is, the rate to which they refer when judging whether market rates will rise or fall. If asset holdings are stable, then the market rate of interest must be the rate at which there are sufficient people who believe rates will rise to hold the available stocks of money and sufficient people who believe rates will fall to hold the available stocks of bonds. Again, the heterogeneity of individuals is preserved. In fact, Keynes argues that the stability of financial markets and the efficacy of monetary policy depends on that heterogeneity (Keynes 1936: 196–9; also 158–61). And again, in the case of liquidity preference for the economy as a whole, Keynes is principally interested in identifying the causal factors that drive its dynamics – in particular, the role of the changing assessments by individuals of the value of the normal rate of interest – rather than in establishing the conditions of static equilibrium.

Keynes's analysis of the labor market and consumption present harder cases. Keynes's account of labor demand follows directly from the optimization problem for the firm: hire labor up to the point that the product real-wage equals the marginal product of labor (Keynes 1936: 5). The problem arises with his denial of the second "fundamental postulate" – that is, his claim that the real wage can exceed the marginal disutility of labor (Keynes 1936: 5–6). The analysis of chapter 2 of the *General Theory* has puzzled critics (friendly, as well as hostile) from the beginning. Leontief (1936), for example, was an early critic. He accused Keynes of violating the orthodox theory of economic choice (p. 94 ff.) and reminds him that monetary neutrality (homogeneity of degree one in prices) is not an axiom of that theory, but a theorem (p. 91). For his part, Keynes (1936: 9) was prepared to believe in money illusion in practice, but was at pains to deny that his system depended on it essentially.

I have argued at length elsewhere that the best interpretation of Keynes's labor market analysis is not that workers value a particular money wage; but that, in addition to valuing what their money can buy, they also value their relative economic position, which is indicated by relative wages

(Hoover 1995).[16] Firms in this story understand the sources of workers' utility and, thus, incorporate relative wages into their production decisions in the manner of modern efficiency wage models. Unlike some modern models, in which efficiency depends on the real wage, firms have a disincentive to reduce *money* wages, since any reduction – unless it is coordinated across the economy – will reduce efficiency. In such a model, the real wage can exceed the marginal disutility of labor without violating homogeneity.

As with Keynes's analysis of investment and liquidity preference, this analysis of the labor market depends essentially on the heterogeneity of workers. And it explains what many have found to be a puzzling feature of Keynes's analysis of unemployment. Despite their heterogeneity, Keynes might have aggregated individual labor supply schedules to produce a labor-supply curve, relating some aggregate wage rate to the total labor forthcoming in the economy. Full employment would then be – as it often is in textbooks – the intersection of the labor supply and demand curves, and involuntary unemployment would then be defined as occurring when the market wage is higher than the equilibrium wage. But Keynes does not define unemployment in that manner.

Instead, he writes:

> Men are involuntarily unemployed if, in the event of a small rise in the price of wage-goods relatively to the money-wage, both the aggregate supply of labour willing to work for the current money-wage and the aggregate demand for it at that wage would be greater than the existing volume of employment. (Keynes 1936: 36)

What Keynes has done is to propose a thought experiment that defines the situation in which men are involuntarily unemployed. Why?

Despite references to "the current money-wage," this test does not require a single money-wage or any aggregation of wage rates. Rather, whatever the actual structure of money wages, any rise in the price of any good purchased by workers will decrease their real purchasing power while increasing the demand for labor on the part of firms. Any situation in which those reactions can result in higher employment is a situation of unemployment. Keynes has once again appealed to notions that do not require collapsing the heterogeneity of economic actors into aggregates and has singled out a specific feature (here, the price of a wage-good) that is relevant both to individual decisions and to a systemic characteristic: unemployment.

The case of the consumption function appears at first to be somewhat different, since Keynes does not present a maximizing account of consumption choice, but the famous "fundamental psychological law" (Keynes 1936: 96). This too may reflect Keynes's appreciation of heterogeneity in that an intertemporal optimizing choice of individual consumption patterns would require complete disaggregation of consumption goods both in the current and future period in the manner of the later Arrow–Debreu contingent-claims framework. It is not just that solving such a problem is formally (much less practically) difficult for the economist; it does not seem to be something that individual agents could approximate in their own behavior. The alternative is to aggregate and optimize over time in the manner of Keynes's younger colleague Frank Ramsey (1928). But that would not show the respect for heterogeneity implicit throughout Keynes's theory. Instead, Keynes sees the consumption decision as a two-stage choice: divide current resources into those to be consumed now and in the future (saving); then allocate current consumption expenditure over particular goods in the usual utility-maximizing manner. Seen this way, consumption expenditure for the economy as a whole is just the sum of individual consumption expenditures.

Keynes does not give up altogether on individual optimization. Much of chapters 8 and 9 of the *General Theory* concerns factors that might affect the propensity to consume, putting to rest the common textbook notion that Keynes's consumption is the simple linear function of current income alone. The factors include changes in real purchasing power (measured in wage-units), as well as windfall capital gains and losses, changes in rates of time-discounting, and expected future income – factors anticipating the considerations of the later permanent-income/life-cycle hypothesis.

The multiplier, whose value depends on the marginal propensity to consume, is also a reflection of heterogeneity. It is another system characteristic that transcends the individual optimization problem and takes as its background an economy in which differentiated agents engage in trade.

Taken together, Keynes's analysis of the fundamental components of aggregate demand and supply display a firm connection between microeconomic choices of firms and individuals and the macroeconomic outcomes. In every case, the causal mechanisms are driven by individual agents. The values of variables salient for the macroeconomic outcomes are traceable directly to individuals. Where aggregation is necessary (for example, in the analysis of consumption and the multiplier), it takes the form of the addition of homogeneous monetary values rather than relying on the arbitrary weighting of a price index. The outcomes for the economy as a whole clearly *emerge* out of individual behaviors. The characteristics of the system – for example, that output is not given, as it is assumed to be for individual allocations – are distinct from the characteristics of individual markets and individual optimization, but are not disconnected or mysterious. *Emergence* is perhaps the most characteristic feature of Keynes's account of the relationship of microeconomic to macroeconomic behavior.[17]

4. HICKS AND THE GENERAL-EQUILIBRIUM PROGRAM

To a large extent, Hicks, as much as Keynes, belongs to the prehistory of microfoundations. The transition between Hicks and the first of the three microfoundational programs that I wish to consider is so seamless that it makes sense to consider them together. What I shall say about Hicks's own microfoundations and indeed much of the general-equilibrium program of microfoundations is schematic, omitting most of the details. Weintraub (1979) provides an excellent history, and there is no need to repeat it.

Hicks was deeply engaged in writing his masterwork, *Value and Capital* ([1939] 1946) when Keynes's *General Theory* first appeared. As Weintraub (1979: 55) observes, it can be seen as an attempt to construct a Walrasian macromodel. The main lines of Hicks's approach are familiar. He begins with individual optimization: a restatement of the theory of subjective value, drawing heavily on Pareto and the device of indifference curves; and an analogous restatement of the theory of firm. He situates the individuals in a Walrasian general equilibrium. He sees Keynesian problems as arising in a dynamic framework. Frisch noted:

> it is always possible by a suitable system of subscripts and superscripts, etc., to introduce practically all factors which we may imagine: all individual commodities, all individual entrepreneurs, all individual consumers, etc... (Frisch, 1933: 172)

Whereas Frisch noted a possibility, Hicks – mainly verbally, to be sure – sketched out the detailed formal theory, moving beyond a Walrasian static, general equilibrium to a general equilibrium in which time is broken into distinct periods, commodities are dated, and not only do decisions today affect decisions tomorrow, but expectations of the future affect decisions today.[18]

Hicks's vision (as well-described by Weintraub) does not find a gulf between microeconomics and macroeconomics. Rather, the characteristically macroeconomic features that Keynes had emphasized – the unemployment of labor and capital as a result of deficient aggregate demand, the non-neutrality of money, and the efficacy of monetary and fiscal policies –

arose because the Walrasian model of perfect coordination was not an adequate model of the world. A dynamic model – one in which expectations, incomplete markets, and adjustment processes were central features – could capture the main Keynesian insights. The dynamic model was based in individual optimization and, thus, was completely compatible with microeconomics.

Like Frisch, Hicks connected macroeconomics to dynamics. But Frisch thought that detailed macrodynamics – a macrodynamics with explicit representation of all agents – was simply too hard to implement in practice. He thus made the pragmatic decision to reformulate macrodynamics in terms of aggregates. Hicks reacted in what seems at first blush a more principled manner. Hicks's

> method of analysis ... enables us to pass over, with scarcely any transition, from the little problems involved in detailed study of the behaviour of a single firm, or single individual, to the great issues of the prosperity or adversity, even life or death, of a whole economic system. The transition is made by using the simple principle, already familiar to us in statics, that the behaviour of a group of individuals, or group of firms, obeys the same laws as the behaviour of a single unit. ... The laws of market behaviour, which we have elaborated for those tenuous creatures, the representative individual and the representative firm, thus become revealed "in their own dimensions like themselves" as laws of the behaviour of great groups of economic units, from which we can readily evolve the laws of their interconnexions, the laws of the behaviour of prices, the laws of the working of the whole system. (Hicks [1939] 1946: 245)

Hicks's theoretical rationale for the assumption that what is true of the individual is true of the group – at least in part, a denial of Keynes's emergent properties of the economy as a whole – is found in what would later be referred to as his "composite-commodity theorem,"

> the very important principle, used extensively in the text, that if the prices of a group of goods change in the same proportion, that group of goods behaves just as if it were a single commodity. (Hicks [1939] 1946: 312–13; cf. 33–4)

On the one hand, the composite-commodity theorem provides a set of conditions under which the aggregate can be treated as an individual. On the other hand, it says nothing about how likely those conditions are to be found – even approximately – in real world cases. Hicks does not address the applicability of the theorem to the real world. Subsequent developments in aggregation theory, however, suggest that its range of applicability is exceedingly narrow. Gorman (1953) showed that an aggregate utility function could take the same form as individual utility functions only in the case of identical, homothetic preferences or, equivalently, when Engel curves are linear and parallel. A series of results, sometimes referred to as the "Sonnenschein–Debreu–Mantel" results shows that under a range of conditions market excess-demand functions exist, but their shapes do not recapitulate the properties imposed by the axioms of rational choice on individual supply and demand functions (see Kirman 1992 for an exposition). Individual relations may give rise to definite aggregate relations, but aggregate relations do not bear any simple analogical relationship to individual ones. Subsequent microeconomic theory itself undermines Hicks's optimistic appeal to the composite-commodity theorem.[19]

One reaction to these results is to acknowledge that aggregation is too difficult and to stick to formal general-equilibrium models in which all agents are named as individuals. Another reaction is to interpret the composite-commodity theorem to provide an existence result: there is some way to formulate a model much simpler than a disaggregated general-equilibrium model that can be used to explore various aspects of the economy in which aggregation itself is not the key feature.

The literature that forms the core of Weintraub's (1979) history of microfoundations takes the first path. His is a history of the general-equilibrium microfoundational program, which is conceived as showing how Keynesian problems can arise directly from the interactions of individual agents. The presuppositions of this path explain Weintraub's contention that the Arrow–Debreu–McKenzie model does not provide microfoundations, if by that we mean "a bridge between two distinct bodies of knowledge"; rather in one variant or other, it encompasses both microeconomics, identified with successful coordination, and macroeconomics, identified with coordination failure (Weintraub 1979: 71, 75).

The two paths are not always kept separate. Patinkin's *Money, Interest, and Prices* ([1956] 1965) is structurally analogous to Hicks's *Value and Capital* in that it starts with individual agents, incorporates them into a general-equilibrium model, and then appeals to the composite-commodity theorem to justify attention to highly simplified systems when addressing Keynesian problems. In chapter 13, Patinkin explores the systemic implications of a failure of the labor market to achieve the Walrasian equilibrium, setting the stage for both the investigation of Walrasian disequilibrium theory, eventually leading to the investigation of non-*tâtonnement* processes and more aggregative general disequilibrium models of the 1970s and 1980s.

In a series of papers, Backhouse and Boianovsky (2005a, b, c) document the rise and disappearance of the aggregative general disequilibrium approach to microfoundations and its relationship to Patinkin's chapter 13. Robert Clower (1965) provided the seminal contribution with the observation that such essentially Keynesian mechanisms as the consumption function cannot arise in a Walrasian general-equilibrium model. The supply and demand schedules generated in such models are all notional, in the sense that they ask what would an agent wish to do if he could buy or sell as much as he likes at a particular set of prices. Contrary to the Keynesian consumption function, an agent's spending decision is not conditioned on income in the Walrasian model, since income is not one of the things, such as the price vector, given in the thought experiment; it is instead an endogenous outcome of decisions conditioned on prices. The Walrasian model assumes that prices are coordinated *deus ex machina* with an "auctioneer" or "recontracting" serving as the avatars of the god in the machine. In a world without such a mechanism, Clower observes, agents will respond to price signals in ways that will not necessarily clear markets. The excess supplies and demands that they face provide additional constraints to their optimization problem. Thus, the expenditure of a worker who cannot sell as much labor as he notionally wishes to do will be constrained by the income that he can actually raise, giving rise to a consumption function.

While Clower's account is largely confined to the individual, he sees implications for the economy as a whole. These are worked out informally in Leijonhufvud's (1968) reinterpretation of Keynes's *General Theory*. What is most interesting in this context is Barro and Grossman's "A General Disequilibrium Model of Income and Employment" (1971) and Malivaud's *Theory of Unemployment Reconsidered* (1977), which popularized the non-Walrasian models as aggregative, general disequilibrium models with representative agents.[20] While not explicitly attending to the issue of aggregation, these models follow the second path from Hicks's composite-commodity theorem to its natural conclusion.

One path from Hicks essentially became the domain of economic theorists – generally regarded as microeconomists, even when they addressed coordination failures – and hardly affected mainstream macroeconomics. The second path ended in a historical dead end – general disequilibrium (or fixed-price) models with representative agents. Backhouse and Boianovsky (2005a, b) speculate that one reason for the disappearance of general disequilibrium microfoundations was that Barro became convinced that price stickiness (for example, from contracts) could be regarded as an optimal, *equilibrium* outcome of a sufficiently complex Walrasian model. The economy was thus Walrasian at the core and was better represented, even when using simplified models, by market-clearing, general-equilibrium models.

While there may be a good deal of truth to this story as a part of Barro's biography, I want to suggest that a more important reason is found in genealogy of the general-disequilibrium models as the product of the second path from Hicks's composite-commodity theorem: they are special theoretical cases, toy models built to display certain principles, but not models that have any claim on the real world. They were thus a poor basis for econometrics. It will be easier to appreciate this claim after we have considered the second microfoundational program.

5. KLEIN AND THE MICROFOUNDATIONS OF MACROECONOMETRICS

Post-World War II macroeconometrics derives in nearly equal measure from Tinbergen's pioneering models of the Dutch and US economies and from Keynes's *General Theory* as seen through the lens of the aggregative formalizations of Hicks ([1939] 1946) and Modigliani (1944). Although Tinbergen and Keynes make strange bedfellows, given Keynes's ([1939] 1983) hostile review of Tinbergen's book on econometric modeling, Lawrence Klein in his *Keynesian Revolution* (1947) and subsequent efforts at applied macroeconometric models was able to forge a common program out of inharmonious roots. Since Kleinian macroeconometrics is the *bête noir* of the mainstream narrative, it is perhaps surprising that Klein lays out a consistent microfoundational program:

> A problem which has never been adequately considered by Keynesians is the derivation of a theory in terms of communities of individuals and groups of commodities from a basic theory in terms of individuals and single commodities. In modern economic terminology this is the problem of passing from micro to macro economics, i.e., aggregation. (Klein 1947: 56)

While Klein's aggregation program is quite different from the general-equilibrium program, deriving from Hicks, it starts in much the same place. Klein (1947: 57) begins with individual agents solving optimization problems, ideally situated in a Walrasian equilibrium. (Formal derivations of each of the key Keynesian functions are provided in an appendix.) Klein, like Frisch, sees a detailed general-equilibrium account as impractical; for the purposes of econometric modeling, individuals have to be replaced by aggregates. But unlike Frisch, he is not willing simply to take his aggregates off the shelf uncritically; and, unlike Hicks, he is not willing to restrict his concerns to special cases suitable for theory. Klein argues by analogy that macroeconomic functions share the properties of microeconomic functions, provided one has used the "appropriate aggregation methods" (Klein 1947: 58).

But what are the appropriate methods? Klein explored this question in detail in two papers published in *Econometrica* in 1946. Klein is not content with the special case of Hicks's composite-commodity theorem, as prices will not stay constant in a dynamic economy with significant income effects – the distribution of income matters.[21] Klein, who contrary to our inter-pretation in section 2, sees Keynes's theory as a theory of the relationship of aggregates, criticizes Keynes for his unjustifiable assumption that aggregate schedules are stable without accounting for distributional factors (Klein 1947: 57).

Two approaches to aggregation were current in the 1946 discussion. First, one could try to work out the implications of individual behavior for the existing price indices and other aggregates in the national accounts, which are generally weighted sums of individual data. Klein sees this as a nearly impossible task. May (1946) and Pu (1946) proposed aggregation schemes of this form that worked on the condition that all equilibrium conditions were fulfilled (see Janssen 1993, ch. 5 for further discussion). Klein (1946b: 303) rejected their approach on the grounds that it was wrong to presuppose equilibrium and that an aggregate had to be suitable in or out of equilibrium.

Klein argued that a more fruitful approach was to take both micro-economic theory and Keynesian economic theory as given, and to work out aggregates that made them compatible with each other. The criterion of compatibility was that analogous marginal conditions held at both the individual and the aggregate levels (Klein 1946a: 94). The criterion is fulfilled if the conditions of Hicks's composite-commodity theorem hold, but only then (p. 95). Common index numbers fail to fulfil the criterion (pp. 100–102). Klein's aggregates would look very different from the atheo-retical aggregates: "we cannot know in advance the form of the aggregates but must accept those forms which satisfy a mathematical requirement" (Klein 1946b: 311).[22] In particular, the appropriate aggregates would not be weighted sums. As Klein remarks: "[t]here is no reason to assume … that there is something sacred about a sum" (Klein 1946b: 310). We should not, in Klein's view, adopt an aggregation scheme (or any concept or definition in any science) simply because it is familiar and widely used. Rather, the standard should be that a conceptual scheme contributes to useful science. And the standard of utility, for Klein, is whether ultimately it contributes to human happiness.

In practice, Klein's strategy has proved to be overoptimistic, since the Sonnenschein–Debreu–Mantel theorem demonstrates that there is no guarantee, as Klein supposes, that aggregates exist such that maximizing for a community function yields the same results as maximizing disaggre-gated individual functions, even if aggregates are "properly measured" (Klein 1947: 199; 1946a: 93). The theorem lay in the future, and Klein was not to know. As an econometrician, he would, as others did, model the economy using published aggregate data. The real force of his approach to microfoundations was the intellectual reassurance that it offered:

> If we want to simplify mathematical models of general equilibrium into a small number of equations, it is useful to know that operationally significant concepts exist which justify such simplifications. It is only in models of macroeconomics that we can see through all the complex interrelationships of the economy in order to form intelligent judgments about such important magnitudes as aggregate employment, output, consumption, and investment. (Klein 1946a: 108)

Beyond the theoretical solace of believing that appropriate aggregation was feasible in principle, Klein also appeals to microeconometrics, to budget studies that show that distribution effects are small and might be neglected without much loss (Klein 1947: 59, 194). He also argues that in practice ordinary published aggregates will correlate so highly with properly computed aggregates "that one set can be substituted for the other" (Klein 1946b: 311).

Empirical practice is paramount in Klein's view, and his approach to microfoundations does not suppose that we build up from secure microdata, but that we start with the available data and a feasible macroeconomic model consisting of "a small number of equations" and constantly work to disaggregate it and to elaborate it in the direction of a complete Walrasian general-equilibrium model. This is the strategy behind the program that developed through various simpler models (Klein 1950; Klein and Goldberger 1955) and ultimately into the famous Brookings macroeconometric model of the US economy with its more than 150 equations (Duesenberry et al. 1965). Whether explicitly engaged in macromodeling or not, much of the macroeconomics from the 1950s to the 1970s can be seen as the implementation of Klein's microfoundational program. Each of the Keynesian functions was analysed at a microeconomic level and its implications for a feasible macroeconometric model considered.

We could easily examine investment, demand for money, labor demand or supply, or the Phillips curve in the same spirit, but let us instead consider two analyses of the consumption function – the relative-income hypothesis of James Duesenberry (1949) and the permanent-income hypothesis of Milton Friedman (1957). Duesenberry was later a collaborator with Klein on the Brookings Model; while Friedman was skeptical of this type of modeling. But both Duesenberry and Friedman represent methodologically similar efforts to ground macroeconomic relationships in microeconomic relations. That they differ on other methodological issues illustrates how widespread their common approach to microfoundations was.

Both studies start with the observation, due to Simon Kuznets, that simple versions of Keynes's consumption function are difficult to reconcile with empirical facts about consumption (Duesenberry 1949: 1–2; Friedman 1957: 3–6). A linear version of the consumption function in which the average propensity to consume exceeds the marginal propensity to consume predicts that the average propensity to consume will fall over time and that it will be lower for richer than for poorer people. Kuznets found that the average propensity to consume in aggregate was higher than the marginal for short spans but was constant over longer periods; while in budget studies the average propensity to consume is higher for individuals with lower incomes.

To reconcile these apparently contradictory findings, Duesenberry proposed that relative socioeconomic position both through time and across individuals matters. If income is steady for any individual, more or less independently of its level, the average propensity to consume will be constant. But there is habit persistence induced by treating current income as a reference point. If income falls, the first response will be to maintain socioeconomic status by maintaining the familiar consumption pattern: consumption falls less quickly than income. If income rises, the first response will again be to continue in familiar patterns: consumption rises less quickly than income. An enduring increase in income, however, raises the reference point and the average propensity to consume readjusts to its typical rate. A similar thing happens – perhaps more slowly – with an enduring fall in income.

The budget studies are explained by the fact that they are point-in-time studies. The value of consumption to an individual depends, in part, on "keeping up with the Joneses." Poorer people have to have a higher average propensity to consume to maintain comparability with richer neighbors. But "a rising tide lifts all boats"; so that an increase in aggregate incomes that leaves income distribution relatively stable raises consumption proportionately (Duesenberry 1949, ch. 3).

Duesenberry's analysis is predicated on the assumed consistency of microeconomics and macroeconomics. Kuznets's facts themselves combined the microeconometrics of budget studies with the macroeconometrics of time series. Duesenberry grounds his analysis in ordinary microeconomic consumer theory with the added hypothesis that preferences are interdependent.

Friedman's permanent-income hypothesis explains the same set of facts without the assumption of interdependent preferences. Like Duesenberry, Friedman supposes that the "long-run" average propensity to consume is constant. He explains variations around it by drawing a distinction between permanent income – essentially the income flow from the annuitized value of one's expected human and nonhuman wealth – and temporary windfall deviations between measured and permanent income. The permanent–temporary distinction involves both the idea that even predictable variations in income will be smoothed (wealth not income is the spending constraint) and that the idea that consumers must form expectations of uncertain future income flows to estimate wealth.

In budget studies, the poor (as measured by current income) show a higher measured average propensity to consume because some are only transiently poor owing to of windfall losses of income. Since such a loss has only a small effect on wealth (roughly the interest rate times the loss), their permanent income is hardly impaired and they maintain the higher level of consumption that it justifies. Symmetrically, some of the rich are only transiently rich and base their consumption on their lower permanent income. These transients raise the average propensity to consume of the poorer groups and lower the average propensity to consume of the richer groups.

The time-series data is explained by the fact that over any shorter period of years temporary shocks to income may be dominantly positive or negative, shifting people on average above or below their permanent income and raising or lowering the average propensity to consume in exactly the same way as in the cross-sectional account; while over a longer run of years, positive and negative temporary shocks will average out, so that measured income and permanent income nearly coincide.

On Duesenberry's account, the short-run consumption function is the real result of a more complex socioeconomic process than contemplated by textbook consumer theory, but just as grounded in the canons of microeconomic rationality. On Friedman's account, the short-run consumption function is a statistical illusion – an epiphenomenon.

As with Duesenberry's analysis, Friedman bases his hypothesis squarely in microeconomic, utility-maximizing consumer theory. Friedman argues for the superiority of his approach over Duesenberry's mainly on the basis of the microeconomic budget studies (Friedman 1957, ch. 6). Neither provides a direct derivation of the aggregate relationship from the individual relationships. Microfoundations in this program is not a matter of deductive certainty but of apparent consistency. Anticipating the Lucas critique, Duesenberry (1949: 72) sees the object to find fundamental invariants. In the manner of Klein, he argues that, in principle, invariant relationships at the individual level deductively imply invariant relations at the aggregate level, though the aggregate's relations are not necessarily simple sums of the individual's ones. But in practice it comes down to empirical facts.

Neither Duesenberry nor Friedman sees the adaptation of hypotheses to facts as undermining the authority of microeconomic theory. Duesenberry (1949: 13), for instance, argues that utility theory has an empirical basis, and it is empirical observation that warrants the notion of interdependent preferences. Friedman's notion of wealth follows from general principles of intertemporal optimization; whereas the constancy of the ratio of consumption to permanent income is a contingent fact, consistent with, but not implied by, consumer theory. Without the microtheoretical analysis, it would be impossible to conceive of the notion of permanent income or to propose its measurement or to test the hypothesis of the constant permanent average propensity to consume.

The role of microeconomics in supporting the various Keynesian aggregate functions has been stigmatized as merely suggesting the variables to be included in a regression. The two analyses of the consumption function demonstrate otherwise. Duesenberry's microanalysis suggests a functional form that includes a ratchet effect – the contextual calibration of the reference level of income. And while Friedman's microanalysis does suggest a new variable, permanent income, this variable is not an observable; and the theory suggests the strategy for its construction. What is more, the theory explains the nature of the relationship between current income and consumption while, at the same time, giving a reason to regard it as nonstructural. The relationship between microeconomics and macroeconomics in these two cases is not one of logical implication, but the microecononomics nonetheless does serious work to support the macroeconomics.

The commitment to microeconomics is not merely theoretical – a well formed aggregate function is consistent with microtheory – but empirical. Duesenberry argues for microeconometric testing:

> we ought to operate on the following principles. First, every hypothesis ought to be stated in terms of the behavior of individual firms or households, even when we are only interested in the aggregate results. ... Second, in so far as it is possible, we ought to test our hypotheses against data which indicate the behavior of individual households or firms. (Duesenberry 1949: 75)

Elaborating and testing the microeconomic basis for the consumption function and the other Keynesian functions is an essential part of Klein's top-down microfoundational approach. The target – though it may never be reached – is the completely disaggregated model:

> In contrast with the parsimonious view of natural simplicity, I believe that economic life is enormously complicated and that the successful model will try to build in as much of the complicated interrelationships as possible. That is why I want to work with large econometric models and a great deal of computer

power. Instead of the rule of parsimony, I prefer the following rule: the largest possible system that can be managed and that can explain the main economic magnitudes as well as the parsimonious system is the better system to develop and use. (Klein 1992: 184)[23]

The Brookings model is the most perfect expression of Klein's approach. In its 1965 version the model includes 32 sectors and more than 150 equations (Duesenberry et al. 1965). The modelers, however, understood the tradeoff implicit in real-world data. On the one hand, aggregation leads to imprecision; on the other hand, data are sparse and disaggregated data have low signal-to-noise ratios (Duesenberry and Klein 1965: 7–8). The tradeoff and the problems of tractability imply that modelers must start with highly aggregated systems and disaggregate them wherever, and to the degree that, it is feasible to do so. Consumption, for instance, is broken down into five categories; firms into five categories; investment in four industrial groups (Duesenberry and Klein 1965: 7–8; Suits and Sparks 1965: 203; Jorgenson 1965: 56). The microeconomics is never far from mind. For example, just as in the case of the consumption function, Jorgenson (1965: 40) maintains that a major failing of earlier aggregative analyses of investment was a failure to apply microeconomic theory to determine not only which factors were important but *how* those factors should be functionally related.

Since the mainstream narrative stigmatizes large-scale macroeconometric models as unidentified, nonstructural reduced forms that substitute correlation for causation, it is noteworthy that the Brookings team gives significant attention to structural modeling, appropriate estimation methods, and to the different information that might be extracted from structural and reduced-form models (Fisher 1965). In this, they continue a line of thought that was already clear in the work of the Cowles Commission (Koopmans 1950; Hood and Koopmans 1953) and related to microfoundations in Duesenberry's work on the consumption function.

In trying to understand the microfoundational elements in Klein's macroeconometric enterprise, we are not offering a defense of its substantive achievements. But we do take note, first, of the fact that macroeconometric models of the same genre persist in government and private policy analysis today; and, second, that contrary to the mainstream narrative, such models were never entirely macroeconomic, but were situated by their creators in a clear microfoundational program.

6.   THE NEW CLASSICAL MACROECONOMICS AND THE REPRESENTATIVE AGENT

Despite the persistence of practical macroeconometric models in the tradition of Klein, the aggregation program of microfoundations has been eclipsed since the early 1980s by the representative-agent program, introduced by new classical economists but now the common property of all mainstream macroeconomists, new Keynesian as well as new classical (see Duarte, this volume). So complete has been the victory of representative-agent program that few economists of a recent vintage have ever been instructed in the elements of the aggregation program – the IS-LM model or the microfoundations of the individual Keynesian functions. Microfoundations as a concept, in the minds of many, has come to exclude the earlier programs altogether. The general-equilibrium program of microfoundations has come to be seen as a respectable area of research, but one that is essentially *microeconomic*; while the aggregation program of microfoundations is falsely characterized as an analysis of aggregates without any substantial connection to microeconomics. Figure 1.2 and Tables 1.1 and 1.2 quantify the narrowing of the association of microfoundations with the representative-agent program, showing how little the term was employed before the advent of the new classical macroeconomics, how much it has grown since, and the close relationship between discussions of microfoundations and the particular issues emphasized by new classical economists.

The publication of *Microeconomic Foundations* (1970a), edited by Phelps, was the watershed event in the establishment of the representative-agent microfoundational program. There is an irony in this since the sensibility that informed the Phelps project and many of the contributions to the volume was more the role of search, which involves many agents, and heterogeneous information than it was the representative agent. But Lucas and Rapping (1970) contributed a key paper, which has strong claims to be the first paper in the new classical macroeconomics and the fount of the representative-agent program. Most references to microfoundations in JSTOR in the years immediately following its publication are to the Phelps volume. As Table 1.1 shows, Phelps is referenced as much in the context of microfoundations as Lucas.[24] The detailed pattern is different, as shown in Table 1.3. Where Phelps is more frequently associated with microfoundations than Lucas in the 1970s, references to Lucas reach parity in the 1980s, and references to Phelps fall sharply behind in the 1990s.

Table 1.3   Phelps, Lucas, and Microfoundations

	Lucas	Phelps
1970–1979	87	259
1980–1989	228	235
1990–1999	212	124
Total 1956–2009	652	653

Notes: Entries are the number of articles in 97 JSTOR economics journals 1956–2009 or subperiods that include terms from the microfoundational family (see main text note 7 for a definition) and each of the economists' names.

The premise of the Phelps volume was that the Keynesian account of the labor market was inconsistent with standard neoclassical microeconomics. Real effects of aggregate demand shifts in the *General Theory* depend on "esoteric non-neutrality" (Phelps 1970b: 1; also Phelps and Winter 1970: 310). While this is an interpretation of Keynes's labor market that we rejected in section 3 above, it is probably the most common interpretation among economists since the *General Theory* was first published. In an important sense, the Phelps volume was conceived in much the same spirit as the microeconomic analyses of other Keynesian functions that dominated the aggregation program.

Lucas and Rapping's contribution was no different. Its central premise is that Keynes gave up too soon on perfect competition in the labor market (Lucas and Rapping 1970; also 1969). Lucas and Rapping generated real effects of demand shocks through expectational errors of the sort that Friedman (1968) and Phelps (1967) had made the centerpiece of their reconstructions of the Phillips curve. To this, Lucas and Rapping introduced intertemporal optimization – the intertemporal elasticity of substitution being the key factor governing the response to transitory shocks. The paper is typical of the earlier aggregative literature in that the "simple theory of a single household *suggests* an aggregate supply function" (Lucas and Rapping 1970: 265, emphasis added). The empirical investigation using aggregate data is not tightly connected to the microeconomic optimization problem.

Although Lucas and Rapping contributed to Phelps's volume, Phelps's direct influence on Lucas derived from what Lucas had learned at the conference of which the volume is a record. In one of his most famous papers, "Expectations and the Neutrality of Money," Lucas (1972a) moves beyond the single-agent optimization of Lucas and Rapping's articles and creates a model of many agents in general equilibrium. This is not a model in the spirit of Keynesian heterogeneity; all agents are fundamentally alike. What differs is not the agents themselves, but the information available to them. Lucas appeals to Phelps's "island model": agents are informationally isolated so that they know local information but can learn aggregate information only with a delay as travel between "islands" is not instantaneous (Phelps 1970b: 6). While Lucas assumes that information is incomplete, he also assumes that agents use it as efficiently as possible, adopting Muth's (1961) "rational-expectations hypothesis." The upshot of Lucas's model is that there is no genuine tradeoff between inflation and real output or employment implicit on common interpretations of the Phillips curve: money is neutral in the long-run and the short-run; the apparent short-run Phillips curve is a statistical illusion, positive demand shocks are associated with signal-extraction errors, so that they are correlated with positive movements of real output; but it is impossible to move systematically along the curve that traces out this correlation. Lucas's strategy is similar to Friedman's strategy in analysing the consumption function – in their views, both the current-income version of the short-run Keynesian consumption function and the short-run Phillips curve were epiphenomenal.

Although Lucas frequently makes reference to general-equilibrium and to the Arrow–Debreu model, he applies very little of the technical work in general-equilibrium theory to his macroeconomic models. His references tend to be casual, in much the same way as Friedman (1968: 8) famously defines the natural rate of unemployment by reference to the Walrasian general-equilibrium model, while never actually deriving a natural rate in such a model. Lucas's "Expectations and the Neutrality of Money" (1972a) is an exception. It is a general-equilibrium model in the spirit of Arrow and Debreu; although, as we noted earlier, it makes highly restrictive assumptions. Programmatically, it serves a function not dissimilar to Klein's articles on aggregation. Each provides a sort of theoretical reassurance that something that we cannot do in practice at least works in principle. In Lucas's case, it allows him to conclude that we could get the desired result out of a fully articulated general-equilibrium model with heterogeneous agents; and knowing that we could, it is OK to short-circuit the process and to work with much simpler models. In "Some International Evidence on Output-Inflation Tradeoffs" (1973), Lucas also derives the epiphenomenal Phillips curve from many agents with differing information, but the real meat of the article is to justify an *aggregate* "surprise-only" aggregate-supply curve, the function that takes the place of the Phillips curve. It is only the aggregate relationships that are tested.

As was widely perceived at the time, the real "revolution" was the use of the rational-expectations hypothesis (see De Vroey, this volume). Rational expectations were closely related to a form of general-equilibrium. The outcomes predicted by the model depended on the expectations held by the agents in the model and rational expectations were defined as those expectations that were consistent with those predictions. Thus, the model required a simultaneous solution of individual and systemic outcomes (for example, the general price level) characteristic of general-equilibrium. But there was no necessary appeal to a *disaggregated* general-equilibrium of *heterogeneous* agents. Rational expectations themselves were a systemic characteristic, which despite Lucas's (1973) account of signal extraction, were not grounded in individual optimization behavior.[25]

Once a microeconomic rationale had been provided for the surprise-only aggregate-supply function, most of the early new classical macroeconomics was devoid of direct reference to microeconomics. Lucas's (1972b) criticism of Friedman's interpretation of the natural-rate hypothesis joined a surprise-only aggregate-supply curve, aggregate demand based on the quantity theory of money, and rational expectations to generate both the ineffectiveness of aggregate demand policy and an early version of the noninvariance or "Lucas critique" of econometric models. Sargent and Wallace's (1975, 1976) more famous papers on policy ineffectiveness were similar, replacing the quantity equation with an IS-LM representation of aggregate demand. Sargent's (1979) macroeconomics textbook emphasizes asset dynamics and rational expectations, but does not introduce an individual optimization problem until chapter 16 – a potpourri of new classical "topics." Few of the articles collected in Lucas and Sargent's (1981) anthology of earlier new classical papers, *Rational Expectations and Econometric Practice*, either involve individual optimization or display explicit concern for microfoundations. As its title suggests, the main focus of the early new classical macroeconomics was on the implications for rational expectations on econometrics – both the problem of estimating macroeconomic models with systemic ("cross-equation") constraints imposed by rational expectations and implications of rational expectations for interpreting the evidence concerning the natural rate of unemployment (supporting claims for policy ineffectiveness). This strand of the new classical literature certainly paid no more attention – and, in fact, it would seem, rather less attention – to microfoundations than did the economists involved with the Brookings Model.

New classical microfoundations originate not so much in the rational-expectations hypothesis *per se* as in the interaction of rational expectations with the intertemporal optimization, starting with Lucas and Rapping's (1969, 1970) investigations of the labor market. Rational expectations requires modeling complete systems, not independent parts. To do so in a fully disaggregated dynamic intertemporal general-equilibrium model is simply too hard. This is exactly the same problem that Frisch faced in 1933.

Lucas and Sargent (1981: xiv) are clear that simplification is essential; the dimensionality of the problem must be reduced through various devices. They do not mention the representative-agent model in this context, but it was already a standard device, especially in optimal growth theory, and had, as we have seen, been used in Barro and Grossman's (1971) general-disequilibrium model. Sargent (1979: 371, fn. 4) refers to the "standard device of 'representative' agents" as needing no special justification and by the time that Sargent's *Dynamic Macroeconomic Theory* (1987) appears – the representative agent model has become the workhorse of the new classical macroeconomics. The new Keynesian graduate textbooks (Romer 1996, and Blanchard and Fisher 1989) also fully incorporate the representative agent.

It is striking, however, that there is little-to-no explicit justification of the representative-agent simplification. This is borne out by Table 1.2, which shows that 380 JSTOR articles after 1970 display the co-occurrence of terms in the representative-agent family and terms in the microfoundations family. In comparison "general equilibrium" co-occurs more than twice as often, and "expectations" and "labor" more than three times as often. Nor does the small co-occurrence reflect merely a low usage generally: in the same period, terms in the representative family occur in 3842 articles altogether.

The fact that no significant defense of the representative-agent assumption *as empirically applicable* is found in the new classical literature bears out the significance of these data. The qualification is important, because the representative-agent assumption poses less of a methodological hurdle when what is wanted is only some case in which aggregation is warranted – essentially Hicks's justification for appealing to the composite-commodity theorem. Sargent (1979: 371, fn. 4) seems to have something like Hicks's justification in mind when he says that the representative-agent assumption merely removes the burden of having to carry around a variable expressing the number of individuals in the model. So, for instance, if one wanted to demonstrate that aggregated relationships were not invariant to changes in taste and technology in a toy model, constructing the special case in which the representative agent is just $N \times$ the individual agents is unproblematic. But there is never any discussion of the conditions under which this assumption is warranted more generally. It is truly just assumed without comment. So, in effect, the new classic macroeconomists sleepwalked into their most characteristic methodological position.

It is easy to imagine that the justification is tractability. Lucas justifies the use of perfect competition on just this basis:

The case for the use of competitive theory in modeling business cycles would, if I were to develop it here, be based entirely on convenience, or on the limits imposed on us by available technology... (Lucas 1980a: 293, fn. 11)[26]

The point is meant to generalize. The essay from which the quotation is drawn, "Methods and Problems in Business Cycle Theory" is an extended methodological defense of drastic simplifying assumptions and the need to recognize the constraints imposed by the technology of scientific investigations (esp. section 1):

The historical reason for modeling price dynamics as responses to static excess demands [as opposed to dynamic optimization with individual agents] goes no deeper than the observation that the theorists of that time did not know any other way to do it. (Lucas 1980a: 286)

Presumably, the same justification would be offered in support of the use of a single representative agent.

The advocates of representative-agent microfoundations face the same barrier to complete disaggregation that Klein and advocates of the aggregation program faced. The difference is that Klein took the data as the binding constraint: disaggregate as far as the data permit, looking for a general consistency with microeconomic theory. In contrast, Lucas and the representative agent program take theory as the binding constraint: work out the theory in a tractable special case and disaggregate as far as the technical advance of microeconomic theory permits, looking for a general, nearly impressionistic, consistency with the available data.

While the cases appear symmetrical, they are not quite. The representative-agent program elevates the claims of microeconomics in some version or other to the utmost importance, while at the same time not acknowledging that the very microeconomic theory it privileges undermines, in the guise of the Sonnenschein–Debreu–Mantel theorem, the likelihood that the utility function of the representative agent will be any direct analogue of a plausible utility function for an individual agent. Kirman's (1992) survey article on the representative agent, which highlights the lack of analogy, is well-cited; yet, it is striking that almost all of the citations are by critics of the representative-agent program; there is little evidence that advocates have even noticed the argument against their approach.

The priority of theory in the representative-agent approach is most striking in the case of calibration methods, first used with real-business-cycle models, but now widespread (Kydland and Prescott 1982, 1991, 1996).[27] Traditional methods of econometric estimation and hypothesis testing are eschewed because the mismatch between models and data nearly always results in rejection of the model. But accepting the verdict of the hypothesis test is to resolve the tension between microeconomic theory and the data in the wrong direction.

Recently, the representative-agent program has begun to push toward models with more heterogeneous agents (for example, Krusell and Smith 2006). The move is analogous to the movement between early macroeconometric models and the more disaggregated Brookings Model. But in one sense the object is different. The object of representative-agent microfoundations is ultimately to eliminate macroeconomics – to derive all results from microeconomic theory. Distinctively macroeconomic phenomena on this view are, like Lucas's analysis of the Phillips curve, merely epiphenomena. In contrast, the object of the aggregation and general-equilibrium programs of microfoundations was to push towards an understanding of how genuine macroeconomic phenomena arise out of microeconomic behaviors. These programs are non-eliminative.

6. MICROFOUNDATIONS – YESTERDAY AND TODAY

The term "microfoundations" dates from the mid-1950s, but the awareness of microfoundations as a methodological program explicitly present in the consciousness of the economics profession really began with Phelps's *Microeconomic Foundations* and the new classical assault on Keynesian orthodoxy – especially on Keynesian macroeconometrics – around 1970. The mainstream microfoundational narrative finds virtue in deductive rigor, the unity of economics, and the invariance of econometric relationships. The rhetoric of microfoundations draws on an image of a macroeconomics grounded in microeconomics – anything we want to know about the economy is derivable from the analysis of individuals, taking only their tastes and the constraints of technology and resources as given. While this vision of microfoundations is newly articulated in the 1970s, it is an essential element of its rhetorical success that it claims to be returning to a sounder, pre-Keynesian conception of economics.

An historical irony is that the earliest surveys and histories of microfoundations (Weintraub 1977, 1979) and methodological investigations (Janssen 1993) played an important part in promoting the rhetoric of microfoundations, but generally did not address the mainstream narrative. Instead, they mainly documented a distinct program in general-equilibrium theory. In doing so, they highlighted the fact that the relationship between microeconomics and macroeconomics was a central issue, starting when these distinctions were first drawn by Frisch in the early 1930s.

The mainstream narrative portrays macroeconomics as a retreat from sound microeconomics and as based in nonstructural associations among aggregated variables. This picture is vastly different from the visions of Frisch or Keynes. Explicitly for Frisch and implicitly for Keynes, microeconomics was the economics of a part of the economy, holding the remainder of the economy constant in the background; while macroeconomics was the economics of the economy as a whole. The distinction was inspired by Marshall. Macroeconomics is general equilibrium, provided that term is broadly conceived to refer to the properties of interdependent systems taken as a whole and not to Walras's or Arrow and Debreu's conception of such systems. This was clearly Frisch's conception of macroeconomics. Aggregation did not define macroeconomics for Frisch; it mattered only practically.

Keynes did not share Frisch's ambitions to develop either an applied econometrics or a *formal* economic dynamics. He was not, therefore, as constrained as Frisch by practical considerations, and he formulated his macroeconomics with essential reference to heterogeneous individuals. Contrary to the characterization of Keynes familiar from Lucas and the mainstream narrative, the individual played an essential role in Keynes's analysis, even though he denied the vision of macroeconomics as having been built upward deductively from self-sufficient, autonomous microeconomic units. Microeconomics on this interpretation of Keynes is the economics of a part in the context of the whole. Microeconomic parts are neither self-sufficient nor autonomous on this view; microeconomics presupposes, and takes, macroeconomics as given. Macroeconomic properties emerge out of and transcend the individual, and provide the background to microeconomic decision-making. Keynes's conception of macroeconomics, I believe, has not been widely appreciated and has not much influenced mainstream macroeconomics.

Frisch used aggregates, but provided no account of the relationship of aggregates to individuals. Keynes sidestepped aggregation problems by providing an account of macroeconomics that was not meant to support econometrics. Both Frisch and Keynes wished to provide dynamic, general-equilibrium accounts of macroeconomics, but neither understood these accounts in terms of the Walrasian model.

In contrast, Hicks, who also wanted a dynamic macroeconomics, was a Walrasian and was concerned with aggregation. Hicks's composite-commodity theorem isolates stringent conditions under which aggregation works. One reaction to the theorem was to accept that the conditions are too stringent and that, therefore, only the analysis of general-equilibrium models in which every individual was specified would be acceptable. Another reaction is to say that the theorem isolates a special case in which aggregation works; and, by sticking to the special case, we can construct aggregate models to investigate other issues. The first reaction is what generated the general-equilibrium program of microfoundations, ably documented in Weintraub's history. The second reaction inspired the large number of representative-agent models (for example, optimal growth models) that became workhorses of macroeconomic theory in the 1960s and 1970s.

In either its disaggregated or aggregated form, the general-equilibrium program of microfoundations avoids the practical problems of empirical macroeconomics. Empirical macroeconomics must come to terms with aggregation. Klein took the issue to be so important that he defined the distinction between micro and macro in terms of aggregation. Klein and others working in the aggregation program of microfoundations took reassurance from the theoretical results of the general-equilibrium program that suggested that micro and macro can be rigorously connected in principle. But their central priority was empirical economics. Thus, microfoundations in the aggregation program was a matter of working down from aggregated data to as much disaggregation as practical, rather than working up from individual optimization deductively. Economists in the aggregation program looked for consistency between individual optimization and aggregate outcomes and between microeconometrics and macroeconometrics, but they did not hope for a formal deductive path from individuals to the aggregate. Later work on aggregation theory reinforced the view that ground-up derivations were not feasible, providing support for Klein's initial strategy.

The new classical macroeconomics was initially a reaction to the aggregation program – indeed, Lucas and other new classicals originally worked within the program. They perceived a weakness in the Keynesian account of labor markets and sought to repair it with a greater emphasis on dynamics and expectations. Their preferred approach to expectations, the rational-expectations hypothesis, invoked a system property, which undermined Klein's piecemeal strategy of investigating different Keynesian functions separately. The analysis of complete systems is difficult, if they are at all complex. So, just as Frisch before them, they began to work with drastically simplified systems. And, just as Klein before them, they faced a tradeoff between theoretical tractability and empirical relevance. Whereas Klein had resolved the tradeoff by giving priority to empirical applicability and aspiring to move toward greater and greater disaggregated detail, the new classicals placed the priority on consistent theory. Whereas Klein had started with aggregates and hoped that their relationships would not prove to be fatally inconsistent with individual behavior, the new classicals started with the special case of the representative agent and hoped that its implications would not prove to be fatally inconsistent with data. The new classicals aspired toward an elaboration of their simplified theory – that is, toward a detailed theory of heterogeneous agents – but did not allow their results to be held hostage to achieving that elaboration any more than Klein allowed his results to be held hostage to disaggregation. Yet, there was an important methodological disanalogy. Klein was explicitly aware of the difficulties posed by aggregation. The new classicals treat it as a non-issue, showing no appreciation of the theoretical work on aggregation and apparently unaware that earlier uses of the representative-agent model had achieved consistency with theory only at the price of empirical relevance.

NOTES

1. Prepared for the First International Symposium on the History of Economic Thought: "The Integration of Micro and Macroeconomics from a Historical Perspective," University of São Paulo, Brazil, 3–5 August 2009. I thank Pedro Garcia Duarte, Gilberto Tadeu Lima, Thomas Mayer, Raul Cristóvão dos Santos, and two anonymous referees for comments on an earlier draft.
2. See Hoover (1988) for an account of the new classical macroeconomics and the role of microfoundations in it.
3. See Harcourt 1977; Horwitz 2000; Weintraub 1977, 1979; Janssen 1993; Hartley 1997.
4. De Vroey, this volume, addresses Lucas's view that the concept of general equilibrium provides an essential disciplinary device for macroeconomics.
5. Smith and Ricardo, of course, spoke of *political economy*, not economics.
6. Duarte, this volume, examines the place of the representative-agent model in forging a consensus in macroeconomics between new classicals and new Keynesians over the past two decades.
7. Tinbergen (1938: 10) also uses "macroeconomic."
8. Frisch's influence is also suggested by the fact that the first four examples of his term "macrodynamic" being used in any of the economics journals catalogued in JSTOR occur in volume 3 of *Econometrica*, the journal he edited. As well as an article by Frisch and a coauthor, the term occurs in Tinbergen (1935), Kalecki (1935), and Theiss (1935).
9. I thank Olav Bjerkholt for his information and a copy of the relevant parts of Frisch's lectures.
10. Data gathered in May and June 2009. The two families of search terms are:*macroeconomics family*: "macroeconomic" or "macroeconomics" or "macro economic" or "macro economics" (the JSTOR search engine treats hyphens as blanks; so these terms cover both adjectival and nominal uses);*microeconomics*: "microeconomic" or "microeconomics" or "micro economic" or "micro economics";
11. Data gathered in May and June 2009. The *microfoundational* family of search terms is: "microfoundation" or "microfoundations" or "micro foundation" or "micro foundations" or "microeconomic foundation" or "microeconomic foundations" or "micro economic foundation" or "micro economics foundations."
12. Thalberg (1998) discusses Frisch's debt to early economists, particularly to Wicksell, as well as his older contemporaries Joseph Schumpeter and Johan Åkerman.
13. On the relationship of Keynes to the national-income accountants, see Mitra-Kahn (2009).

14. This is, of course, a conjecture. Plausible, but equally conjectural, is a referee's suggestion that Keynes was responding defensively to Hayek's attacks on the use of index numbers in the *Treatise*.

15. A referee urges me not to exaggerate the degree to which the dynamics of the *Treatise on Money* are carried over into the *General Theory*, arguing that, in comparison to the *Treatise* or any Swedish work of the time, the *General Theory* is static. I am unrepentant. If dynamics is defined to be attention to time sequences, then the referee would be right. My argument, however, is that, for Keynes, dynamics is more about causal processes – whether or not one is explicit about time periods – and that Keynes by no means abandons that concern in the *General Theory*.

16. "the struggle for money-wages is ... essentially a struggle to maintain a high *relative* wage..." (Keynes 1936: 252).

17. Keynes ([1933] 1988: 262) was perfectly aware of the necessary concept of emergence. In this essay on Edgeworth, Keynes writes: "Mathematical Psychics [the topic and title of a book by Edgeworth] has not, as a science or study, fulfilled its early promise... The atomic hypothesis which has worked so splendidly in physics breaks down in psychics. We are faced at every turn with the problem of organic unity, of discreteness, of discontinuity – the whole is not equal to the sum of its parts, comparisons of quantity fail us, small changes produce large effects, the assumptions of a uniform and homogenous continuum are not satistifed." (I thank Gilberto Tadeu Lima for pointing out this passage.)

18. Hicks ([1939] 1946: 2–3), sees his approach as that of Walras modified by Marshall.

19. Hands, this volume, stresses that the relationship of microeconomics to macroeconomics was a two-way street. Some developments in microeconomics – for example, the stress on gross substitutability – were motivated by their relevance to macroeconomics, while the Sonnenschein–Debreu–Mantel results, thought the product of microeconomic investigation, nonetheless undermined the general-equilibrium program in microeconomics by calling that relevance into question. On the Sonnenschein–Debreu–Mantel result, also see the chapters by Duarte and Mirowski in this volume.

20. Whether these should be seen as "disequilibrium" models or as "equilibrium" models with additional constraints is a semantic question that appeared from time to time in the literature, but which need not detain us.

21. Cf. Hands, this volume.

22. Nelson (1984) discusses the alternative aggregation strategies from the point of view of methodology or philosophy of science. A more recent, though theoretical example, is provided by the equation defining the aggregate price level in Blanchard and Fischer (1989: 376) which is an aggregate price level related to underlying prices set by monopolistically competitive firms according to a highly nonlinear function nothing like the typical Laspeyres or Paasch indices. See Hoover (2010) for a discussion.

23. It is worth noting that, although we have identified Friedman as a fellow traveler with Duesenberry in seeking the microeconomic basis of individual Keynesian functions, Friedman dissented strongly and early from Klein's complexity-is-best notion and never supported large-scale macroeconometric modeling (Friedman 1940, 1951; see also Hammond 1996: 67–68).

24. References to Phelps are often not personal but to papers by other authors in the volume.

25. Janssen (1993: 134) sees them as analogous to the price-vector in the Arrow–Debreu general-equilibrium model – a macro property for which no individual microeconomic account is provided, the "auctioneer" being merely a *façon de' parler*; see also Hoover (2009: 404).

26. Lucas's position may surprise followers or critics who take market clearing to be a *fundamental* principle of new classical macroeconomics – anything not demonstrating market-clearing being rejected as *ad hoc*. But Lucas is not a nihilist who would hold economics hostage to an ideal. He criticizes Keynes's notion of involuntary unemployment, not because it is wrong, but because he sees it as a hypostatization of a methodological strategy (Lucas 1978: 353). It is consistent to regard market clearing in the same

way, even while arguing that it is the currently best methodological strategy. And one of Lucas's arguments in favor of rules over discretion is, in fact, that we ought to be circumspect in the claims that we make for our success as economic modelers: "As an advice giving profession we are in way over our heads" (Lucas 1980b: 209).

27. Hartley, Hoover, and Salyer (1998) provide a critical account of the real-business cycle model.

REFERENCES

Backhouse, Roger E., and Mauro Boianovsky (2005a). Disequilibrium Macroeconomics: An Episode in the Transformation of Modern Macroeconomics. Unpublished typescript, version 4, August 2005.

Backhouse, Roger E., and Mauro Boianovsky (2005b). Whatever Happened to Microfoundations. Unpublished typescript, version 1, August 2005.

Backhouse, Roger E., and Mauro Boianovsky (2005c). Generalizing General Equilibrium: From Arrow to Malinvaud. Unpublished typescript, version 1, August 2005.

Barro, Robert J. (1984). *Macroeconomics*. New York: Wiley.

Barro, Robert J., and Herschel I. Grossman (1971). A General Disequilibrium Model of Income and Employment. *American Economic Review*, 61 (1):82–93.

Blanchard, Olivier (2000). What Do We Know about Macroeconomics that Fisher and Wicksell Did Not? *Quarterly Journal of Economics*, 115 (4):1375–409.

Blanchard, Olivier, and Stanley Fischer (1989). *Lectures on Macroeconomics*. Cambridge, MA: MIT Press.

Bjerkholt, Olav (1998). Ragnar Frisch and the Foundation of the Econometric Society. In *Econometrics in the 20th Century: The Ragnar Frisch Centennial Symposium*. Edited by Steinar Strøm. Cambridge: Cambridge University Press.

Clower, Robert (1965). The Keynesian Counterrevolution: A Theoretical Appraisal. In *The Theory of Interest Rates: Proceedings of a Conference Held by the International Economic Association*. Edited by F.H. Hahn, and F.P.R. Brechling. London: Macmillan.

Duesenberry, James S. (1949). *Income, Saving and the Theory of Consumer Behavior*. Cambridge, MA: Harvard University Press.

Duesenberry, James S., and Lawrence R. Klein (1965). Introduction: The Research Strategy and Its Applications. In Duesenberry et al. (1965), pp. 3–34.

Duesenberry, James S., Gary Fromm, Lawrence R. Klein, and Edwin Kuh (eds) (1965). *The Brookings Quarterly Econometric Model of the United States*. Chicago: Rand McNally.

Fisher, Franklin (1965). Dynamic Structure and Estimation in Economy-wide Econometric Models. In Duesenberry et al. (1965), pp. 589–636.

Fleming, J.M. (1938). The Determination of the Rate of Interest. *Economica*, N.S. 5 (19):333–41.

Friedman, Milton (1940). Review of *Business Cycles in the United States of America, 1919–32* by Jan Tinbergen. *American Economic Review*, 30 (3):657–60.

Friedman, Milton (1951). Comment on 'A Test of an Econometric Model of the United States, 1921–1947' by C. Christ. In *Conference on Business Cycles*. New York: National Bureau of Economic Research.

Friedman, Milton (1957). *A Theory of the Consumption Function*. Princeton: Princeton University Press.

Friedman, Milton (1968). The Role of Monetary Policy. *American Economic Review.* 58 (1):1–17.

Frisch, Ragnar (1933). Propagation Problems and Impulse Problems in Dynamic Economics. In *Economic Essays in Honor of Gustav Cassel: October 20th 1933.* London: George Allen and Unwin.

Frisch, Ragnar (1933/34). *Forelesninger holdt 1933^II og 1934^I over Makrodynamikk,* mimeographed lecture notes.

Gorman, William. M. (1953). Community Preference Fields. *Econometrica,* 21 (1):63–80.

Hammond, J. Daniel (1996). *Theory and Measurement: Causality Issues in Milton Friedman's Monetary Economics.* Cambridge: Cambridge University Press.

Harcourt, Geoffrey C. (ed.) (1977). *The Microfoundations of Macroeconomics: Proceedings of a Conference Held by the International Economic Association, at S'Agaro, Spain.* Boulder: Westview Press.

Hartley, James E. (1997). *The Representative Agent in Macroeconomics.* London: Routledge.

Hartley, James E., Kevin D. Hoover, and Kevin D. Salyer (1998). The Limits of Business Cycle Research. In *Real Business Cycles: A Reader.* Edited by James Hartley, Kevin D. Hoover, and Kevin D. Salyer. London: Routledge.

Hicks, John R. ([1939] 1946). *Value and Capital: An Inquiry Into Some Fundamental Principles of Economic Theory.* 2nd ed. Oxford: Clarendon Press, 1946 [1st ed. 1939].

Hoover, Kevin D. (1988). *The New Classical Macroeconomics: A Sceptical Inquiry.* Oxford: Blackwell.

Hoover, Kevin D. (1995). Relative Wages, Rationality, and Involuntary Unemployment in Keynes's Labor Market. *History of Political Economy,* 27 (4):653–85.

Hoover, Kevin D. (2006). Dr. Keynes: Economic Theory in a Diagnostic Science. In *The Cambridge Companion to Keynes.* Edited by Roger Backhouse, and Bradley Bateman. Cambridge: Cambridge University Press.

Hoover, Kevin D. (2009). Microfoundations and the Ontology of Macroeconomics. In *Oxford Handbook of the Philosophy of Economic Science.* Edited by http:// www.econ.duke.edu/~kdh9/Source Materials/Research/The CVAR Approach with abstract.pdf Harold Kincaid and Donald Ross. Oxford: Oxford University Press.

Hoover, Kevin D. (2010). Idealizing Reduction: The Microfoundations of Macroeconomics. *Erkenntnis,* 73 (3):329–47.

Horwitz, Steven (2000). *Microfoundations and Macroeconomics: An Austrian Perspective.* London: Routledge.

Janssen, Maarten C.W. (1993). *Microfoundations: A Critical Inquiry.* London: Routledge.

Jorgenson, Dale W. (1965). Anticipations and Investment Behavior. In Duesenberry et al. (1965), pp. 35–94.

Kalecki, Michael (1935). A Macrodynamic Theory of Business Cycles. *Econometrica,* 3 (3):327–44

Keynes, John Maynard ([1909] 1983). The Method of Index Numbers with Special Reference to the Measurement of General Exchange Value. In *Collected Writings of J.M. Keynes,* vol. XI. Edited by Donald E. Moggridge. London: Macmillan.

Keynes, John Maynard ([1930] 1983). *Treatise on Money,* vol. 1. In *Collected Writings of J.M. Keynes,* vol. V. Edited by Donald E. Moggridge. London: Macmillan.

Keynes, John Maynard (1936). *The General Theory of Employment, Interest and Money*. London: Macmillan.

Keynes, John Maynard ([1933] 1988). Francis Ysidro Edgeworth. In *Essays in Biography, Collected Writings of J.M. Keynes*, vol. X. Edited by Donald E. Moggridge. London: Macmillan.

Keynes, John Maynard ([1939] 1983). Professor Tinbergen's Method. In *Collected Writings of J.M. Keynes*, vol. XIV. Edited by Donald E. Moggridge. London: Macmillan.

Kirman, Alan (1992). Whom or What Does the Representative Agent Represent? *Journal of Economic Perspectives*, 6 (1):126–39.

Klein, Lawrence R. (1946a). Macroeconomics and the Theory of Rational Behavior. *Econometrica*, 14 (2):93–108.

Klein, Lawrence R. (1946b). Remarks on the Theory of Aggregation. *Econometrica*, 14 (4):303–12.

Klein, Lawrence R. (1947). *The Keynesian Revolution*. New York: Macmillan.

Klein, Lawrence R. (1950). *Economic Fluctuations in the United States, 1921–1941*. New York: Wiley.

Klein, Lawrence R. (1992). My Professional Life Philosophy. In *Eminent Economists: Their Life Philosophies*. Edited by Michael Szenberg. Cambridge: Cambridge University Press.

Klein, Lawrence R., and Arthur S. Goldberger (1955). *An Econometric Model of the United States: 1929–1952*. Amsterdam: North-Holland.

Koopmans, Tjalling C. (1950). *Statistical Inference in Dynamic Economic Models*, Cowles Commission Monograph 10. New York: Wiley.

Krusell, Per, and Anthony A. Smith, Jr. (2006). Quantitative Macroeconomic Models with Heterogenous Agents. *Advances in Economics and Econometrics: Theory and Applications, Ninth World Congress*, vol. 1, Econometric Society Monographs No. 41. Cambridge: Cambridge University Press.

Kydland, Finn E., and Edward C. Prescott (1982). Time to Build and Aggregate Fluctuations. *Econometrica*, 50 (6):1345–70.

Kydland, Finn E., and Edward C. Prescott (1991). The Econometrics of the General Equilibrium Approach to Business Cycles. *Scandinavian Journal of Economics*, 93 (2):161–78.

Kydland, Finn E., and Edward C. Prescott (1996). The Computational Experiment: An Econometric Tool. *Journal of Economic Perspectives*, 10 (1):69–85.

Leijonhufvud, Axel (1968). *On Keynesian Economics and the Economics of Keynes*. New York: Oxford University Press.

Leontief, Wassily (1936). The Fundamental Assumption of Mr. Keynes's Monetary Theory of Unemployment. *Quarterly Journal of Economics*, 51 (1):192–7.

LeRoy, Stephen F. (1983). Keynes' Theory of Investment. *History of Political Economy*, 15 (3):397–421.

Louçã, Franciso (2007). *The Years of High Econometrics: A Short History of the Generation that Reinvented Economics*. London: Routledge.

Lucas, Robert E., Jr. (1972a). Expectations and the Neutrality of Money. Reprinted in Lucas (1981), pp. 66–89.

Lucas, Robert E., Jr. (1972b). Econometric Testing of the Natural Rate Hypothesis. Reprinted in Lucas (1981), pp. 90–103.

Lucas, Robert E., Jr. (1973). Some International Evidence on Output-Inflation Tradeoffs. *American Economic Review*, 63 (3):326–34.

Lucas, Robert E., Jr. (1976). Econometric Policy Evaluation: A Critique. Reprinted in Lucas (1981), pp. 104–30.

Lucas, Robert E., Jr. (1977). Understanding Business Cycles. Reprinted in Lucas (1981), pp. 215–40.

Lucas, Robert E., Jr. (1978). Unemployment Policy. *American Economic Review*, 68 (2):353–7.

Lucas, Robert E., Jr. (1980a). Methods and Problems in Business Cycle Theory. Reprinted in Lucas (1981), pp. 271–96.

Lucas, Robert E., Jr. (1980b). Rules, Discretion, and the Role of the Economic Advisor. In *Rational Expectations and Economic Policy*. Edited by Stanley Fischer. Chicago: University of Chicago Press.

Lucas, Robert E., Jr. (1981). *Studies in Business-Cycle Theory*. Oxford: Blackwell.

Lucas, Robert E., Jr. (1987). *Models of Business Cycles*. Oxford: Blackwell.

Lucas, Robert E., Jr. (2004). My Keynesian Education. In *The IS-LM Model: Its Rise, Fall, and Strange Persistence. History of Political Economy* 36 supplement. Edited by M. De Vroey, and K.D. Hoover. Durham, NC: Duke University Press.

Lucas, Robert E., Jr. and Leonard A. Rapping (1969). Price Expectations and the Phillips Curve. *American Economic Review*, 59 (3):342–50.

Lucas, Robert E., Jr. and Leonard A. Rapping (1970). Real Wages, Employment, and Inflation. In Phelps (1970a), pp. 257–308.

Lucas, Robert E., Jr., and Thomas J. Sargent (1981). *Rational Expectations and Econometric Practice*. London: George Allen and Unwin.

Malinvaud, Edmond (1977). *The Theory of Unemployment Reconsidered*. Oxford: Blackwell.

May, Kenneth (1946). The Aggregation Problem for a One-Industry Model. *Econometrica*, 14 (4):285–98.

Mitra-Kahn, Benjamin (2009). How Keynes Convinced the British to Re-define the Economy, unpublished working paper (http://webspace.newschool.edu/~kahnb081/Mitra-Kahn-ch08.pdf2).

Modigliani, Franco (1944). Liquidity Preference and the Theory of Interest and Money. *Econometrica*, 12 (1):45–88.

Muth, John F. (1961). Rational Expectations and the Theory of Price Movements. *Econometrica*, 29 (3):315–35.

Nelson, Alan (1984). Some Issues Surrounding the Reduction of Macroeconomics to Microeconomics. *Philosophy of Science*, 51 (4):573–94.

Patinkin, Don ([1956] 1965). *Money, Interest, and Prices*. 2nd ed. New York: Harper & Row.

Phelps, Edmund S. (1967). Phillips Curves, Expectations of Inflation and Optimal Unemployment over Time. *Economica*, N.S. 34 (135):254–81.

Phelps, Edmund S. (ed.) (1970a). *Microeconomic Foundations of Employment and Inflation Theory*. New York: Norton.

Phelps, Edmund S. (1970b). Introduction: The New Microeconomics in Employment and Inflation Theory. In Phelps (1970a), pp. 1–26.

Phelps, Edmund S., and Sidney G. Winter, Jr. (1970). Optimal Price Policy Under Atomistic Competition. In Phelps (1970a), pp. 309–37.

Pu, Shou Shan (1946). A Note on Macroeconomics. *Econometrica*, 14 (4):299–302.

Ramsey, Frank P. (1928). A Mathematical Theory of Saving. *Economic Journal*, 38 (152):543–59.

Romer, David (1996). *Advanced Macroeconomics*. New York: McGraw-Hill.

Sargent, Thomas J. (1979). *Macroeconomic Theory*. New York: Academic Press.

Sargent, Thomas J. (1987). *Dynamic Macroeconomic Theory*. Cambridge, MA: Harvard University Press.

Sargent, Thomas J., and Neil Wallace (1975). 'Rational' Expectations, the Optimal Monetary Instrument, and the Optimal Money Supply Rule. *Journal of Political Economy*, 83 (2):241–54.

Sargent, Thomas J., and Neil Wallace (1976). Rational Expectations and the Theory of Economic Policy. *Journal Monetary Economics*, 2 (2):169–83.

Suits, Daniel B., and Gordon R. Sparks (1965). Consumption Regressions with Quarterly Data. In Duesenberry et al. (1965), pp. 203–26.

Thalberg, Bjørn (1998). Frisch's Vision and Explanation of the Trade Cycle Phenomenon: His Connections with Wicksell, Åckerman, and Schumpeter. In *Econometrics and Economic Theory in the 20th Century: The Ragnar Frisch Centennial Symposium*. Edited by Steinar Støm. Cambridge: Cambridge University Press.

Theiss, Edward (1935). Dynamics of Saving and Investment. *Econometrica*, 3 (2):213–24

Tinbergen, Jan (1935). Annual Survey: Suggestions on Quantitative Business Cycle Theory. *Econometrica*, 3 (3):241–308.

Tinbergen, Jan (1936). Sur la Determination Statistique de la Position d'Equilibre Cyclique. *Revue de l'Institut International de Statistique/Review of the International Statistical Institute*, 4 (2):173–88.

Tinbergen, Jan (1938). *A Statistical Test of Business-Cycle Theories: A Note on Method*. Geneva: League of Nations.

Hood, W.C., and Tjalling C. Koopmans (eds) (1953). *Studies in Econometric Method*. Cowles Foundations Monograph no. 14. New York: John Wiley & Sons.

Weintraub, E. Roy (1977). The Microfoundations of Macroeconomics: A Critical Survey. *Journal of Economic Literature*, 15 (1):1–23.

Weintraub, E. Roy (1979). *Microfoundations: The Compatibility of Microeconomics and Macroeconomics*. Cambridge: Cambridge University Press.

Weintraub, Sidney (1956). A Macroeconomic Approach to the Theory of Wages. *American Economic Review*, 46 (5):835–56.

Weintraub, Sidney (1957). The Micro-Foundations of Aggregate Demand and Supply. *Economic Journal*, 67 (267):455–70.

2. From foundational critique to fictitious players: the curious odyssey of Oskar Morgenstern

Robert Leonard*

1. INTRODUCTION

For the contemporary economist, the names of John von Neumann and Oskar Morgenstern are so tightly associated together that it is difficult to prise them apart. By virtue of their association with the creation of game theory, the two have become somehow "fused" together in our perception, and the considerable differences between them lost to view. Nonetheless, while we refer unthinkingly today to the "von Neumann-Morgenstern utility function", or to their joint authorship of the *Theory of Games and Economic Behavior* ([1944] 1947), the fact remains that while one was a Hungarian mathematician of extraordinary calibre, the other was a philosophically-inclined Austrian economist with little or no mathematical training. In what follows, I would like to consider the life and work of that economist in particular, Morgenstern, paying special emphasis to the role of foundational critique in the Vienna and early Princeton phases of his career. This will also allow us to appreciate his distinct character and outlook, and the considerable intellectual distance he travelled in becoming a co-author of von Neumann's.

From the mid-1920s until 1938, Morgenstern was active in a Vienna that bristled with intellectual activity and political tension. Lapsed Austrian economist, Othmar Spann, preached a form of Romantic idealism, intentionally whipping up his students against rationalist economics, against Marxism and against Freud. Students participating in Ludwig von Mises' seminar encountered a resolute attachment to political liberalism; strong views on the nature, potentialities and limits of economic theory; and scepticism concerning the potential role of mathematics in providing theoretical insight. Those who congregated around Hans Mayer encountered an Austrianism that sought to define itself, not so much by its political vision as by critical confrontation with the formal work of Jevons, Cournot and Walras, with special emphasis on their supposed inability to account theoretically for the central role in economic life played by time. Amongst the members of the Vienna Circle, Otto Neurath focused on poverty, needs and harsh realities, calling for the massive public organization of economic life, and conveying his views through rich visual displays at the Social and Economic Museum of Vienna. The political context, too, was charged and, throughout the interwar period, largely inhospitable to the liberalism championed by the Austrian economists. From 1923 until 1934, under a Social Democratic municipal government, the Austrian capital was "Red Vienna", site of Europe's most signficiant interwar experiment in socialist transformation. The city was racked by conflict between the socialists and the conservative national government in 1927 and again in 1934, the latter culminating in shelling and military conflict in the streets of the capital. From 1934 until 1938, the country was run by a corporatist government, with the restriction of political freedom and regulation of economic life. In 1938, Austria was annexed by Hitler's Germany, which brought an extraordinary chapter in intellectual and artistic history to an end.

In this rich context, Oskar Morgenstern came of age and achieved professional maturity. While, for most of the 1930s, he was director of the Austrian Institute for Business Cycle Research, with many public involvements, his role as critic of economic theory was fundamentally important to him. From his *Habilitation* thesis right up to his collaboration with von Neumann, these were the writings that engaged him most and that connected him to the broader academic world. Throughout the 1930s, he sought to "modernize" economics, clearing aside what he regarded as the "rubble" of traditional wisdom. When he moved to Princeton in 1938, it was his disposition as critic of economic theory that facilitated his relationship with the mathematician and their collaboration on the theory of games.

While, viewed in this synoptic manner, there appears to be a smooth harmony to Morgenstern's development as critic, a little probing reveals various complications and intricacies, the exploration of which will be the subject of this chapter. For the moment, I will mention three.

The first is that while the role of critic came naturally to Morgenstern as a product of the "Austrian" school, the effect of his engagement with foundationalist criticism in the 1930s was to carry him *away* from Austrianism. At the beginning, in the late 1920s, he was a school economist of good standing, shaped by Hans Mayer and Ludwig von Mises, and counted among his peers Hayek, Haberler, Strigl and Rosenstein-Rodan. His emphasis on the need to account for time, knowledge and expectations was very much part of the Austrian approach. By the mid-1930s, however, while he maintained this critical stance, he was distancing himself from his Austrian contemporaries, insisting in his writings upon the heterogeneity of the Viennese economists, and, to a degree markedly greater than that of any of his local peers, allying himself with mathematicians with a view to addressing theoretical weaknesses in economics. By the time he left Vienna in 1938, despite remaining typically Austrian in his critical stance, for example towards Walrasian general equilibrium theory, he had broken with Vienna, both literally and figuratively, and was something of a intellectual maverick in search of a new home.

The second observation concerns the complicated role that foundation-alist criticism played in his collaboration with von Neumann. While Morgenstern's ideas here were essential in forming the bond between himself and the mathematician, and in Morgenstern's writing an introduction to the *Theory of Games*, they do not appear to have been essential to the bulk of what von Neumann himself did in creating game theory.

Related to this, and thirdly, with von Neumann, Morgenstern now found himself, for the first time, caught up in a mathematical maelstrom. As a Modern, Hilbertian mathematician, von Neumann drew him into a strange new world. On the one hand, it offered a strategic agent that was much simpler in conception than any Austrian ideal. On the other, it also involved granting great autonomy to the mathematics: concocting empirical heuristics in order to justify mathematical results obtained by deduction, inventing purely formal devices such as the "ficitious player" in order to be able to extend the apparatus of the stable set to non zero-sum games. Drawn into this world, Morgenstern was severed completely from Austrianism, and had to re-evaluate, and distance himself from, some of his earlier critical work.

2. THE ECONOMIST AS CRITIC

As I re-read the interwar articles, letters and diaries of Morgenstern in preparation for this essay, I was struck not only by the centrality of critique to his theoretical activity in Vienna, but also by the sheer doggedness he displayed in the matter. Whether confronting the sceptical responses of Hayek or Knight to his work, or being gently castigated by kinder correspondents such as Eve Burns, Morgenstern showed himself to be consistently stubborn. For example, having been chided by Burns for his nihilism, he retorted:

> I am very sorry to have disappointed you with my book [*Die Grenzen der Wirtschaftspolitik*, 1934a], due to its negativism, but I have the feeling that what

is really necessary today is pitiless criticism, and I can tell you in confidence that I have only just begun. My second book will also be overwhelmingly critical. Because only through that can the rubble of traditional wisdom be put aside. And the way is free for new [ideas]... and modernization. (OM to Burns, March 6, 1934, Oskar Morgenstern Papers, Special Collections Library, Duke University, hereafter OMDU)

While during the 1930s Morgenstern was a policy economist and research director of considerable influence, the writings for which he is best remembered, and which he seems to have regarded as quite important, were those concerned with theoretical critique. He wrote about business cycle theory; from what he regarded as its inevitable inability to provide useful prediction to its inadequacy in accounting for the passage of time. He also wrote about the imprecision in the treatment of the foresight of economic agents in contemporary neoclassical and general equilibrium theory. Throughout, he insisted on the need for greater logical rigour in economics in general.

Morgenstern's intellectual style here was a reflection of two distinct, and in some ways opposed, influences; and a great deal of the tension pervading his oeuvre can be understood in the terms of this opposition. The first was his "Austrian" inheritance, with the work of Othmar Spann, Hans Mayer and Ludwig von Mises all being influential.[1] Particularly important, it seems to me, was Mayer's Austrian critique of the inadequacy of orthodox theory in accounting for time, and Mises' emphasis on the primacy of theory in opposition to German Historicism and American Institutionalism. The second set of influences was the mathematicians and philosophers with whom Morgenstern early cultivated a relationship. Morgenstern differed from his Austrian teachers in the openness he showed to developments in mathematics and scientific philosophy. His contact with various mathematicians, including Karl Menger and Abraham Wald, and his reading of other mathematicians and philosophers, including Carnap, Schlick, Russell and Hilbert, meant that he orientated his Austrian theoretical critique in a direction quite different from most of his economist peers.

Morgenstern's engagement with mathematics was a complicated matter. In Vienna, it became shot through with considerations of power. For example, by allying himself with the mathematicians, he distinguished himself from his economist mentors and asserted his professional independence. His emphasis on clarity and rigour also stemmed from a desire to cleave a separation between the realms of economic analysis and politics: for he saw the field of economics as infiltrated with, and distorted by, the political preferences of theorists. He was explicit about this with regard to Mises, and there are hints that he regarded Keynesian policy as being based on sloppy theoretical foundations. There is also the fact that Morgenstern was himself ill-trained in mathematics, relying for guidance on seminars with Menger, tutorials with Wald and Franz Alt, and private reading. All of this made for a psychologically interesting situation, with Morgenstern showing, in papers that were often less than rigorously clear, an obsession with clarity, purity and rigour.

In 1925, Morgenstern had finished his doctoral degree, with a thesis on marginal utility, and was about to leave Vienna for three years on a Laura Spelman Rockefeller Fellowship.[2] Up to that point, he had been subject to several local influences, ranging from the holistic doctrines of "lapsed Austrian" Spann to the theoretical critique of his teacher Hans Mayer.[3] A one-time disciple of Carl Menger, and successor to von Böhm-Bawerk's chair at the university, Spann had abandoned the methodological individualism of Austrian economics and developed what he termed Universalism. This admixture of German Romanticism and Idealistic philosophy took the social whole, not the individual, as the point of departure in understanding social evolution. Only when individuals adopted the role for which they were destined by nature could social harmony be ensured. Spann's corporatist outlook was essentially a neo-feudal one, inspired by the early 19th-century writings of German Romantic Adam Müller and inflected by the mysticism of Novalis and Augustine. As far as I can determine, Spann left no lasting traces in Morgenstern's later work, but he was significant for at least two reasons. First, his work is a reminder that, in the mid-1920s, Morgenstern's eventual commitment to an economics based upon a foundation of methodological individualism was not a foregone conclusion: the Austrian theory of Menger, Wieser and von Böhm-Bawerk was just one of a number of competing forms of socio-economic analysis, the others ranging from Spann's holism through Austro-Marxism to Bolshevism. Second, it is not impossible that Morgenstern's experience with Spann, in which infatuation was quickly followed by rupture, marked the beginning of the young economist's suspicion of any incursion of politics into social science. The theme of normative "purity", the search for an economics unbesmirched by political tastes, would become central to Morgenstern's work in the next decade.

If Spann's writings concerned social scientific foundations in the very broadest sense, the second formative influence upon Morgenstern squarely confronted foundational issues in economic theory. As successor to Wieser at the University of Vienna from 1923, first editor of the *Zeitschrift für Nationalökonomie*, and, later, President of the *Nationalökonomische Gesellschaft* when that society was recreated in 1928, Hans Mayer was an important presence in Vienna. His foundational critique of the 1920s culminated in his substantial 1932 paper, "The Cognitive Value of Functional Theories of Price", which focused upon certain incongruities in mathematical economics, in particular its inability to deal with *time*.

A worthy economic theory, said Mayer, one that was in-keeping with the scientific ambitions of Carl Menger, would acknowledge that tastes emerged in time. Rather than taking preferences as given, present from the outset of the analysis, as did the theories of Cournot, Jevons and Walras, an appropriate theory would recognize the fact that some tastes were actually finite and that new ones appeared only when others were satisfied. Any theory that proposed to explain not just the existence but the appearance and evolution of prices had to take account of the temporal nature of preferences. By presuming that all tastes were present from the beginning, Walrasian general equilibrium theory excluded time from its framework, providing an artificially static portrait of a situation that was inherently temporal in nature.

If Mayer's detailed essay expressed the interwar Austrian resistance to the mathematical economics being promoted abroad in Lausanne and England, so too did the work of Ludwig von Mises, particularly in his 1933 collection of essays, *Epistemological Problems of Economics*. The structures of mathematical economics, said Mises, in their rigidity and their focus on equilibrium, portrayed economic activity in unduly static, stilted terms. Economic life was fluid and ever-changing, and no mathematical treatment could adequately capture this.[4]

The critique advanced by Mayer and Mises also highlighted the limitations of Austrian theory. While it was relatively easy to insist upon the need for a theory that would recognize time, change, and the *tendency* towards equilibrium rather than its attainment, it was not at all obvious how to accomplish this. As long as no alternative theory was forthcoming, the constructive element in Austrianism would be overshadowed by its critical negativism.

While, for various personal and political reasons, Morgenstern would rarely acknowledge the extent to which he inherited the critical mantle of Mayer and Mises, it shaped him, and resonated in his essays of the 1930s. Where he differed significantly from both was in his readiness to engage sympathetically with mathematics and logic: if his teachers criticized formalism and turned away, he criticized and eventually embraced it.

3. *WIRTSCHAFTSPROGNOSE*

His 1928 Habilitation thesis, *Wirtschaftsprognose*, or "Economic Prediction", was written after three years of study abroad on the Rockefeller

Fellowhip. Most significant for that essay was the year spent in the USA, first at Columbia University, close to Wesley Mitchell and Henry Moore, and then at Harvard, with Charles Bullock and Warren Persons. Pointing to the significant forecast errors of the 1920s, Morgenstern advances theoretical arguments against the very possibility of economic prediction, such as that then being conducted by agencies such as the Harvard Economic Service, the Babson Statistical Organization and Moody's Investor Service.

The central idea is that, because economic actors react to forecasts, the latter will always be undermined. This undermining can be mild, such as when the effect of agents' reactions is to accelerate in time realization of the predicted phenomenon (for example, a prediction of price rises), or severe, when the reactions of agents have the effect of reversing, or annulling, the prediction completely.

Morgenstern's argument is very "Austrian" in style, and is replete with foundational considerations. In the "static economy" of general equilibrium, economic choice and action no longer have any meaning: "the rationality of economic acts has reached such a high degree of perfection that the economic acts have disappeared" (1928: 7). Everything stands still. The supposedly dynamic general equilibrium model of H.L. Moore is not fundamentally different, says Morgenstern, insofar as actors are presumed to know the "coefficients of movement" of the economy, thereby preserving "perfect subjective rationality" (ibid.).

In the real economy, however, there is great heterogeneity. Economic subjects and entrepreneurs each have a set of "orientation points", which comprises the knowledge, beliefs and expectations that they use to make their way through economic life. The knowledge, beliefs and expectations of different individuals are closely related insofar as the behaviour of each actor affects that of others. When a prediction is made, each actor and entrepreneur must integrate it into his knowledge set and change his behaviour accordingly. How he changes his behaviour will depend on how he believes others to have assimilated the prediction and decided to change *their* behaviour.

In the relatively simple case of a predicted rise in the price level, the effect will be to induce agents to act in a manner the effect of which is to accelerate the predicted price increase, viz. buyers purchasing now rather than later; sellers holding stocks in anticipation of the rise. A prediction that does not apply to the time period for which it was intended, says Morgenstern, is a useless prediction.

Might the authority attempt to revise its prediction in order to pre-empt the reaction of the public? The effect would be to cause confusion among the public, with subjects and entrepreneurs postponing action until their knowledge and expectations had been stabilised. Such a situation, in which the public and the authority each try to divine the actions and reactions of the other, Morgenstern likens to the famous anecdote from Sherlock Holmes, in which Moriarty is pursuing Holmes who has just left on a train from London to Dover. What Moriarty should do depends on whether he believes Holmes will go all the way to Dover or will alight at the sole intermediate stop. And what Holmes will do to evade him will depend on his estimation of Moriarty's likely action. The result is an infinite regress of guess and counter-guess, with no obvious solution.

In more realistic situations, where several agencies are making competing predictions, the way in which the public assimilates them, and thereby contributes to undermining them, will depend on a range of factors that no economic science can hope to comprehend – for example, differences as regards optimism and pessimism; varying capacities of assimilation of economic information; and differing beliefs about the prejudices underlying the forecasts of the different agencies. So great is the number of individuals involved, and so great their heterogeneity, says Morgenstern, that it is impossible to comprehend the fate of a particular prediction beyond the moment it is announced. Agencies should thus confine themselves to presenting economic information, and cease making false claims about the efficiency of their mathematical methods in predicting the future.

With *Wirtschaftsprognose*, Morgenstern set the tone and, to a certain extent, the content of his theoretical writings in the decade that followed. Emphasizing heterogeneity and complexity in economic life, he would amplify his criticism of the standard "static" theory. In the absence of coherent, logical foundations, he argued, the very idea of equilibrium stood in jeopardy. Unlike the 1928 essay, however, Morgenstern's writings of the 1930s reflect significant changes that had occurred in his life in the interim. First, as research manager, prominent citizen and, soon, journal editor, his world expanded. Already disinclined psychologically to be part of any particular "school", Morgenstern was now in correspondence with Knight, Keynes and others of similar standing, circumstances which saw him draw away even further from his Austrian economist peers. Second, for reasons themselves not unconnected to politics, he drew closer to the world of logic and mathematics, and developed an increasingly non-Austrian response to his Austrian foundationalist critique.

4. POLITICS AND PRECISION

In 1929, after a delay of a year caused by Spann's political wrangling, Morgenstern was appointed *Privatdozent* at the University of Vienna.[5]

That same year, he became co-director, with Hayek, of the Austrian Business Cycle Institute, which had been set up several years previously by Mises. In 1930, the organization received five years' funding from the Rockefeller Foundation, and, a year later, Hayek left Vienna for the London School of Economics, leaving Morgenstern in charge. For the next eight years, he ran the Institute, overseeing the publication of economic reports and monographs, participating in various committees, and attending local scientific meetings or seminars. The latter included the Economic Association, frequently; Karl Menger's Mathematical Colloquium, occasionally; and, at least once, the *Schlick Kreis*, or Vienna Circle. Morgenstern wrote his theoretical/philosophical contributions in the context of this broad, multifarious activity.

If, in the public sphere, he had to show professionalism and diplomacy, in his private ruminations, Morgenstern tended to be candid:

> Friday was the Economics Association. Mises spoke about worn-out methodology, and his concluding talk especially was just impossible. Lots of Jews. Alvin Hansen is here, quite nice, but didn't impress me too much. (Diary, March 25, 1929)

While there is no evidence that Morgenstern's anti-semitism, then typical of many Austrians, had any concrete impact upon his intellectual life, it is manifest in his diaries, especially through the early 1930s. As collaborator with Abraham Wald and John von Neumann, he would learn to outgrow it. As for the division hinted at with Mises, while it seems to have had nothing to do with prejudice, it would only grow with time. In the course of the 1930s, Morgenstern learned to reject much of what he associated with Mises: his imprecision; his attachment to "*a priorism*" in economic philosophy; his idiosyncratic dismissal of the use of mathematics; and his seeming inability to separate economic analysis from the promotion of "laissez-faire". As a result of his growing immersion in the world of logic and mathematics, Morgenstern increasingly insisted on precision and the excision from economics of normative or political preferences.

The beginning of his "break" with Austrianism may be found in his 1934 book, *Die Grenzen der Wirtschaftspolitik*, translated in 1937 as *The Limits of Economics*. Announcing it to Hayek, he wrote that he was "just finishing a little book that deals with the problem of adapting economics to problems in the economy. In many ways, I was inspired by reading Robbins' book ([1932] 1935), but it is mainly a summary of discussions I had with practitioners. It is particularly for a wider audience, and won't go much into methodological details" (OM to Hayek, July 11, 1933). In his diary, however, he was more frank: "I can already imagine what kind of echo the book is going to have. Lots of people are going to be in a huff, because somehow everybody is going to feel affected. But that's the way it is" (Diary, Sept. 17, 1933).

Subsequently dismissed by Hayek as "a collection of, often brilliant, aphorisms, but [lacking] the consistent argumentation with which one can start a discussion",[6] *Limits* is Morgenstern's attempt to insist upon the native "purity" of economic science: theory is completely separate from political stances such as liberalism, socialism or collectivism. At significant points throughout the book, Mises is clearly the target. Thus, "*a priorism*", Mises' view that the essential insights of economics are immediately obvious truths, not requiring empirical verification, is dismissed by Morgenstern as a claim that can be neither confirmed nor refuted. *A priorism* has nothing to do with the real world, he says.[7]

Morgenstern similarly rejects all attempts to ground the defence of capitalism in economic science – a feature of Mises' writings throughout the 1920s and reiterated in his 1933 collection, *Epistemological Problems of Economics*. Political preferences are the reflection of feelings and tastes, says Morgenstern, and, as such, cannot find support in economic analysis. Liberalism, he continues, argues against interventionism, yet remains silent about the intervention required in order to maintain free competition (p. 20). Liberalism has always looked to the classical economics of Smith and Ricardo, he says, thereby ignoring changes in economics that have occurred in the interim. Similarly, there may be changes in *mentality*, such as the growth of a popular desire for public provision; something that rigid "systems", such as liberalism, tend to ignore. This is *not* to say that economic theory is no longer capable of providing an explanatory framework, he adds, or that the historical method need be resurrected. It is, however, a reminder that liberal proponents of the *a priori* method are wrong when they "see in every appeal to experience and reality the ghost of the negation of theoretical, i.e., scientific, work" (p. 28).

In keeping with what he had previously advanced in *Wirtschaftsprognose*, Morgenstern maintains, in *Limits*, his nihilistic insistence upon complexity, difficulty, frictions and disequilibrium, all of which are ultimately related to the "time" factor. Thus, he says, analysing the effects of economic policy measures is made difficult by the fact that the immediately visible effects of a policy have a greater psychological impact than dispersed ones. The economy, furthermore, may not be in equilibrium to begin with. In Chapter VI, he insists upon the need to analyse the effect of "power" in economic life. Von Böhm-Bawerk, in his *Macht oder ökonomisches Gesetz* (1914), had shown how the use of economic power through, for example, unionization, led to increased indeterminacy; but time, says Morgenstern, tends to weaken the effect of power. There is need for greater analysis of power, he concludes.

His chapter on "The Dangers of Economics" gives a sense of the way in which his thinking in the early 1930s was being shaped by diverse influences. One of the dangers arising from attempts to apply economics, he says, is that it is incomplete as a science. Only an *a priori* science (which economics is not), deductively worked through completely by a supermind, could theoretically hope for completeness. But not even in logic has this occurred. Here, he refers to a recent lecture by Karl Menger on "The New Logic", in which Menger outlined recent developments in logic, such as Russell and Whitehead's response to antinomies of set theory and Gödel's proofs concerning incompleteness. If logic is far from complete, says Morgenstern, then how much more incomplete must be the empirical science of political economy.

* * *

In the evenings, I read Carnap, which is very difficult, but from which I gain a lot. I am slowly learning to think, and by doing that I come more and more into a mathematical way of thinking, or command myself into it. (Diary, March 30, 1929)

Signs of Morgenstern's interest in analytical philosophy and mathematics were evident during his years as a Rockefeller Fellow. During his time in Boston, he was a frequent participant at Alfred Whitehead's "at-home", and in Italy, in 1928, he wrote in his diary about looking forward to hearing David Hilbert and Hermann Weyl speak at the International Congress of Mathematicians in Bologna. Upon returning to Vienna and settling down, he continued to read widely, including Carnap, Hilbert and Ackermann, and Frankel.

At the same time, he cultivated his contacts with mathematicians in Vienna, the most important by far being Karl Menger, son of the founder of the Austrian School. There was a certain complementarity between Menger and Morgenstern. Although a mathematician by training, Menger was very well-educated in economics, having edited in 1923 the second, posthumously published, edition of his father's *Grundsätze*. Like Morgenstern, he spent time abroad as a post-doctoral student, in his case at the University of Amsterdam in the company of Dutch intuitionist, L.E.J. Brouwer. When he returned to a post in geometry at the University of Vienna, Menger became occasionally involved in economist circles. Like Morgenstern, however, he was not a "club man", and, being a somewhat difficult personality, he tended to remain at the margins. Thus, while he was initially close to the core members of the Vienna Circle – which included his advisor, Hans Hahn; Moritz Schlick, whom he revered; Otto Neurath, whose radicalism he disliked; and Rudolf Carnap – Menger soon distanced himself from the group, choosing to describe himself as, not a member, but an associate of the Wiener Kreis. He may be seen as a querulous figure, an insider neither in the Circle nor among the economists.

Menger's influence upon Morgenstern was exerted in several ways. First of all, as Director of the Austrian Business Cycle Institute, the economist was in a position to offer financial support to the mathematician's impoverished students. These included Abraham Wald, most famously, and Franz Alt, both of whom provided some combination of research work for the Institute or mathematics instruction for Morgenstern. The latter developed a close relationship with Wald, in particular, consulting him on his interpretation of Keynes' *Treatise on Money* (1930a, b) and other critical writings. Second, Menger's own writings in economics and social science, and certain of his public lectures, such as the one on logic mentioned above, became required reading for Morgenstern. The key articles here included Menger's "St. Petersburg Paradox" (1934a), "The New Logic" (1933), "Remarks on the Law of Diminishing Returns" (1936), his lecture on "Einige Neuere Fortschritte..." ("Recent Progress in the Exact Treatment of Social Scientific Problems"), and his 1934 book on mathematical sociology, *Moral, Wille und Weltgestaltung.*

Without going into each of these contributions in depth, we can mention some of their significant characteristics. Menger's paper on the St. Petersburg Paradox showed how various attempts to theoretically resolve that paradox had all failed. The paradox in question could be explained only by taking account of the fact that people differed in the manner in which they evaluated risk or future returns. His "Diminishing Returns" paper was a scathing critique of putative "proofs" of the Law of Diminishing Returns, including one by Mises. It deconstructed several such proofs, showing how their arguments were ill-conceived, their conclusions not following from their postulates. His "New Logic" lecture of 1933 was an outline of the history of logic, with special emphasis on the paradoxes in set theory associated with Russell and the effect of the recent proofs by Gödel on the Hilbert Programme in metamathematics. Finally, his book of 1934 on sociology was an attempt to provide a logic of social compatibility, analysing the formation of groups without any normative stipulations whatsoever by Menger himself.

Underlying much of Menger's foray into social science was the conviction that, in matters of logic and proof, many economists were less than rigorous. Morgenstern, hearing these views from someone who was both a true mathematician *and* son of the founder of the Austrian School, gained confidence in his own critical attitude. Thus, when Menger challenged the looseness of Mises' arguments, or the inexactness of his references to logic and proof, Morgenstern was energized in his breaking away from this father figure.[8] When Hans Mayer refused to publish Menger's "St. Petersburg Paradox" analysis, supposedly because it was too mathematical, this contributed to the frustration felt by Morgenstern with this other mentor. Thus Morgenstern's continued embrace of mathematics was not a purely scientific matter, but was bound up with considerations related to self-assertion and the creation of an independent identity.[9]

Stimulated by this new mathematical company, Morgenstern confronted foundational matters more directly than he had in *Limits*. Thus in early 1935 he wrote to Frank Knight: "I myself am very critical of orthodox views of the Vienna School. Have you read my article on 'The Time-moment in Value Theory'? I would be interested in comments" (OM to Knight, January 4, 1935).

Inspired by Mayer's insistence on the centrality of time, and influenced by Morgenstern's own reading of Schlick and Menger, "The Time-Moment" (1934b) expresses his dissatisfaction with the mechanical way in which time has thus far been integrated into general equilibrium analysis. In potted fashion, and without offering any constructive alternative, Morgenstern criticizes the Walrasian theory for assuming infinitely fast adjustment of prices, suggesting the likelihood that speeds of adjustment will differ across markets. He also dismisses H.L. Moore's introduction of a time coefficient into the Walrasian system to create a "moving equilibrium". Much of Morgenstern's dissatisfaction seems to stem from the fact that the effect of time is likely to be felt differently in different parts of the economy. For example, tastes can be expected to vary over time in an unpredictable and irregular manner. Lack of concrete suggestions notwithstanding, Morgenstern insists that these questions will be best tackled by mathematical means. He concludes:

> From the management of time by the consumer and the entrepreneur, then, results a genuine inclusion of the time element in the theory of the exchange economy. Such an approach penetrates the problem much more than some introduction of time-parameters into some system of equations and the tagging of all economic processes with time indices.... The time element presents one of the most urgent problems with which economic theory is faced. About the immense difficulties there can be no doubt. For this reason the intensive collaboration of many investigators has become very necessary. (1934b: 167)

Frank Knight did not think much of this paper, saying that he found the whole argument to be "of such a degree of refinement of conception and doctrine that [he] did not get the feeling of very great importance in the contribution" (Knight to OM, undated). Undeterred, Morgenstern pressed ahead with his critique of time and general equilibrium, penning his more successful "Perfect Foresight and Economic Equilibrium" of 1935. Not only did this paper gain the applause of correspondents such as Knight and Haberler, but it appears to have stimulated further work by Hayek, some features of which help illustrate Morgenstern's deviation from Austrianism as it was evolving along Mises–Hayek lines.

In it, Morgenstern criticizes Walras and Pareto for failing to be clear about the degree of foresight assumed of agents in general equilibrium theory, and he levels particular criticism at Hicks for suggesting that such agents are endowed with "perfect foresight". Similarly, Keynes, in the *Treatise on Money*, refers to "correct forecasting" or "accurate forecasting". This, says Morgenstern, "need not absolutely coincide with complete foresight, although the accompanying text borders upon this interpretation" (p. 170). Morgenstern's central message is that, unless it is made clear what exactly agents are presumed to know – about price mechanisms, and the actions, knowledge and intentions of other agents – the conceptual underpinnings of general equilibrium are flawed. What is meant by "perfect foresight"?, he asks. If, as appears to be the case, it means complete knowledge of the economic process, then the knowledge and analytical powers presumed of the individual are simply extraordinary, for he has assimilated nothing less than a completed science of economics.[10] It is not even clear that such agents, or "demi-gods", could exercise such foresight, since planning future actions requires taking account of the actions of others. The attempt by each individual to refine his intended actions in response to his evaluation of the intended actions of others would lead to an infinite regress, in which no agent would have the last say. Here, Morgenstern resorts to the Holmes–Moriarty example once again, this time in order to illustrate the intractability of such interactive outguessing.

Just as the Holmes–Moriarty episode had been used to illustrate the impossibility of economic prediction in *Wirtschaftsprognose*, here it is used to suggest the impossibility of general equilibrium, in the absence of greater clarification of what exactly is assumed of theoretical agents. It is worth emphasizing the nihilistic tone that pervades Morgenstern's account: "Unlimited foresight and economic equilibrium are… irreconcilable with one another" (p. 174). Without a formal specification of states of knowledge and how they relate to one another through time, the very idea of general equilibrium is without foundation.

As usual, Morgenstern is vague about what is to be done. His interest in paradoxes having been stimulated by his reading in set theory, he suggests that it might be possible to overcome outguessing paradoxes by using something akin to Russell's theory of types. Knowledge about basic facts (prices, quantities) would be of the lowest type; knowledge about others' knowledge would be of a higher type; and so on. Such a gradation, he suggests vaguely, might be used to clarify the relationship between knowledge and equilibrium.

The other source to which Morgenstern points, and with greater assuredness, is the above-mentioned book on mathematical sociology by Karl Menger (1934b). The analytical core of this book explored the compatibility of theoretical agents who had different characteristics or had taken various stances with respect to simple social norms. Thus, for example, one's sensitivity to others, combined with one's decision to smoke or not, had logical implications for the formation of compatibility groups among the combined population of smokers and non-smokers. Menger's simple geometry of social interaction was seen by Morgenstern as the potential beginnings of a mathematics adequate to the analysis of interacting agents: "the only examination of a strictly formal nature about social groups ... which, it is hoped, will become known to economists and to sociologists because of its importance in laying the foundation for further work" (pp. 174–5).[11]

Morgenstern's reaching out to Menger here unwittingly revealed the mere two degrees of separation that stood between his meditations on general equilibrium and the tumult of Viennese politics. For Menger had begun creating his formal sociology in 1933, when political tensions between the clerical conservatives under Dollfuss and the socialists of Red Vienna became so unbearable as to force him to abandon his work in mathematics proper. He turned for solace to the formal analysis of social compatibility, and his examples of smokers and non-smokers were, in fact, slightly disguised explorations of social relationships more important to him, such as those between Left and Right, or Jews and non-Jews.

There were, of course, significant differences between the theoretical difficulties of concern to Morgenstern and the simple analysis of Menger, the most important, perhaps, concerning the role of time. Menger's simple examples were entirely static: individuals took stances with regard to norms and this gave rise to various (logically) possible compatibility groups. Time played no role: there was no consideration of either evolution of attitudes or experience. Morgenstern's concern for the foresight and expectations of agents had originated in, and remained imbued with, considerations concerning the passage of time. Thus, with the benefit of hindsight, it could be said that, in reaching out to Menger's static structures, Morgenstern was unwittingly sowing the seed of a capitulation of sorts, in which his rich, and impossibly demanding, Austrian critique would be reined in and diminished in order to accomodate the limited possibilities offered by mathematics.

Such a reading is in keeping with another aspect of the story surrounding the "Perfect Foresight" paper. In early 1936, Hayek wrote to him from the LSE: "It will interest you that we recently had an interesting discussion about your essay in our seminar. Since I consider the results were really valuable and enlightening [*sic*]". Hayek went on to say that he was considering writing up the results of their seminar discussion for publication in the *Zeitschrift für Nationalökonomie* (Hayek to OM, Feb. 9, 1936).

Coming from the same Austrian background, Hayek shared Morgenstern's interest in these questions of the relationship between time, foresight and economic equilibrium. Indeed, in his own paper, Morgenstern had quoted disapprovingly an earlier article by Hayek, in which the latter, perhaps referring to Hicks, had written:

> It has become clear that in place of a simple negligence of the time-motive, well-defined assumptions must deal with the attitude of the persons concerned as regards the future. *Assumptions* of this kind, which the analysis of equilibrium must make, *are substantially that all persons concerned correctly foresee the relevant events in the future*, and this foresight has to include not only the change in objective data *but also the behaviour of all other persons*. (Hayek 1935, quoted in Morgenstern [1935] 1976: 171, italics Morgenstern's)

The response by Hayek to Morgenstern took the form of, not a ZfN publication, but his famous "Economics and Knowledge" article of 1937, in *Economica*. Here, Hayek clarified his thinking on the matter of the relationship between anticipations and equilibrium. Unlike Morgenstern, who was prepared to jettison the notion of equilibrium in the absence of a rigorous description of the behavioural underpinnings, Hayek emphasizes the observed coordinative abilities of the economy and tendency towards equilibrium, and then asks what account of foresight would be congruent with it. The existence of equilibrium simply meant that the foresight of all agents was "correct", insofar as all plans were in harmony and based upon the same knowledge and expecations.

> Correct foresight is then not, as it has sometimes been understood, a precondition which must exist in order that equilibrium may be arrived at. It is rather the defining characteristic of a state of equilibrium. Nor need foresight for this purpose be perfect in the sense that it need extend into the indefinite future, or that everybody must see everything correctly. We should rather say that equilibrium will last so long as the anticipations prove correct, and that they need to be correct only on those points which are relevant for the decisions of the individuals. (1937: 41-42)

Hayek went on to downplay the importance of empirical investigation, concluding, somewhat ambiguously, that it was more important to be clear about the principles involved.

From here on, Morgenstern and Hayek would take quite different paths. Although both were Austrian critics of neoclassical orthodoxy and general equilibrium, in their responses, beginning in the late 1930s, they diverged increasingly from one another. While Hayek developed his unique brand of social science, criticizing "scientism" in economics and promoting a liberal politics, Morgenstern embraced formal, mathematical work and became ever more suspicious of those, to the Left or the Right, who sought to make political use of economic analysis. By the time he had fallen under von Neumann's spell at Princeton, Morgenstern would become very dismissive indeed of Hayek.[12]

5. KEYNES

During the 1930s in Vienna, the figure of Keynes is clearly important for Morgenstern, but he remains spectral, hovering in the background and never fully brought into the open. In May 1934, in reference to Keynes's *Treatise on Money*, Morgenstern's friend Haberler wrote to him:

> I am convinced that you will find contradictions on every page of Keynes' book. The book is incredibly sloppily written. For instance, he always falls back onto the ordinary, same definition of saving and investment, and forgets his artificial definition, according to which losses... which one has never gotten are counted among the savings. As I hear, he is working on a new edition of the first part. I would wait with the criticism until it appears. (Haberler to OM, May 22, 1934)[13]

Morgenstern clearly drafted an article critical of the *Treatise*, but, thus far, I have been unable to find any trace of it. In September 1935, he wrote in his diary about finding his "long lost notes on Keynes":

> I am going to have them copied and then go through them with Wald. I am still positive that there is much more to be said about them than has been said up to now. For example, that (PI) should contain all prices, but P only consumption goods, P' investment goods. Where are the old ones, and the wages?! and many other absurdities. For example, his impossible definition of saving, which again is only the *additional* saving. (Diary, September 9, 1935)

The following month, he wrote that Wald found his article on Keynes to be "mathematically alright", and that he was going to send it for publication "to Chicago".[14] To Knight, at the *Journal of Political Economy*, he announced the submission as an amended verion of his "Perfect Foresight" article, with added observations on risk. "I have a certain interest to have this article appear in English because Mr. Keynes is preparing a book on the theory of money based largely on the element of expectation and anticipation" (OM to Knight, Dec. 18, 1935). Not only was the proposal rendered nugatory by the appearance of the *General Theory* (1936), but Knight loved the "Perfect Foresight" article as it stood, describing it as "a major piece of work", and even translating it himself, releasing it as a Chicago mimeo.[15]

Among Morgenstern's correspondents, Keynes's new book met with cursory abuse. "Have you read Keynes already?", wrote Haberler. "There are rather ghastly things in the book [so] that a purely logical critic would, I believe, have a field day! For example, the story of the multiplier seems to me utter nonsense" (Haberler to OM, March 7, 1936). By April, the book had become "simply horrible". From Chicago, Knight wrote that, while he only begun reading it, "a couple of my friends whom I consider pretty competent judges say outright that Keynes is losing his mind" (Knight to OM, May 1, 1936).

In 1937, in an eight-page appendix added to *Limits*, that year's translation of *Die Grenzen*, Morgenstern connected his critique of "time" and "expectations" to the *General Theory*:

> Mr. Keynes has given a prominent place to the role of expectations. But his analysis relating to this point is so vague that I think we shall have to wait for further elucidations from his pen before delivering final judgement on it. Obviously it is not sufficient merely to refer to expectations and anticipations. We need to know how they are determined, on what factors they depend and the ways in which they are mutually interdependent. Mr. Keynes gives no real analysis of these points." (pp. 158–9).

By the time he was collaborating on the *Theory of Games*, Morgenstern would become as dismissive of Keynes as he had been of Hayek, privately regarding him as a "scientific charlatan".[16]

For the five or six years leading up to 1938, the intellectual stance held by Morgenstern in Vienna forbids our classifying him in any familiar manner. Although a product of the Austrian school, he was increasingly critical of it and reluctant to have himself branded as such. Although essentially liberal in his economic outlook, he nonetheless retained his position of influence under Dollfuss's anti-liberal corporatist regime, until finally breaking with it in late 1937 over the question of agricultural regulation. Although mathematically trained only through private reading and tutorials with Wald and Alt, he was an energetic promoter of the kind of mathematical economics of which his Austrian teachers were sceptical.

On the matter of microfoundations, the subject of this collection, several aspects of Morgenstern's thinking are worth emphasizing. To the extent that he attached critical importance to finding what he deemed a logically coherent and empirically appropriate conception of the rational economic agent, Morgenstern was very much concerned with "microfoundations". It was in this spirit that he criticized general equilibrium theory and Keynes's economics, and his emphasis on formal rigour was one of the features that distanced him from Hayek. Yet the very breadth and variety of the objects of his criticism, not to mention the newness of Keynes's work, mean that it would be wrong to see Morgenstern in the 1930s as being concerned with the foundations of "macroeconomics". The meaning of the latter had not yet become stable, and nowhere does Morgenstern write as if he understood his work in terms of the now acceptable micro–macro dichotomy. To put it bluntly, his work questioned the foundations of every kind of economics that came his way, and it speaks to the disciplinary flux and instabilities of the period.

Throughout the mid-1930s, Morgenstern intended to collect these critical/theoretical articles in the form of a book, to be called *Time, Profit and Economic Equilibrium*, and he was still considering it after he moved to Princeton in 1938. Then, he was deflected in this when he fell in with John von Neumann.

6. TO PRINCETON

Having already done so elsewhere, I shall not enter in detail into the collaboration in the years leading up to the *Theory of Games*. Rather, I would like to discuss the extent to which foundational criticism was important to that partnership, and the way in which that collaboration marked the death of Morgenstern as an "Austrian" economist.

Morgenstern and von Neumann met at a time when both were slightly vulnerable. The former had left Vienna in early 1938, just before the *Anschluss* of Austria and, with that, the takeover of his research Institute by Ernest Wagemann, director of the Berlin equivalent. While many Viennese intellectuals and academics, especially Jews, had begun leaving the city after 1933, Morgenstern had hung on till the end, enjoying influence as a public economist, even co-existing with the Austrofascist regime from 1934 till 1938. Then, he found himself at Princeton, stripped of all such power and influence, and he had to invent himself anew. No longer being concerned with Austrian policy issues, he was free to concentrate fully on theory.

Von Neumann had been at Princeton – first the University and then the Institute for Advanced Study – since the early 1930s, and was thoroughly settled in America. The late 1930s, however, was a particularly unsettling time for him. His first wife abandoned him in December 1937, so he spent much of 1938 in Hungary and other European countries, trying to arrange the exodus of his future wife, Klara Dán. These personal difficulties were compounded by the turns being taken in Hungarian politics, with the institutionalization of anti-Semitism and consequent pressure on both his and his in-laws' families. While both families did escape Hungary during this time, von Neumann's exiled father-in-law then committed suicide at Princeton in December 1939. All in all, this was a difficult time for von Neumann and it had the effect of destroying his scientific output for two years.

This commotion, however, was also what brought him back to game theory. By the late 1930s, von Neumann had done essentially nothing in game theory since publishing the 1928 paper, in which he had proved the minimax theorem for the two-person, zero-sum game and briefly surmised that larger games might be analysed in terms of the payoffs available to coalitions of players. Now, over ten years later, when confronted with political developments in Hungary and Europe, von Neumann was drawn towards the analysis of social and political alliances, in a manner not unreminiscent of Karl Menger in Vienna in 1933. That is why the 1944 *Theory of Games* is taken up with, above all, the analysis of equilibria in coalitional games, with a central, stabilizing role being played by social norms as regards discrimination towards certain players or groups.

In early 1940, therefore, Morgenstern found the mathematician necessary to fill the gap after separating from his Viennese colleagues, and in von Neumann an interlocutor open to his re-nascent theory. There were also affective factors involved, with Morgenstern acting as buffer between the sometimes tense Hungarian couple. Together, Morgenstern and the von Neumanns were part of Princeton's *Mitteleuropa* community-in-exile, which included Einstein, Hermann Weyl, Carl Siegel, Gödel, and, on occasion, Thomas Mann. All were concerned by what was happening back in wartime Europe. These circumstances lent a degree of intimacy and humanity to the game theory collaboration that went beyond mere professional academic co-authorship.

The initial effect of Morgenstern's encounter with von Neumann was to bring renewed energy to his campaign as critic. This can be felt in his harsh review of Hicks' 1939 *Value and Capital*, a book he described as one of "the most unreadable works... on economic theory" (1941a: 364). Pointing to Wald's (1936) and von Neumann's (1937) proofs in general equilibrium, Morgenstern dismisses Hicks's assumption that the counting of equations and unknowns is sufficient to guarantee the determinateness of a linear system. He also condemns the "indiscriminate use of the word 'equilibrium'"... "If the respective equilibrium is not qualified further as being either stabile, labile or indifferent, the whole statement hangs in the air, adding to the usual vagueness of the usual procedure... Some of these equilibrium conditions need not at all conform to the ordinary simple maximums or minimums. They are most likely of the so-called 'minimax' type, the analysis of which requires instruments of great subtlety" (pp. 374–5, footnote). In-keeping with what we have seen earlier, Keynes is criticized for his imprecise treatment of expectations, and it is quite likely that it is to Hayek that Morgenstern is referring when he condemns the lack of clarity in the discussion of "consistency of plans" and equilibrium:

> It is obvious that ... it has not been decided whether there exists only one single grouping of plans which is compatible with equilibrium or whether there are many possible ones, each of which would be "consistent". In order to decide a problem of this kind it is, naturally, necessary to be more specific about the character of the plans or, in other words, to define them more specifically. The problems involved are of quite exceptional difficulty and resemble closely those of the theory of games. (p. 380)

Throughout this phase, Morgenstern's thinking was dominated by what he called the "Prediction-Time Complex". In 1940, stimulated by these new discussions with the Hungarian, he began writing his "Quantitative Implications of Maxims of Behavior" (1941b), in which, albeit in a purely discursive manner, he attempts to extend the analysis of interacting decisions beyond what he had seen achieved in Menger (1934b). Unlike the latter, he is particularly concerned with what he terms *restricted maxims* – that is, actions which cannot be executed regardless of how others behave with respect to them, such as drawing deposits from the bank. "The individual's decision to act according to such a maxim will depend upon their evaluation of how others are likely to act, all of which places great demands upon the intelligence of the acting individuals" (Morgenstern 1941b: 8).

Making the connection between this embryonic analysis and politics, Morgenstern argues that such situations highlight the potential for positive interventionism, in order to substitute for individual subjective rationality: for example, the imposition of a moratorium on bank withdrawals, in order to protect deposits, would accomplish what each individual would desire if they were in a position to take full account of the intended actions of other account holders. Such intervention, by providing a "substitute for the corrective which superior information and intelligence would offer", would not be vulnerable to the "criticisms which are voiced against every intervention by the adherents of a purely laisser-faire attittude" (p. 17). It was another step away from Austrian liberalism and once again, as in the Hicks essay, von Neumann's recent work on games is cited as a possible approach to such situations.

7. ENTERING VON NEUMANN'S UNIVERSE

While von Neumann read several of Morgenstern's Vienna papers, including "The Time Moment" (1934b), and now the Hicks review and "Maxims", he independently extended his theory of games to situations of three, four and more players. The result was what became the *Theory of Games and Economic Behavior* (von Neumann and Morgenstern [1944] 1947), a 630-page exploration of games of different sizes, with an elaborate introduction that was written by Morgenstern and corrected and amended by von Neumann.

Philip Mirowski has written about what he calls the two conflicting "voices" in the *Theory of Games*, the "other" voice being that of the Austrian economist concerned about time and dynamics. While I agree, and have suggested above, that the latter was a defining part of Morgenstern's background, my sense is that, come the publication of the *TGEB*, there was no conflict as such, because Morgenstern had, with little resistance, made all the necessary concessions. By that, I mean that the closer he drew to von Neumann, and to the realities of actual, mathematical creativity, the more he found himself tailoring his theoretical ambitions and rescinding his vestigial Austrianism.

Three vignettes from the *TGEB* allow us to explore various facets of the work in relationship to Morgenstern's foundational critique. I will consider the book's Introduction, its resolution of the Holmes–Moriarty dilemma, and von Neumann's sophisticated analysis of coalitional games.

The Introduction represents the meeting of the two minds, motivating the *TGEB* by reference to the lacunae of orthodox neoclassicism. Simple utility maximisation and Walrasian general equilibrium are rejected as the primitive, uninventive application of rational mechanics to the social domain. This comes from von Neumann who, as Mirowski has pointed out, viewed the work of Hicks, and later Samuelson, with great disdain. The Austrians, of course, including Mayer, Mises and Hayek, would have agreed with the dismissal of mechanical general equilibrium, but not through a conviction that a better mathematical economics was possible. It is thus a measure of the distance travelled by Morgenstern that he was now viewing the matter from von Neumann's perspective – without, of course, the latter's back-ground or accumulated mathematical training. This, in turn, explains the numerous references in his diary to the deep transformation he was under-going: learning, nay struggling, to see the world in an (appropriate) math-ematical way. Similarly, the introductory chapter also rejects the idea that there is any fundamental distinction between social and natural science, between *Geisteswissenschaft* and *Naturwissenschaft*. This was an affirma-tion of what Morgenstern had begun thinking during the 1930s, at Karl Menger's instigation, and it, too, represented a shift away from the found-ing Austrian ideas of Menger Sr.[17]

The reason why the mathematics of constrained utility maximisation was irrelevant was because it failed to address the fundamental conceptual starting points: decisions were very often dependent upon the evaluation, not of fixed constraints, but of the likely decisions of others. Hence the similarity between social interactions and games, and, with that, the need for a new mathematics, crafted especially for the domain. Nor was it clear, they write, that the analysis of games of increasing numbers of players would automatically lead to a re-emergence of a coalition-free, perfectly competitive situation.

Behind this measured expression of doubt about the relevance of perfect competition lay von Neumann's gut conviction of the importance of multiple social equilibria: a single physical background could give rise to many different possible social structures, something that had been brought home to him through his confrontation with politics in the 1930s. The discussion of foundations, therefore, and thus the introductory chapter, came *after* the creative mathematical work had been done by von Neu-mann. It was a *post hoc* construction in which Morgenstern could join, essential in motivating, for the reader, the difficult theory that followed, yet of secondary importance to it from the point of view of von Neumann's scientific creativity. "One of these days", wrote Morgenstern on New Year's Day, 1943, "I have to write down a few things about the story of the book (and my minimal share; but I seem to have acted as a kind of catalytic factor)".

On pages 176–8, the *Theory of Games* resolves the Holmes–Moriarty dilemma, presenting it as a two-person, zero-sum game and solving it through the application of mixed strategies. It is assumed that, to Moriarty, catching Holmes is worth 100; missing him at the intermediate station worth –50 (since he gets all the way to the Dover port); and missing him at Dover worth 0 (since he remains somewhere in the country and doesn't escape to the Continent). With these payoffs, Moriarty should go to Dover with a probability of 60%, and Holmes should get off at Canterbury with a probability of 60%.

In a footnote to this analysis, Morgenstern explains that he no longer holds the "pessimistic views" he expressed when he first cited this Holmes–Moriarty dilemma, in *Wirtschaftsprognose*, or in his "Perfect Foresight" article of 1935 (p. 176, n.2). Simple though it may be, this is a particularly "pregnant" footnote. For while the minimax analysis solves the decision-making task of Holmes and Moriarty, it offers little by way of response to the problems of prediction that originally motivated Morgenstern's use of the story in *Wirtschaftsprognose*. Recall that Morgenstern was concerned there with showing why complexity could only result in the defeat of an economic prediction. In particular, a government that tried to revise its prediction in order to anticipate the public reactions to its first forecast would cause so much disturbance amongst the multiplicity of economic agents that "the economic equilibrium would be disturbed profoundly" (Morgenstern, 1928: 98). All actions would stop and "economic subjects and entrepreneurs would wait for a stabilization of the system of orientation points which was shifted in an artificial way. All economic plans – and intentions are contined in the plan and its duration – would be postponed. Only misery and lightmindedness would govern" (*ibid.*). That this nihilistic 1928 emphasis on confusion amongst multiple, heterogeneous subjects is now being dismissed as unduly "pessimistic", is a measure of Morgenstern's evolution from Austrian critic in 1928 to analytical co-author 15 years later.

Similarly, in "Perfect Foresight and Economic Equilibrium", the Holmes–Moriarty example was used to illustrate the difficulties raised by the assumption of perfect foresight in agents in general equilibrium. Under such an assumption, the individual has perfect foresight into all aspects of the economic process: prices, production, revenue. Given the extent to which all economic phenomena are interdependent, this logically implies incredible powers on the part of the economic agent:

> The individual exercising foresight must thus not only know exactly the influence of his own transactions on prices but also the influence of every other individual, and of own future behaviour on that of the others ...
> ... The impossibly high claims which are attributed to the intellectual efficiency of the economic subject immediately indicate that there are included in this equilibrium system not ordinary men, but rather ... demi-gods, in [the] case [where] the claim of complete foresight is fulfilled. (p. 173)

With its two players and two strategies, the Holmes–Moriarty situation once again represents a drastic simplification, this time of the general disequilibrium complexities emphasized by Morgenstern in "Perfect Foresight". Only having been swept away by von Neumann's knowledge and wizardry could he choose to emphasize the technical solution and dismiss as unduly pessimistic his complex critique of a decade earlier.

In mid-April, 1942, having watched von Neumann spend two hours constructing the axiomatics of cardinal utility, Morgenstern marvelled in his diary: "It gave me great satisfaction, and moved me so much that afterwards I could not think about anything else. I feel more and more the aesthetic pleasure linked with mathematics. I believe that this is one of the main characteristics" (Diary, April 14, 1942).

This emphasis upon aesthetics was very much von Neumann's, and he explained its place in his philosophy of mathematics in an essay, "The Mathematician", published in 1947. What did one look for in mathematical practice?, von Neumann asked:

> Ease in stating the problem, great difficulty in getting hold of it and in all attempts at approaching it, then again some very surprising twist by the approach, or some part of the approach, becomes easy, etc. Also, if the deductions are lengthy, or complicated, there should be some general principle involved, which "explains" the complications and detours, reduces the apparent arbitrariness to a few simple guiding motivations etc. These criteria are clearly those of any creative art, and the existence of some underlying empirical, worldly motif in the background – often in a very remote background – overgrown by aestheticizing developments and followed into a multitude of labyrinthine variants – all this is much more akin to the atmosphere of art pure and simple than to that of the empirical sciences" (1947: 9).

I have argued elsewhere that this style of mathematical creativity is in evidence in the *TGEB*. In particular, von Neumann explicitly adopts a "Modern" style, which involves alternating, in a largely opportunistic manner, between purely mathematical deduction and heuristic justification of the resulting insights. The guiding belief is that unearthing the formalism can reveal truths about the world.

While the mathematics in the *Theory of Games* tends to be laborious rather than beautiful, von Neumann's exploration of stable set solutions to cooperative games provides many examples of this opportunistic mathematical philosophy in action. One is in Chapter XI, where, faced with the task of applying the stable set solution to non zero-sum games, he invents the device of the "fictitious player", in order to transform non-zero sum games into zero-sum. Another is in Chapter VII (pp. 314–20), where his exploration of the solutions to the zero-sum, four-person game involves some subtle discussion, linking mathematical properties and features of social organisation. I cannot convey the exact details here without entering upon several pages of technical presentation. Suffice it to say that heuristic consideration of the game leads to the suggestion of imputations (that is, coalitions with their associated payoffs). These, however, are shown to be mathematically insufficient to constitute a solution (that is, one that respects the technical criteria of the stable-set, which, as a formal entity has power for von Neumann). Thus, he adds the technically-necessary imputations, and resorts, on his own admission, to somewhat contrived arguments in order to justify their inclusion. He admits freely that it is now the *mathematics* that is generating the plausibility arguments, and that he is not entirely convinced by the latter, but that this free-flight of the mathematics is a well-known occurrence in mathematical–physical theories. In another variant further on, identifying a group of imputations that constitute a stable set, he even goes so far as to suggest that the complexity and delicacy of the particular social inter-relations described are "due to the solution rather than to the game itself" (p. 320). Parts of von Neumann's commentary in the *Theory of Games* seem to be pervaded by a metaphysical faith in the formalism being constructed.

With this, Morgenstern was carried into mathematical terrain for which not even his most difficult lessons with Wald, or discussions with Menger, had adequately prepared him. It was one thing to look to Menger for exactitude in the law of diminishing returns, or for hints as to how to treat restricted maxims formally. It was quite another to enter a world in which empirics, deduction and aesthetics were freely combined, where the mathematics became not merely a language for the representation of social relations but a source of hidden knowledge about them. Morgenstern was the first of many to be astonished by the *Theory of Games*.

In his writings on game theory after 1944, Morgenstern, in general, stuck closely to several basic ideas: that game theory overcame the mistaken dependence on rational mechanics; that it provided a way of modelling strategic interaction (for example, where the player does not control all the variables); that it provided a way of understanding the emergence of coalitions (here, he tended to emphasize the applications to monopolistic behaviour); and that it remained to be seen whether increasing the number of players in a game permitted the reassertion of perfect competition (see, for example, Morgenstern 1948; 1949a, b). In these writings, he orientates the theory of games towards possible economic applications, such as to imperfect competition. There is relatively little discussion of what had, for von Neumann, constituted a key impetus, namely the determination of social organization, with different equilibria depending upon social norms. Also, there is very little mention of the more philosophically "adventurous" parts of the *TGEB*, such as von Neumann's fictitious players or sophisticated exploration of the mathematics of the stable set.

8. CONCLUSION

Morgenstern's engagement with foundational critique was a defining feature of his intellectual identity. He began as a near-typical product of the Austrian School, formed by Mayer and Mises, and concerned to show the impossibility of prediction, given the complexity of the interaction between the expectations, beliefs and decisions of heterogenous economic actors. His engagement with foundational critique continued, even when he himself began to pull away from his Austrian heritage.

There were at least two elements to his withdrawal from Austrianism. Firstly, the more he became involved with colleagues in mathematics, the more he learned to respect precise language, and, consequently, the more suspicious he became of the Austrian tendency, particularly amongst Mises and Hayek, to identify economics with a liberal politics. Secondly, while his essays of the 1930s, on the need to properly account for time in economic theory, and on the need to specify the degree of foresight of agents in general equilibrium, are very much "Austrian"-inspired, the manner in which Morgenstern sought clarification in mathematics was not. Because of the difficulties of responding to Austrian criticisms with formal, mathematical methods, Morgenstern's Austrianism was inevitably compromised.

A key source of the tension pervading his writings, and private reflections, is the fact that while he made appeals to mathematicians for theoretical help, he himself was not mathematically trained, despite lessons and considerable efforts on his part. While in his dealings with Menger and Wald he remained at arm's length from the mathematics, this changed when he was sucked into von Neumann's vortex. He now had to engage fully with a mathematician in the throes of creating a new work. Morgenstern's introduction to the *Theory of Games and Economic Behavior* emphasizes foundational matters. While this expresses the reasons why Morgenstern found the theory of games to be so attractive, it was a *post hoc* rationalization as far as von Neumann was concerned. His creation of game theory was sparked by personal engagements, not by foundational critique. Because the theory of games was not only mathematical but concerned with providing a static analysis of coalitions, whose agents were homogeneous as far as their knowledge and reasoning powers are concerned, it necessarily involved the disappearance of any remaining traces of Morgenstern's Austrianism.[18] Looking back at Vienna from Princeton, he said as much himself:

> I have the impression that my former scientific life was just full of vague presentiments. I have probably always expected a lot from mathematics and

logic, but I was so mistrustful in some aspects, partially under the influence of K. Menger, and rightly so. Since I have known Johnny, everything has changed, and a completely new *era* has started for me. I am not at all sad that I haven't some (many!) papers, because they would mean nothing to me today. (Diary, December 5, 1943)

NOTES

* For stimulating comments on an earlier draft, I would like to thank an anonymous referee, Pedro Garcia Duarte, Gilberto Tadeu Lima, Fabio Barbieri, and the other participants and discussants at the Sao Paulo conference on which this volume is based. I would like to thank Duke University for access to, and permission to quote from, the Oskar Morgenstern Papers. The research underlying this chapter was made possible by a research grant from the Canadian Social Sciences and Humanities Research Council. The full, book-length story of which this paper is part may be found in Leonard (2010).

1. I write "Austrian" here to signify the heterogeneity it implied: although Mayer and Mises regarded themselves as members of the Austrian School, their critical contributions differed in many ways. As for Spann, he was far removed from Austrianism, describing the evolution of society in terms of a holistic, dialectical teleology.

2. It appears that no trace of Morgenstern's thesis is to be found in the archives.

3. For a closer discussion of the early influences on Morgenstern, see Leonard (2004).

4. While Mayer's and von Mises' critiques of equilibrium economics shared common features, there was so much personal antipathy between the two men that any form of cooperation was impossible. The hostility seems to have been related to professional jealousy, with Mises having been denied a chair at the University of Vienna. It was further compounded when Mayer was complicit in the dismissal of Jews from the Economic Society in 1938. This would cast Mayer into the historical shadows for a good two generations.

5. An unpaid lecturing position, the Dozentship represented the first rung on the university teaching scale.

6. Hayek to Morgenstern, April 2, 1934.

7. In an appendix to the 1937 translation, Morgenstern explicitly mentions Mises' *a priorism* as "one of the points where he diverges fundamentally from the view point put forward in the foregoing chapters" (1937: 156).

8. Other considerations also appear to have affected his relationship with his former teachers, including a failed bid by a group, including Mises and Mayer, to gain Rockefeller funding for a research group in the social sciences, parallel to Morgenstern's Institute. By the end of 1934, the latter could write that Mises and Mayer were not going to be asked to the Institute anymore (Diary, Dec. 9, 1934). On this episode, see Leonard (2011).

9. For all that, Morgenstern never achieved any significant mastery of mathematics himself, remaining, above all, a critic keen to engage with mathematicians. It may have been that this "distance" from mathematics contributed to his effectiveness, allowing him to concentrate on the broader theoretical picture without becoming absorbed in the technical details.

10. In this, Morgenstern comes as close as was possible in the mid-1930s to dismissing what several decades later would become the hypothesis of "rational expectations".

11. Schlick ([1930] 1939) was a significant stimulus for Menger's 1934 book. As for Morgenstern's "Logistics and the Social Sciences" of 1936, suffice it to say that it is essentially a repetition, for economists, of Menger's 1932 public lecture, "The New Logic". Only a formal approach to economics can overcome the pitfalls posed by the use of ordinary language. Menger's "logic of wants or wishes" is held up as a starting point for the rigorous analysis of economic wants (Morgenstern 1936: 404).

12. Thus, by 1942, Hayek's *Pure Theory of Capital* was "higher nonsense". Hayek keeps "talking about an 'Investment Function', but there is no question of stating the concept with any precision. He does not seem to know what a function really is. This type of 'economic theory' *must* vanish" (Diary, March 15, 1942). A year and a half later, "Yesterday a letter from Hayek. He hates science as he always has. He claims to have heard 'many curious rumours' about the book. Funny. He is going to find it even more 'curious' when he sees it. . . He is in a dead end. The Pure Theory of Capital is not worth reading" (Diary, September 1, 1943). "Reading Hayek's Serfdom. It's not worth a lot. Only wonderful in its love of freedom. He should look up what is said in our book about symmetry and fairness! There is nothing profound in it. Naturally I don't like planning either, but the intellectual situation is much more complicated" (Diary, Oct. 25, 1944).
13. This was followed by another letter in which Haberler wrote, "As my wife told me, you also believe now that your Keynes criticism is justified. I am looking forward to the new version" (Haberler to OM, July 11, 1934).
14. Diary, Oct. 26, 1935
15. Knight to OM, May 1, 1936.
16. See Diary, May 2, 1943.
17. In his "Neuere Fortschritte", Karl Menger rejects this distinction, thereby distancing himself from the Austrian tradition inspired by his father. Elsewhere, he would write about the tussle between the "two souls within his breast" (Goethe): that of the mathematician and that of the Austrian economist.
18. In keeping with our earlier claim that Morgenstern was not concerned with the microfoundations of "macroeconomics" per se, it is worth noting that the culmination of his quest, von Neumann's game theory, was not directed towards understanding unemployment, inflation or other aggregates. Concerned with equilibrium coalition-formation in games of varying size, it was a new mathematics of social organisation, intended to take account of the existence of discrimination and power.

REFERENCES

Baumol, William J. and Stephen M. Goldfeld (eds) (1968) *Precursors in Mathematical Economics: An Anthology*. LSE Series Reprints of Scarce Works on Political Economy, No. 19. London: LSE.
von Böhm-Bawerk, Eugen (1914). *Macht oder Okonomisches Gesetz*. Wien: Manzsche k. u. k. Hof-Verlags und Universitats-Buchhandlung, pp. 205–71.
Hayek, Friedrich (1937). Economics and Knowledge. *Economica*, 4 (N.S.):33–54.
Hicks, John (1939). *Value and Capital*. Oxford: Clarendon Press.
Hicks, John R. and Wilhelm Weber (eds) (1973). *Carl Menger and the Austrian School of Economics*. Oxford: Clarendon.
Keynes, John Maynard (1930a). *A Treatise on Money*. Vol. 1: *The Pure Theory of Money*. Reprinted in Keynes (1971–88), Vol. 5.
Keynes, John Maynard (1930b) *A Treatise on Money*. Vol. 2: *The Applied Theory of Money*. Reprinted in Keynes (1971–88), Vol. 6.
Keynes, John Maynard (1936). *The General Theory of Employment, Interest and Money*. London: Macmillan.
Keynes, John Maynard (1971–88). *Collected Writings*. London: Macmillan, for the Royal Economic Society.
Leonard, Robert (2004). Between Worlds: or an Imagined Reminiscence about Equilibrium and Mathematics in the 1920s. *Journal of the History of Economic Thought*, 26 (3):285–310.

Leonard, Robert (2010). *Von Neumann, Morgenstern and the Creation of Game Theory: From Chess to Social Science, 1900–1960.* Cambridge: Cambridge University Press.

Leonard, Robert (2011). The Collapse of Interwar Vienna: Oskar Morgenstern's Community, 1925–50. *History of Political Economy*, 43 (1):83–130.

Mayer, Hans ([1932] 1994). Der Erkenntniswert der funktionellen Preistheorien. In *Die Wirtschaftstheorie der Gegenwart.* Translated and reprinted as "The Cognitive Value of Functional Theories of Price, Critical and Positive Investigations Concerning the Price Problem". In *Classics in Austrian Economics, A Sampling in the History of a Tradition.* Edited by Israel Kirzner. London: William Pickering.

Menger, Karl (ed.) (1928–1936). *Ergebnisse eines Mathematischen Kolloquiums.* Seven Volumes. Leipzig and Vienna: Deuticke.

Menger, Karl (1933). Die Neue Logik. In *Krise und Neuaufbau in den Exakten Wissenschaften. Fünf Wiener Worträge.* Leipzig and Vienna: Deuticke. Translated by H.B. Gottlieb and J.K. Senior as "The New Logic" in *Philosophy of Science*, 4:299–336. Reprinted in Menger (1979), pp. 17–45, with prefatory notes on "Logical Tolerance in the Vienna Circle", pp. 11–6.

Menger, Karl (1934a). Das Unsicherheitsmoment in der Wertlehre. Betrachtungen in Anschluss an das sogenannte Petersburger Spiel. *Zeitschrift für Nationalökonomie*, 5:459–85. Translated as "The Role of Uncertainty in Economics" in Menger (1979), pp. 259–78.

Menger, Karl (1934b). *Moral, Wille und Weltgestaltung. Grundlegung zur Logik der Sitten.* Julius Springer: Vienna. Translated as *Morality, Decision and Social Organization. Towards a Logic of Ethics.* Dordrecht: Reidel, 1974.

Menger, Karl (1936). Bemerkungen zu den Ertragsgesetzen. *Zeitschrift für Nationalökonomie*, 7:25–6, and Weitere Bemerkungen zu den Ertragsgesetzen, *ibid*, pp. 388-97. Translated as "The Logic of the Laws of Return. A Study in Meta-Economics" in Morgenstern (ed.) (1954), pp. 419–81. Revision of translation as "Remarks on the Law of Diminishing Returns. A Study in Meta-Economics" in Menger (1979), pp. 279–302.

Menger, Karl (1979). *Selected Papers in Logic and Foundations, Didactics, Economics.* Dordrecht: Reidel.

von Mises, Ludwig ([1933] 1960). *Epistemological Problems of Economics.* Princeton: Van Nostrand.

Morgenstern, Oskar (1928). *Wirtschaftsprognose: Eine Untersuchung ihrer Voraussetzungen und Möglichkeiten.* Vienna: Julius Springer.

Morgenstern, Oskar ([1934a] 1937). *Die Grenzen der Wirtschaftspolitik.* Vienna: Julius Springer. Translated and revised by Vera Smith as "The Limits of Economics" (1937).

Morgenstern, Oskar ([1934b] 1976). Das Zeitmoment in der Wertlehre. *Zeitschrift für Nationalokonomie*, 5 (4):433–58. Translated as "The Time Moment in Economic Theory" in Schotter (ed.) (1976), pp. 151–67.

Morgenstern, Oskar ([1935] 1976). Vollkommene Voraussicht und Wirtschaftliches Gleichgewicht. *Zeitschrift für Nationalkonomie*, 6 (3):337–57. Translated as "Perfect Foresight and Economic Equilibrium" by Frank Knight, mimeo, Univ. of Chicago. Reprinted in Schotter (ed.) (1976), pp. 169–83.

Morgenstern, Oskar (1936). Logistics and the Social Sciences. *Zeitschrift für Nationalokonomie*, Vol. 7, No. 1, pp. 1–24, translated in Schotter (ed.) 1976, pp. 389-404.

Morgenstern, Oskar (1937). *The Limits of Economics*. London: W. Hodge. Translation of Morgenstern (1934a), by Vera Smith.

Morgenstern, Oskar (1941a). Professor Hicks on Value and Capital. *Journal of Political Economy*, 49 (3):361–93.

Morgenstern, Oskar (1941b). Quantitative Implications of Maxims of Behavior. Unpublished manuscript, Princeton University.

Morgenstern, Oskar (1948). Oligopoly, Monopolistic Competition, and the Theory of Games. *American Economic Review*, 38 (2, Papers and Proceedings):10–32.

Morgenstern, Oskar (1949a). The Theory of Games. *Scientific American*, 80:22–5.

Morgenstern, Oskar (1949b). Economics and the Theory of Games. *Kyklos*, 3 (4):294–308.

von Neumann, John (1928). Zur Theorie der Gesellschaftsspiele. *Mathematische Annalen*, 100, 295–320. Translated by S. Bargmann as "On the Theory of Games of Strategy" in Tucker A. W. and R. D. Luce (eds) (1959), pp. 13–42.

von Neumann, John (1937). Über ein ökonomisches Gleichungssystem und eine Verallgemeinerung des Brouwerschen Fixpunktsatzes, *Ergebnisse eines Mathematischen Kolloquiums*, 8: 73–83. Translated as (1945) A Model of General Economic Equilibrium. *Review of Economic Studies*, 13: 1–9.

von Neumann, John (1947). The Mathematician. In *The Works of the Mind*. Edited by R. B. Heywood, pp. 180–96. Reprinted in Taub (ed.) (1963), Vol. I, pp. 1–9.

von Neumann, John and Oskar Morgenstern ([1944] 1947). *The Theory of Games and Economic Behavior*. Princeton: Princeton University Press.

Robbins, Lionel ([1932] 1935). *An Essay on the Nature and Significance of Economic Science*. London: Macmillan.

Schlick, Moritz ([1930] 1939). *Fragen der Ethik*. Vienna: Springer. Translated as *Problems of Ethics*. New York: Prentice Hall.

Schotter, Andrew (ed.) (1976). *Selected Economic Writings of Oskar Morgenstern*. New York: NYU Press.

Taub, Alfred H. (ed.) (1963). *John von Neumann, Collected Works*, Vols. I-VI. New York: Macmillan.

Tucker, A. W. and R. D. Luce (eds) (1959). Contributions to the Theory of Games. Vol. IV, Princeton: Princeton University Press.

Wald, Abraham (1935). Uber die Produktionsgleichungen der ökonomischen Wertlehre", in Karl Menger (ed.) (1936), *Ergebnisse eines Mathematischen Kolloquiums*, Vol. 7, 1934–35, Leipzig and Vienna: Franz Deuticke, pp. 1–6. Translated as "On the Production Equations of Economic Value Theory", in Baumol and Goldfeld (1968), pp. 289–93.

3. The rise and fall of Walrasian microeconomics: the Keynesian effect[1]

D. Wade Hands[2]

We may digress to point out that the general point of view and habit of mind reflected in the Hicks–Slutzky analysis has wide ramifications in recent literature and has led to utter confusion in the whole body of economic thought. We refer, of course, to the huge corpus of discussion beginning with Keynes's *General Theory* and following the lead of that work. (Frank Knight, 1944: 300)

1. INTRODUCTION

Pronouncements of the death of Walrasian microeconomics have become quite common in recent years. For a growing number of economists, the research program that was once the discipline's showpiece of rigor and technical sophistication "has finally run out of gas" (Rizvi, 1998, 274) and should be moved from the front lines of economic research to the back-burner of retrospective reflection (Bowles and Gintis 2000). In many cases the target for the narrative of demise is narrowly-focused on the most abstract version of Walrasian general equilibrium theory, and in such cases the story is usually that it succumbed to a host of internal technical difficulties, particularly those associated with stability analysis and the Sonnenschein–Mantel–Debreu (SMD) theorems on excess demand functions (Kirman 1989, 2006, Rizvi 1998, 2003). In other cases the target is much broader – neoclassical economics or rational choice theory in general – and here the downfall is often associated with the theory's questionable empirical record and the recent development of alternative approaches such as behavioral economics, experimental economics, and the economics of complexity (Colander 2000, 2006; Colander, Holt and Rosser 2004a, 2004b, Davis 2006, 2008). Commensurate with, although relatively independent of, these narratives about the fall of Walrasian microeconomics, a body of historical literature has developed during the last few decades

which gives us a deeper understanding of the various forces that contributed to the rise of Walrasian economics and how the resulting theory came
to take the particular form that it did. A few of the many books covering
aspects of this recent historical literature include Amadae (2003), Giocoli
(2003), Ingrao and Israel (1990), Mirowski (2002), and Weintraub (1985,
1991, 2002), but the relevant research is quite extensive and this is only the
tip of the iceberg.[3]

This chapter will also discuss the rise, and to a lesser extent the fall, of
Walrasian microeconomics, but it will focus on an aspect of the story that
has received very little attention: the role of *Keynesian economics*. Of
course, there already exists an extensive literature on the relationship
between the Walrasian and Keynesian research programs. For example, the
histories of macroeconomics offered by the Cambridge-centered critics of
IS-LM Keynesianism that Alan Coddington once labeled the "Fundamen-
talist Keynesians" (Coddington 1983), clearly emphasize the relationship
between Walrasian and Keynesian economics. They argue, as do post-
Keynesians of a variety of stripes, that Walrasian ideas – initiated by John
R. Hicks's original IS-LM paper (Hicks 1937) – influenced, and ultimately
corrupted, the central message of John Maynard Keynes's *General Theory*
(1936).[4] The economists Coddington labeled "Reconstituted Reduction-
ists" (Clower 1965, Leijonhufvud 1968) have a different take, but they too
have drawn attention to, and criticized, the Walrasian influence on textbook Keynesianism. But identifying the Walrasian imprint on standard
Keynesian theory is not exclusive to those who would call themselves
Keynesians. Milton Friedman's Marshallianism was associated in part with
his identification and criticism of Walrasian theoretical influences within
Keynesian macroeconomics (see DeVroey 2009, Hoover 1988, or Mayer
2009 for example). Finally, even Hicks himself, when explaining the origins
of the IS-LM model, stressed the influence of Walrasian ideas on the
Keynesian theoretical framework he set in motion: "the idea of the IS-LM
diagram came to me as a result of the work I had been doing on three-way
exchange, conceived in a Walrasian manner" (Hicks 1980-81: 142).

Although there is an extensive literature on the relationship between
Walrasian and Keynesian economics, none of it really focuses on the issues
examined here. All of these authors, and most others who have examined
the relationship between Walrasian and Keynesian theory, have directed
the explanatory arrow from the former to the latter. The two main questions have traditionally been: How did Walrasian ideas influence, condition, or possibly determine, what came to be the standard textbook
Keynesian theory? and, Was that Walrasian influence a good thing or a bad
thing (with respect to either the scientific adequacy of the resulting theory
or its fidelity to Keynes's own thinking)? My focus will be quite different.

First and most importantly, I will run the explanatory arrow in the opposite direction: from Keynesian to Walrasian ideas. I want to explain not how Walrasian ideas played a role in shaping what became standard textbook Keynesian macroeconomics, but rather how Keynesian ideas played a role in shaping what came to be the standard textbook Walrasian micro-economics (with Arrow and Hahn 1971 as the canonical text). Secondly, my interest will be more explanatory than evaluative; I will focus on identifying influences and revealing the profession's theoretical preferences, not on evaluating whether those influences and preferences were scientifically a good thing or a bad thing (or whether they were exegetically faithful).

The chapter is organized in the following way. The first section lays out some definitions and presuppositions relevant to the overall discussion. Given that the argument cuts across such a wide swath of time, individuals, and ideas, it is useful to be clear right up-front how important terms will be used and to point out some of the things that will be taken as given throughout the chapter. The second section is the heart of the argument and the chapter's main contribution. This section argues that Keynesian ideas played a role in the Walrasian rise to dominance and also influenced the content of the particular "Walrasian" theory that ultimately emerged. The neoclassical synthesis was a two-way street with influence between Walrasian and Keynesian ideas flowing both ways, and the particular versions of both "Keynesian macro" and "Walrasian micro" that stabilized during the mid-twentieth century were joint products of that synthesis. The third section discusses the connection between the neoclassical synthesis and the fall (or at least demotion) of Walrasian microeconomics. The final section contains a brief summary and a review of the main themes of the chapter.

2. A FEW PRESUPPOSITIONS AND STAGE-SETTING FOR WHAT FOLLOWS

I will talk about Walrasian economics and Keynesian economics as if they were research programs that can clearly be distinguished from other theoretical frameworks and are sufficiently stable to be identified, and re-identified, across various points in time.[5] Although I do assume that both research programs contain certain core or paradigmatic propositions/conceptualizations, this does not mean that I have captured the "essential nature" of these programs, or that such an essence even exists. These propositions are simply empirically-identifiable features of a particular sort – reliable identifiers of family resemblance – and their stability is always subject to particular time constraints. Roy Weintraub's six core propositions (Weintraub 1985: 109) do a reasonably good job identifying the key features of the Walrasian research program, and the core of the Keynesian program would include propositions such as: the short run aggregate level of output and employment are determined by aggregate expenditure; the interest rate is determined by the supply of and demand for liquidity; the marginal propensity to consume is positive and less than one; etc. Notice that accepting such core propositions – reliable identifiers of family resemblance – leaves a lot of room for variation and debate within the two research programs.

It is also useful to identify two presuppositions about the history of twentieth-century economics that will be assumed throughout the discussion. Both seem relatively uncontroversial, but it is useful to state them explicitly since they are taken as given in all of what follows. The first is that mainstream economics was dominated by the *neoclassical synthesis* from sometime during the mid-1950s until roughly the mid-1970s.[6] The neoclassical synthesis was a product of contributions by a number of different economic theorists – key texts include Hicks (1937, [1939] 1946), Lange (1944), Lerner (1944), and Samuelson (1947) – and although there were clearly differences among the various contributors, one of the main results of the synthesis was that the discipline came to be seen as an amalgam of two separate – but consistent and non-antagonistic – parts: macroeconomics and microeconomics.[7] As Paul Samuelson put it in the third edition of his famous *Economics* textbook: "the economist is justified in saying that the broad cleavage between microeconomics and macroeconomics has been closed" (Samuelson 1955: 360). The synthesis was the "instrument of reconciliation" (Pearce and Hoover 1995: 211) between these two branches of economic theory; its macroeconomics was Keynesian and its microeconomics (at least the "high theory") was Walrasian. By the 1960s the synthesis manifested itself in essentially every economics textbook in the United States (Pearce and Hoover 1995), it produced the "micro" and "macro" curricular structure that continues to dominate economics instruction, and for many years it formed the theoretical backdrop for effectively all research in economic theory.[8] As Brian Snowdon and Howard Vane explain:

> The synthesis of the ideas of the classical economists with those of Keynes dominated mainstream economics at least until the early 1970s. The standard textbook approach to macroeconomics from the period following the Second World War until the early 1970s relied heavily on the interpretation of the *General Theory* provided by Hicks (1937) and modified by the contributions of Modigliani (1944), Patinkin (1956), and Tobin (1958). Samuelson's best selling

textbook popularized the synthesis ... making them accessible to a wide readership and successive generations of students. It was Samuelson who introduced the label 'neoclassical synthesis' into the literature in the third edition of *Economics* in 1955. The synthesis of classical and Keynesian ideas became the standard approach to macroeconomic analysis, both in textbooks and in professional discussion ... (Snowdon and Vane 2005: 23)

The second historical presupposition is the *pluralism* and *diversity* that existed within microeconomics during the interwar period. Although this period was a bubbling cauldron of diverse economic ideas from Institutionalist, Marxist, and Austrian economics, this wide-ranging inter-programmatic diversity is not the diversity that will be emphasized here. The diversity emphasized in this chapter is a more intra-programmatic diversity – the diversity among various economists who were broadly marginalist or neoclassical (although not all would label themselves as such) and shared a common commitment to certain modeling strategies, mathematical tools, and types of evidence – yet who promoted and defended quite different economic theories.[9]

Focusing on demand theory, a partial list of these various approaches would include: defenders of the Marshallian tradition in either cardinal utility (Robertson 1952) or compensated demand (Friedman 1953) form; those who, Cournot- or Cassel-like, started from demand functions rather than individual choice (these took different forms including, among others, statistical (Moore 1914, Schultz 1928) and mathematical (Evans 1930) versions); Slutsky ([1915] 1952); Bernardelli (1952); Knight (1944); Gilboy (1930); Hicks and Allen (1934); Allen's non-integrable interpretation of Hicks and Allen (Allen 1936); Nicholas Georgescu-Roegen's psychological threshold (Georgescu-Roegen 1936) and directed choice (Georgescu-Roegen 1950) models; Harold Hotelling's entrepreneurial demand function model (Hotelling 1932); Ragnar Frisch's conditional preferences approach (Frisch 1926); Oskar Morgenstern's reconstituted demand theory (Morgenstern 1948); Paul Samuelson's radical behaviorism in his first "revealed preference" paper (Samuelson 1938); and W. E. Armstrong's just-perceptible-differences theory (Armstrong 1939). By the late 1950s this diversity of ways of explaining consumer choice and demand had been replaced by a Walrasian theory originating in the work of Leon Walras (1954) and Vilfredo Pareto (1971), but given its final (calculus-based) form in Hicks and Allen (1934) and Slutsky ([1915] 1952). Early influential book-length statements include Hicks's *Value and Capital* ([1939] 1946), Samuelson's *Foundations* (1947), and Henry Schultz's *Theory and Measurement of Demand* (1938); these n-good multivariate calculus-based versions of the theory formed the basis for the standard graduate microeconomics textbooks of the 1960s and 1970s (lower-level textbooks offered the same theory, but presented it in one- and two-dimensional diagrams). The argument will be that Keynesian economics had something to do with Walrasian demand theory emerging as *the* (rather than *a*) theory of demand as well as why certain aspects were emphasized and particular theoretical formulations emerged as they did.

The last two remarks I would like to make in this section are comments on, rather than presuppositions for, what is to follow. The first is that when I argue that particular aspects of Walrasian economics were "consistent with" Keynesian economics, I only mean to the architects of the neoclassical synthesis. These remarks – in fact, my entire argument – in no way implies an endorsement of the view that "Walrasian economics" and "Keynesian economics" are in any substantive sense consistent or could co-exist in a theoretical partnership indefinitely. In fact I generally agree with those who argue that the neoclassical synthesis exhibited a certain "theoretical schizophrenia" (Snowdon and Vane 2005: 21). The "fit" that formed the backbone of the neoclassical synthesis was at a best a temporary equilibrium. It existed because of the particular way the two research programs co-evolved, the historical situation (politically, economically, and epistemologically), the persuasive power of certain individuals and their self-conscious efforts to downplay differences, and many other historically contingent factors.[10]

Finally, I think it is useful right up-front to be clear about what I am not arguing. My argument is *not* that Keynesian economics was the *only* reason that the Walrasian version of neoclassicism emerged triumphant or that Walrasian microeconomics took the particular form that it did during its heyday. The reason research programs rise to dominance and the transformations they go through during their evolution is always a very complex story. In the first paragraph I cited a number of authors/texts who have recently made contributions to our understanding of the ascent and character of Walrasian general equilibrium theory. The argument here is not an alternative to those and other narratives;[11] it simply provides an additional, unrecognized, factor that deserves to be considered.

3. WHY AND WHICH WALRASIAN ECONOMICS?

This section will discuss four ways (sections 3.1–3.4) in which the compatibility between the versions of Walrasian and Keynesian theory that stabilized during the neoclassical synthesis helped the former win out over its immediate competitors and how the theoretical structure of Walrasian theory was pulled in various directions that enhanced the fit.

3.1 The Centrality of Market Demand

It should be uncontroversial that demand (as opposed to supply, production, or cost) is central to Keynesian economics. There are many different interpretations of the *General Theory*, but common to all is the idea that aggregate demand (aggregate expenditure, aggregate spending, ...) is the major determinant of output and employment.

Of course, demand theory is also fundamental to Walrasian microeconomics. The core idea is that demand functions are the result of consumers solving a particular constrained optimization problem: choosing the most preferred (utility maximizing) bundle from the set of affordable bundles. The consumer's preference-ordering is the key primitive in the analysis; preferences are assumed to be well-ordered (complete, transitive, etc.) and thus can be represented by an ordinal utility function $U(x)$.

Writing out the standard consumer choice problem we have:

$$\text{Max}_{x} U^h(x) \tag{CCP}$$

$$\text{Subject to: } M^h = \sum_{i=1}^{n} p_i x_i,$$

where $p_i > 0$ is the price of good i and $M^h > 0$ is consumer h's money income. Given the standard assumptions on preferences and the linearity of the budget constraint, the utility function will have sufficient mathematical structure to guarantee the existence of a well-behaved solution.

The solutions to the consumer choice problem are the n individual *demand functions*. The demand for good i by individual h is given by:

$$x_i^h = d_i^h(p, M^h) \text{ for } i = 1, 2, \ldots, n \tag{ID}$$

where $p = (p_1, p_2, \ldots, p_n)$. *Market demand functions* are obtained by adding up the individual consumer demand functions, so assuming there are H individuals, the demand for good i is given by:

$$x_i = D_i(p, M^1, M^2, \ldots, M^H) = \sum_{h=1}^{H} d_i^h(p, M^h)^{12} \tag{MD}$$

As noted above, this Walrasian demand theory – now simply the theory of demand – comes down to contemporary textbooks from Pareto, through Slutsky ([1915] 1952) and Hicks and Allen (1934), and the influential presentations in Hicks ([1939] 1946), Samuelson (1947), and Schultz (1938).

In relating this microeconomic theory of demand to Keynesian macro-economics, it is useful to note that there are really *three separate parts to the micro side*: rational choice (the behavior of individual economic agents), individual demand (an individual's demand for a particular good), and market demand (the total market demand for the good). The market demand functions should then relate in some non-inconsistent way to the aggregate demand function of macroeconomics. The discussion in this section will focus on the three different parts of the micro side.

Consider Figure 3.1, which illustrates the relationship between macro-economic aggregate demand (far right side) and the three different parts of microeconomic demand theory (left side). Almost all microeconomic theories of demand have some version of all three of these aspects, but most *also emphasize one of these aspects more than others*. For example, going back to the partial list of various pre-synthesis demand theories given in section 1, some of these focused primarily on the psychological specifics of human decision making (for example, Armstrong, Bernardelli, Georgescu-Roegen, and to a lesser extent Allen and Frisch). Although such theories frequently came up with something like a market demand function, their main focus was on individual choice (that is, the far left-hand side of Figure 3.1). In some ways this individual-choice-theory-first tradition has recently been revived by the work of experimental and behavioral economists (although it is seldom recognized as a revival since the experimental and expected utility aspects of the recent literature tend to blur its relationship to 1930s demand theory[13]). On the other hand, other theorists tended to focus primarily on market demand functions and had only a very thin, and in some cases non-existent, theory of individual behavior (for example, Cournot, Cassel, Evans, Moore, Schultz 1928 but not 1938, and others). Those theorists tended to focus more on the right-hand side of the micro-economic portion picture (and some, Cassel and Moore in particular, did not have, or believe it was necessary to have, a theory of individual behavior at all).

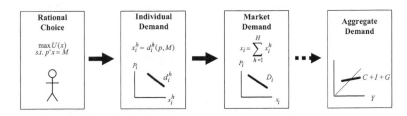

Figure 3.1 Three versions of microeconomic demand theory, and aggregate demand

Given this differentiation between choice-centered and market demand-centered theories, it is important to recognize that the version of Walrasian general equilibrium theory that became dominant during the 1950s and 1960s was much more of a market-focused theory than an individual behavior-focused theory. Of course Walrasian models of the time typically assumed rational economic agents with well-ordered preferences acting under constraint, but explaining *individual* behavior was never the main task. Synthesis-era Walrasian general equilibrium theory was primarily a market-focused approach where all the theoretical heavy-lifting was done by restrictions on *market excess demand functions*. The analysis of stability, uniqueness, and comparative statics – the program's primary theoretical output – was routinely conducted in terms of models specified entirely in terms of market excess demand functions. As Kenneth Arrow and Leonid Hurwicz explained in their influential work on stability theory:

> This work is characterized, in the main, by being based on models whose assumptions are formulated in terms of certain propensities of the individual economic units, although in the last analysis it is the nature of the aggregate excess demand functions that determine the properties of equilibria. (Arrow and Hurwicz 1958: 522)

For example, if the market excess demand for each good i is given by $z_i(p)$ and the model assumes a sufficient amount of continuity and interiority, the only two assumptions needed on the $z_i(p)$s to do "general equilibrium analysis" are zero degree homogeneity (H) and Walras's Law (W):

$$z_i(p) = z_i(\lambda p) \text{ for all } \lambda > 0 \text{ and for all } i = 1, 2, \ldots, n, \tag{H}$$

$$p^T z(p) = \sum_{i=1}^{n} p_i z_i(p) = 0 \tag{W}$$

Granted, the reason why one might think market excess demand functions have these two properties comes from the behavior of the underlying agents, but given (H) and (W), it is possible (and became standard practice) to kick away the rational choice ladder and conduct analysis entirely in terms of market-level excess demand functions. In fact, this is the main message of so-called Sonnenschein–Mantel–Debreu (SMD) theorems on excess demand functions (Debreu 1974; Mantel 1974, 1977; Sonnenschein 1972, 1973).[14] Basically these results say that any continuous function that satisfies (H) and (W) can be an excess demand function for a Walrasian economy. In other words, the SMD results demonstrate that Walrasian general equilibrium theory actually has very weak microfoundations. The standard assumptions on individual consumers do not put much structure on market excess demand functions because the theory has almost nothing to say about the behavior of individual economic agents.

One way to read the argument in this section is to reduce it to simply praising Hicks (1937) for having a good eye for finding the best micro-economic theory to hook up with Keynesian macroeconomics. If it is the late 1930s and one is looking for a microeconomic theory to connect up with Keynesian economics, then choosing the Walrasian program with its focus on market demand and its lack of emphasis on the behavior of individual economic agents (for Keynes a notoriously unreliable source of insight about macroeconomic policy and aggregate economic behavior) does seem to be a very wise move. But one can say more than this.

The Walrasian program in the hands of Pareto (1971) and later Schultz (1938) was more focused on individual choice than the Walrasian theory that came later; in fact Pareto had no market demand functions at all in the *Manual*.[15] These economic theorists never sought the serious psychological underpinnings that concerned some of the competitors to Walrasian theory during the 1930s, but their approach certainly focused "more" on individual behavior than the Walrasian framework that characterized general equilibrium theory at its peak. This would suggest not only that Hicks did in fact have a good eye, but also that Walrasian theory ultimately came to emphasize market demand as a result of the neoclassical synthesis and its co-evolution with Keynesian economics.

3.2 Tâtonnement Stability and Related Issues

Walras's main focus in the *Elements* was the formal characterization of competitive equilibrium: specifying the basic equations of the general equilibrium model and proving the existence of a solution (which for him meant demonstrating that the number of equations was equal to the number of unknowns). Walras did however also attempt, throughout the various editions of the *Elements*, to show how the theoretical solution would actually be reached by the competitive market process. As Walras himself explained in the 4th definitive edition: "Now let us see in what way this problem of the exchange of several commodities for one another to which we have just given a scientific solution is also the problem which is empirically solved in the market by the mechanism of competition" (Walras 1954: 169).[16] His approach to this "empirical" question was to specify an adjustment mechanism where prices changed "by a process of groping ['par tâtonnement']" under the rule that if "the demand for any one commodity is greater than the offer, the price of that commodity in terms of the *numéraire* will rise; if the offer is greater than the demand, the price will fall" (Walras 1954: 170).

To the post-synthesis reader, Walras's words may suggest the system-of-ordinary-differential-equations version of the tâtonnement popularized by Samuelson (1941, 1942, 1944, 1947):

$$\frac{\partial p_i}{\partial t} = H_i\left[z_i[p_1(t), p_2(t), \ldots, p_n(t)]\right] \text{ for all } i = 1, 2, \ldots, n, \tag{T}$$

(where $p_i(t)$ is the price of the ith good at time t, $z_i[\cdot]$ is the excess demand function for the ith good, and $H'_i > 0$), but Walras did not employ this version of the adjustment process or anything like it. Walras's own explanation involved a fairly elaborate "sequential" process of clearing one market at a time based on changing only the price of the good in that market. From any initial disequilibrium position the price of good 1 is adjusted on the basis of the rule that if excess demand is positive the price would be raised and if it is negative it would be lowered until the excess demand for good 1 is equal to zero. Then the same procedure is applied to the market for good 2, then good 3, and on and on in sequence. Obviously in the standard case where the excess demand for each good depends on the prices of all goods, there is no reason to believe that the first iteration will be sufficient to reach equilibrium, so the process would need to be repeated again and again. But under the assumptions of Walras's original model this sequence of iterations need not converge to the general equilibrium.[17]

Walras's sequential tâtonnement was very different from the way the price adjustment mechanism was characterized in the post-Samuelson literature (that is, T). As Walras's translator William Jaffé explained: "The current reformulations of the theory, though they proudly bear the Walras patronymic, display only a distant family resemblance to their ancestral prototype, for the infusion of new technical refinements has all but obliterated any recognizable similarity between the descendant theories and their progenitor" (Jaffé 1967: 1). To see why this difference is important for the issue of the relationship between Walrasian and Keynesian economics, it is useful to rewrite the later version of the tâtonnement (T) in its common "speed of adjustment" form:

$$\frac{\partial p_i}{\partial t} = k_i z_i[p_1(t), p_2(t), \ldots, p_n(t)] \text{ for all } i = 1, 2, \ldots, n, \tag{T'}$$

where $k_i > 0$ is the speed of adjustment for the ith market (Arrow and Hurwicz 1958: 525; Arrow and Hahn 1971: 285). As will be discussed in more detail below, this form makes it possible for some markets to be "slower" or "stickier" in the process of adjustment than others, allowing for Keynesian-type behavior in certain markets while staying broadly within the Walrasian framework. Of course, one can ask whether this characterization of disequilibrium accurately captures what Keynes had in mind, but that is not the issue. The point to note here is that (T') – and thus (T) since it is just a more general version of (T') – accommodates certain ideas associated with Keynesian economics much better than Walras's original sequential process. According to Walras's version, each market will be in equilibrium at a certain point (and generally multiple times during the iterative process), a framework that makes it much more difficult to accommodate the idea that some particular markets are consistently slower or stickier in their adjustment than others.

In addition to and perhaps even more important than the fact that Walras's original sequential formulation of the tâtonnement was difficult to combine with Keynesian theory, is that between Walras's *Elements* and Samuelson (1941), general equilibrium theory systematically moved away from any discussion of the competitive price adjustment mechanism. As Jaffé explains (Jaffé 1967, 1981), Walras recognized that the "realistic" or "empirical" dynamics[18] that he was attempting to model would involve trading at "false prices" which in turn would involve "income" or "endowment" effects that could potentially change the equilibrium price vector. This is a problem even in the pure exchange case, but it is more problematic in the production version of the model. Walras eventually adopted a "no trade outside of equilibrium" condition for both the pure exchange and production models, but this solution is entirely counter to his original purpose for introducing the tâtonnement process. In Jaffé's words: "It is, in fact, an abandonment of realism and with this abandonment the initial purpose of the theory of tâtonnement is lost from sight" (Jaffé 1967: 12). These problems – and here is the point for the Keynesian story – led Pareto to completely abandon any discussion of the tâtonnement mechanism. There was a brief mention in the *Cours*, but it is totally absent from the *Manual* (Donzelli 2006: 12–19). Thus if one considers the evolution of "Walrasian" general equilibrium theory from the early editions of the *Elements* to the *Manual*, the tâtonnement goes from being an important part of the story but modeled differently than (T), to being very problematic, to being entirely abandoned.

Moving forward in time to Hicks and Samuelson, Hicks discussed multiple market stability in *Value and Capital* ([1939] 1946) by generalizing the stability condition for a single market. Samuelson (1941) argued that Hicks's conditions did not represent "true dynamic stability." Samuelson's tâtonnement adjustment mechanism (T) and his stability condition – negative real parts of the characteristic roots of the excess demand Jacobian evaluated at equilibrium prices – became the standard tool for talking about *local* stability in Walrasian theory. The literature on the local stability of the Walrasian tâtonnement that appeared in a steady stream during the next twenty years focused primarily on trying to find reasonable economic restrictions that would be sufficient for Samuelson's matrix condition. The analysis of global stability came later during the late 1950s as a result of applying Liapunov theory; the canonical results were provided in Arrow and Hurwicz (1958) and Arrow, Block, and Hurwicz (1959). These papers proved that the Walrasian general equilibrium price vector (p^*) would be unique and globally stable under a variety of specific restrictions (gross substitutes being the most important).

Samuelson's initial papers on local stability were published in 1941 and 1942, but they were included in Part II of *Foundations* as chapters nine and ten. It is significant that *Foundations* was divided into two separate parts. The first part discussed economic models where the equilibrium was a maximum or minimum of some function (extremum problems). The examples in Part I were the topics that would come to dominate microeconomic textbooks during the next few decades: consumer choice (demand) theory, cost and production, profit maximizing firm behavior, welfare economics, etc. Part II was also about comparative statics, but it examined models where the equilibrium could not be associated with the maximum or minimum of any function. Comparative statics results are more difficult in such cases because of the weaker mathematical restrictions in such problems (in particular, no second order conditions). For these non-optimization-based models Samuelson proposed the *correspondence principle*. It employed similar mathematical techniques, but used the *stability* of the model, rather than optimality, to obtain comparative statics results. The explicit motivation for discussing this class of models and subsuming them under the same formalism was the fact that Keynesian models (business cycle theories) are of this second, non-optimization-based, kind. As Samuelson explains in the introduction to *Foundations*:

> However, when we leave single economic units, the determination of unknowns is found to be unrelated to an extremum position. In even the simplest business cycle theories there is lacking symmetry in the conditions of equilibrium so that there is no possibility of directly reducing the problem to that of a maximum or minimum. Instead the dynamical properties of the system are specified, and the hypothesis is made that the system is in 'stable' equilibrium or motion. By means of what I have called the *Correspondence Principle* between comparative statics and dynamics, definite *operationally meaningful* theorems can be derived from so simple a hypothesis. (Samuelson 1947: 5)

Important to the story here is the fact that Samuelson's discussion of the stability of the Walrasian tâtonnement (in fact all of his explicit discussion of the Walrasian model) was contained in Part II (the non-optimization-based Keynesian part) of *Foundations*. Chapter nine – which was Samuelson (1941) – starts out discussing the correspondence principle, moves to the stability of two-dimensional market models, then the stability of Walrasian multiple-market general equilibrium (his criticism of Hicks, his main stability result, etc.), and finally analyses a 3-variable, 3-parameter, Keynesian model. For Samuelson, the analysis of Walrasian dynamics was more like the analysis of a Keynesian model than the microeconomic theory discussed in Part I of *Foundations*. Of course, Samuelson, like others working on Walrasian models during this period, was assuming that utility maximizing consumers and profit maximizing firms were in some sense "behind" the excess demand functions of in the tâtonnement (T), but Walrasian dynamics was nonetheless directly linked, by formal structure and in its dependency on the correspondence principle, to Keynesian economics.

Another important contributor to the neoclassical synthesis – perhaps even more self-conscious about forging a synthesis than Samuelson – was Oskar Lange. The goal of Lange's *Price Flexibility and Employment* (1944) was to restate general equilibrium "in a way which explicitly takes account of money" (Lange, 1944: ii). The second paragraph of Lange's preface lists the economists who most influenced the study and it reads like a who's who of the neoclassical synthesis: Keynes (on the "substitution between money and goods"), Hicks (for providing the "most up-to-date formulation of the theory of general economic equilibrium"), and Samuelson (for the "dynamic theory of stability of economic equilibrium"). Key to Lange's analysis in *Price Flexibility* is Samuelson's version of the Walrasian tâtonnement (T). Prices which obey (T) exhibit price flexibility (p. 2). The purpose of his analysis was to investigate the relationship between price flexibility in this sense and "employment and economic stability" (p. 1). The book was thus an attempt to combine Walrasian general equilibrium theory – particularly the stability analysis of the Walrasian tâtonnement – with a Keynesian analysis of unemployment and economic stability (in the macro sense). Although the argument was far from tight, the often-repeated theme in the book was that "flexibility of factor prices fails to assure full employment of factors of production" (p. 51) unless a number of additional conditions are satisfied. For Lange, like Keynes, full employment was a rare event in a competitive market economy: for Lange this even applied to Walrasian general equilibrium.

Lange also used Walrasian theory to make Keynesian theoretical points in his paper on Say's Law (Lange 1942). He makes the distinction between Walras's Law (valid in a general equilibrium system) and Say's Law (invalid in such a system). Again the Walrasian formalism was being used to make

Keynesian political–economic points. Since this section is getting quite long, I will simply note that many others who participated in the theoretical literature of the neoclassical synthesis – Alvin Hansen (1949), Abba Lerner (1944), Don Patinkin ([1956] 1965), James Tobin (1958, 1969) and others – also combined elements of general equilibrium theory with elements of Keynesian economics and did so using much the same formula as Lange (though often with more moderate politics).[19] The Walrasian model formed the theoretical backbone – with a strong emphasis on stability analysis – and the Keynesian influence entered on the money/interest and policy sides.

Some of the argument presented in this section, regarding the close relationship between Walrasian stability and the neoclassical synthesis, has been presented in Roy Weintraub's *Stabilizing Dynamics* (1991). Weintraub argues that prior to the neoclassical synthesis terms like "equilibrium" and "stability" had a variety of different meanings – the discourse was not stabilized – with different economists and texts using the terms in different ways. He argues that one of the driving forces behind the ultimate stabilization that took place during the 1950s and 1960s (basically that "dynamic" meant that the system was specified explicitly in terms of differential or difference equations and "stability" meant convergence to equilibrium as $t \rightarrow \infty$) was the effort to reconcile the idea of general equilibrium with ostensibly "disequilibrium" phenomena of involuntary unemployment. As he explains:

> The literature associated with Frisch, Tinbergen, Hicks, and finally Samuelson was associated with understanding the conditions under which an equilibrium would be stable, so as to permit the conjunction of equilibrium theorizing and unemployment analysis. (Weintraub 1991: 123)

This means that the neoclassical synthesis played an essential role in stabilizing dynamics (in general equilibrium theory and in economics more generally).

> The mathematization of equilibrium and stability, the papers from Samuelson on through Arrow and Hurwicz, stabilized that discourse ... The restriction of 'dynamic' to 'dynamical system,' and the construction of 'stable' to 'locally stable equilibrium motion of a dissipative dynamical system,' permitted concurrence ... on the meaning of the claim that unemployment was a disequilibrium position associated with a 'usually' stable competitive equilibrium. The neoclassical synthesis was literally unthinkable before the availability of the mathematization of equilibrium and stability. (Weintraub 1991: 125)

Although my argument is not inconsistent with Weintraub's, I emphasize a different aspect of the story. There were no "stabilized dynamics" before the neoclassical synthesis. The sequential tâtonnement of Walras was quite different from the (more Keynesian accommodating) tâtonnement process of the later literature (T) and discussion of the tâtonnement had all but disappeared from the Walrasian literature by Pareto's most mature work. The "price adjustment mechanism" was not a significant part of general equilibrium theory in the period immediately preceding the work of Hicks and Samuelson; it *became* a significant part of the Walrasian research program during the 1940s and it became so in part because of the neoclassical synthesis and the concerns of Keynesians economics.

In closing this section I would like to emphasize how *important* the topics of stability and Walrasian dynamics were to general equilibrium theorizing during the heyday of the 1960s. For example, Arrow and Hahn's *General Competitive Analysis* (1971) – the canonical summary of the literature – dedicated far more pages to stability than any other topic. The book had fourteen chapters (and a number of mathematical appendices); there was one chapter on consumer choice, one chapter on production theory, and one chapter on existence, but there were *three* chapters on stability analysis (two on the traditional tâtonnement and one on alternative ways of modeling general equilibrium dynamics). Add to this the fact that there was an entire chapter on "The Keynesian Model" and it becomes clear how important stability analysis and its connection to Keynesian economics was for Walrasian microeconomics during this period. The purpose of this section has been to show that that would not have been the case if the Walrasian economics of the day had not been a product of co-evolution with Keynesian economic theory.

3.3   Reversibility, Path-Dependency, and All That

This topic is related to the stability discussion in the previous section, but it can be separated from the way that Walrasian tâtonnement dynamics jelled together with Keynesian notions of disequilibrium and unemployment. One feature of Walrasian models (of any sort) and Keynesian models (of the IS-LM sort) is an absence of path-dependencies, irreversibilities, reference-dependence, hysteresis, endowment effects, or any other properties where the path or initial position influences the characteristics of the equilibrium (or which equilibrium is) reached. Disequilibrium adjustment can be characterized in both models, but the process/mechanism by which the equilibrium is reached has no impact on the resulting equilibrium position.

The story on the microeconomic side is fairly familiar. In recent years a vast amount of empirical evidence from experimental and behavioral economics suggests that such path-dependencies and irreversibilities are pervasive features of human choice (in laboratories and in markets) – see for example Camerer and Loewenstein (2004), DellaVigna (2009), Kahneman (2003), Kahneman, Knetsch, and Thaler (1990), Knetsch (1989, 1992), or Thaler (1980) – but such effects are entirely absent from Walrasian choice theory. For Walrasian theory, the individual consumer has well-ordered preferences (and thus a well-behaved ordinal utility function) and chooses the most preferred bundle (maximizes utility) from the affordable set. The consumer is assumed to have fixed preferences, infinitely fast computational ability, and to move instantaneously to the optimal bundle – as Nicholas Georgescu-Roegen once put it, the agent's behavior is like a "bird" that drops down instantaneously on the optimal bundle, rather than like a "worm" that actually moves through the choice space in real time to arrive at the optimal choice (Georgescu-Roegen 1968: 255). Of course, if the behavior were worm-like, the particular path taken might matter to the final choice (path-dependency) and reversing the parameter change that initiated the choice might not return the consumer to the initial position (irreversibility). Obviously, this feature is common to many neoclassical-based models of individual choice and is not restricted to Walrasian choice theory, but – and here is the point – such path-dependencies and irreversibilities *were* common features of many of the demand theories the Walrasian program was competing against during the 1930s and 1940s.[20] Many of the different competing approaches to choice/price theory listed above in the discussion of interwar pluralism, were motivated by the idea that economic agents do not have stable and reversible preferences, infinitely fast computational abilities, act instantaneously, and so forth. These issues, present in the recent literature on experimental and behavioral economics, disappeared with the ascension of the Walrasian version of choice theory. The question is: How does all this relate to Keynesian economics?

The fact is that Keynesian economics – at least in the form it came to take during the neoclassical synthesis – was also characterized by hermetic separation of the equilibrium position from any dependency on, or influence from, the process/path by which that equilibrium is reached. In "What was Lost with IS-LM?" Roger Backhouse and David Laidler (2004) discuss a number of problems associated with the passage of time and related issues that concerned macroeconomists during the interwar period, but disappeared from discussion once the profession came to accept the IS-LM framework. As they explain: "All of these matters had received widespread attention in the interwar literature, but the wholesale adoption of the static IS-LM framework form the 1940s onward led to their falling into neglect" (Backhouse and Laidler 2004: 31). At the same time that the Walrasian program was rising to dominance in microeconomics and thus facilitating the profession's dismissal of many of the issues of time and path that

concerned microeconomists during the interwar period, the rise to dominance of textbook Keynesianism facilitated a similar dismissal of time-
related issues within macroeconomics. Micro and macro both stabilized
around theoretical frameworks where the "dynamic structure of the world
plays no role in determining the equilibrium toward which the economy
converges" (Backhouse and Laidler 2004: 32).

So, given the argument in the preceding paragraphs, it does seem that
neoclassical synthesis micro and macro were very similar on the issues of
path and time – and perhaps defeated competitors that allowed for path-
dependency and irreversibility on both the micro and macro side – but how
does this show that Keynesian ideas influenced Walrasian theorizing? To
answer this, notice how the literature on the Walrasian tâtonnement is
based on an entirely different strategy for answering the question of *how the
competitive market* reaches equilibrium than Walrasian theory employs
when answering the question of *how the individual economic agent* reaches
equilibrium (optimal choice). In the case of the individual economic agent
(intra-agent equilibrium), Walrasian theory makes equilibrium instantaneous and avoids all issues associated with time, path, initial position,
irreversibility, or the dynamic process of "getting there." The Walrasian
consumer does not grope around in, or converge to, the optimal bundle by
moving through the choice space; they are essentially always in equilibrium.
One can of course do comparative statics exercises in such models and
compare one equilibrium to another, but no time passes (even logical or
virtual time) between the two equilibrium positions, the change does not
affect either equilibrium, and reversing the initial parameter change would
simply take the consumer back to the original point. Notice how different
this is from the Walrasian tâtonnement.

The tâtonnement is also timeless in the sense that no trade takes place
until the equilibrium price vector (p^*) is reached, but the variables are
tracing out paths in "time." This "time" has a natural direction; it makes no
sense to talk about "reversing" the dynamic system (T). In (inter-agent)
equilibrium the motion simply stops – $dp_i / dt = 0$ for all $i = 1, 2, ..., n$. Since
stability implies $\lim_{(t \to \infty)} p(t) = p^*$, and no trade takes place until p^* is reached,
this process may take a very long "time." It is analytical (or virtual) "time"
and not real time, but there is still a big difference between this notion of
"getting to" equilibrium and the instantaneous choice of the Walrasian
agent. The "behavior" of the Walrasian auctioneer is conceptually quite
different than the "behavior" of the Walrasian agent and in particular, the
tâtonnement (T) allows for "stickiness" or "disequilibrium" in a way that is
inconceivable for the Walrasian agent. If, contrary to the Walrasian models
of the neoclassical synthesis, the equilibrium in the Walrasian market were

modeled in the same way as the equilibrium of the Walrasian consumer there would be no tâtonnement "adjustment"; the competitive price system would always be in equilibrium. In fact, in the late 1970s when the New Classical macro of Robert Lucas (1981) replaced Keynesian macro this is exactly the way general equilibrium was discussed. There was no "adjustment"; the economy was always in equilibrium in the same way that the Walrasian agent is always in equilibrium. As Kevin Hoover explains, general equilibrium in the Lucas model means that "self-interested economic agents successfully maximize their utility or profits subject to constraints on their budgets and, crucially, on available information" (Hoover 1988: 42). The Lucas model is strictly Walrasian in that the representative agent does what Walrasian agents have always done. No tâtonnement is needed. As Lucas himself says: "the idea that an economic system in equilibrium is in any sense 'at rest' is simply an anachronism" (Lucas 1981: 287). Yes, an anachronism of the neoclassical synthesis.

So, in the end, it seems that this discussion of individual versus market behavior has left us at a point similar to where we were at the end of section 3.2. The conception of "dynamics" that stabilized in Walrasian general equilibrium theory during the 1950s was in part driven by a desire to find a notion of multi-market competitive equilibrium that was consistent with a version of Keynesian unemployment. What this section has added is that the stabilization was not only about equilibrium and stability in a competitive market, but also about the characterization of the behavior of the individual economic agent. Walrasian economics overcame (or circumvented, or suppressed, depending on your point of view) the path-dependency and irreversibilities that were a concern of a number of non-Walrasian theories of demand during the interwar period, and it also overcame these same issues concerning time and position in the theory of market adjustment, but the two "solutions" were quite different; and different in part because of *Keynesian concerns on the market side*. Later, freed from these Keynesian concerns, New Classical Walrasians such as Lucas endorsed a more consistent Walrasian view where equilibrium in agents and markets meant essentially the same thing.[21] It seems reasonable to conclude that the combination of instantaneously optimizing agents and tâtonnement adjusting competitive markets that characterized microeconomics during the period of Walrasian high theory – present in Walrasian theory neither before, nor after, the neoclassical synthesis – was a product of its co-evolution with Keynesian theory.

3.4   Income Matters

As discussed in section 3.1, the "Walrasian" demand theory that emerged triumphant during the neoclassical synthesis descended more from Pareto than Walras, and it was put in essentially its final (calculus-based) form in Slutsky ([1915] 1952) and Hicks and Allen (1934). Out of all the various contributions and contributors during the half-century stabilization of demand theory, Slutsky ([1915] 1952) – translation published in 1952 – is generally considered to be the key development. Over the last decade there has been a substantial amount of historical research on Slutsky and we now know quite a lot more about his life and work (for example, Barnett 2004, Chipman 2004, Chipman and Lenfant 2002, Weber 1999a, 1999b), but the one question that does not seem to have been adequately answered is: Why has the Slutsky equation – the "fundamental equation of value theory" (Hicks [1939] 1946: 309) – had such a prominent position within microeconomic theory and economic education since the 1950s? The argument in this section will be that this is in part because of the neoclassical synthesis and the impact of Keynesian economics.

If one is thinking about which of the various theories of demand from the 1930s and 1940s would best "fit" with Keynesian macroeconomics, the Walrasian formulation has one obvious advantage: Walrasian demand functions have nominal income as arguments. If one is trying to meld consumer choice theory and Keynesian economics then one needs to be able to explain how changes in nominal income have real effects on individual behavior. Income matters in Keynesian economics and income must matter in any demand theory that is going to live comfortably with Keynesian theory.[22] This feature of Walrasian demand theory certainly gave it a big advantage over various demand theories that did not have such income effects; for example Hotelling (1932) with no income term at all, or various versions of Chicago price theory where income effects are compensated away (Friedman 1953). Although this explains why Walrasian theory made the short-list for the neoclassical synthesis – it fulfilled an important necessary condition – it does not provide much explanation for the particular emphasis on the Slutsky equation. But there is a synthesis-based story for that as well.

Perhaps at this point it would be useful to write down the Slutsky equation,[23]

$$\frac{\partial x_i^h}{\partial p_j} = S_{ij}^h - d_j^h \frac{\partial d_i^h}{\partial M^h} \qquad (S)$$

and the main results: the own Slutsky substitution terms are strictly negative ($S_{ii}^h < 0$), the cross-substitution terms are symmetric ($S_{ij} = S_{ji}$ for all $i \neq j$), and the $n \times n$ matrix of Slutsky substitution terms $S^h = [S_{ij}^h]$ is negative semi-definite ($x^T S^h x \leq 0$ for all $x \neq 0$). The substitution terms (S_{ij}^h) show the change in the consumption of the good caused exclusively by a change in relative prices; the remainder of the expression is the income effect which shows the change in the consumption of the good caused by a price-induced change in real income.

Notice that (S) is in many ways the perfect expression of the neoclassical synthesis. It decomposes observed changes in consumption into a micro part (the change based on only relative prices) and a macro part (the change based on a change in the purchasing power of money). According to the macroeconomic/monetary theory preceding (and following) the dominance of Keynesian macroeconomics we should keep these two things strictly separate: changes in relative prices are an issue for value theory while changes in the purchasing power of money are an issue for monetary theory, and a strict dichotomy should be maintained between these two types of economic theory. The Slutsky equation not only violates this strict dichotomy, it harmonizes micro and macro into one simple expression.

As the Frank Knight quote in the epigraph demonstrates, this was precisely the criticism of the Walras–Hicks–Slutsky demand theory raised by certain members of the Chicago school during the 1940s and 1950s and one of their main reasons for advocating an alternative – more purely micro – theory of demand. As Knight explains:

> The treatment of the Slutzky school adopts the assumption that the price of X varies under the condition that the prices of all other goods (and the consumer's money income) are constant. Hence real income must change ... It throws together two distinct effects upon consumption, the "price effect" and the "income effect." The treatment then proceeds to separate these by means of an ingenious analysis. The cleverness of it all must be conceded. But it is called for only because of an initial confusion in the statement of the problem which is wholly unnecessary and should clearly be avoided ... The "income effect" of Slutsky et al. is merely a particular case or mode of change in the purchasing-power of money, or the price level: and it is this problem as a whole that should be isolated and reserved for special treatment. (Knight 1944: 299)

> An approach to any particular price problem which "jumbles" effects of change in the purchasing-power of money (however caused) with effects of change in the relative value for purchasing different things is mere gratuitous confusion. (*ibid.*: 300)

Friedman also made similar (though less dramatic) comments in a number of works. For example, his paper on the Marshallian demand curve argued that "the separation of the theory of relative prices from monetary theory" was extremely important and it was one of "Marshall's basic organizing principles" which led him to use "a constant purchasing power of money as a means of impounding monetary forces" (Friedman 1953: 66). Friedman argued that Marshall, unlike Walrasian theorists, correctly "recognized the desirability of separating two quite different effects and constructed his demand curve so that it encompassed solely the effect that he wished to isolate for study, namely, the substitution effect" (*ibid.*: 64–5).[24] Similar discontent with the standard Walrasian–Slutsky distinction between sub-stitution and income effects was expressed in Friedman's famous "Provisional Text":

> To summarize, general considerations suggest the desirability of having two functions. One function should be so defined as to summarize the forces affecting the demand for the commodity in question operating via relative prices. In this function, real income should be held constant. The other function should be so defined as to summarize the forces affecting the demand for the commodity in question via real income. In this function, relative prices obviously should be held constant. A function of this latter type is the Engel curve, which relates quantity demanded and real income. The ordinary demand function is intended to provide a function of the former type but does not do so, because changes in real income are not rigorously excluded. (Friedman 1962: 30)

So the bottom line is that the elevation of (S) to the fundamental equation of value theory, like the elevation of (T) to the fundamental equation of Walrasian dynamics, was a product of the neoclassical synthesis. Having nominal income as an argument in demand functions helped the Walrasian theory win out over its immediate competitors, but the context of the neoclassical synthesis – with its mandate for micro–macro harmonization – also helps us understand how the Slutsky equation came to be so important in demand theory. Of course, like all of the other topics discussed in sections 3.1–3.3, the argument is not that the Keynesian connection was the only reason for the prominence of the Slutsky equation, but it is an additional factor not discussed in traditional explanations of the equation's influence (for example, Chipman and Lenfant 2002). All things considered, (S) does seem to be an elegant way to demonstrate that "the broad cleavage between microeconomics and macroeconomics has now been closed" (Samuelson 1955: 360).

4. EVERY GOOD THING MUST END (OR THE DOWN-SIDE OF CO-EVOLUTION)

This section will extend the argument about the influence of Keynesian ideas on the rise and character of Walrasian economics to the question of the Keynesian contribution to the fall of Walrasian microeconomics. The discussion here will be less detailed and more suggestive than the argument in the previous section. One reason is simply that this is already a long paper and a serious analysis of the fall would require a lot more space than is available here, but there are other reasons as well.

First, it is still an open question whether there really has been, or the degree to which there really has been, a "fall" in Walrasian microeconomics during the last few decades. Although many consider it to be obvious that the profession has moved on (for example, Colander 2000, 2006; Colander, Holt and Rosser 2004a, 2004b; Davis 2006, 2008; Rizvi 2003; and many others), it is also clear that Walrasian microeconomics is still an active research program[25] and it remains the standard framework in textbooks at every level.

Second, it might be argued that the profession has in fact "moved on," but the movement reflects more the "maturity" of the Walrasian research program than its failure (Colander 2000, Davis 2006). It may be that Walrasian general equilibrium theory is simply a "completed" research program; the task was to investigate the full implications of the assumption that all economic agents behave in a perfectly competitive manner and that task has now been completed. From this point of view economics is now post-Walrasian, but simply because the profession has successfully completed the research project that had been its main focus for the previous two hundred years.

Third, in addition to the question about the existence of the fall is a broader question about the future of neoclassical economics and rational choice theory more generally. Walrasian microeconomic theory is a particular version of neoclassical economics and to some extent utilizes rational choice theory in its characterization of individual agents. But the extensive literature in experimental and behavioral economics that finds repeated systematic empirical violations of rational choice theory and/or the stability and reversibility that is characteristic of preferences in neoclassical models, clearly has implications for the future of Walrasian microeconomics. If rational choice theory somehow comes to be replaced as the core organizing framework for the way that economists think about, model, and formalize individual behavior, then certainly Walrasian economics is in for an even bigger downturn than it has experienced during the last few years. Of course these issues are still in flux and that severely limits what one can say about the "fall" of Walrasian economics at the current time.

Finally, there is the question of the current status of Keynesian economics. Twenty-five or so years ago it was quite clear that Keynesian economics had fallen from grace within the economics profession (although not necessarily from policy makers and undergraduate instruction[26]), but now, with the recent financial crisis and world economic recession, this is less clear. It is possible there will be a Keynesian revival in macroeconomics and finance within the profession during the next few years, but then again, maybe not. The point is simply that we may be in a period of significant change within the discipline of economics – change that involves both Walrasian and Keynesian theory – and that presents a serious challenge to an attempt to provide an historical analysis of the fall of Walrasian theory.

Taking into consideration all that was said in the previous three paragraphs, I do think it is possible to say a few things about the "fall" of Walrasian microeconomics and its relationship to Keynesian theory and the neoclassical synthesis. First of all, whether Walrasian economics has taken, or will take, a terminal fall or not, it is clear that it has been demoted during the last few decades. Second, whether Keynesian economics stages a comeback or not, during the late 1970s and 1980s it definitely fell from the position it held during the heyday of the neoclassical synthesis. Not only does it seem reasonable to accept these stylized facts of the history of modern economics, it also seems reasonable to agree about some of the causes for both of these events. On the Walrasian side it is clear that the failure of *stability analysis* – starting in the 1960s with the counterexamples by David Gale (1963) and Herbert Scarf (1960), and exacerbated by the SMD results which opened the floodgates for more counterexamples[27] – and the associated failure to prove uniqueness raised serious challenges to the hegemony of the Walrasian program. As Alan Kirman explained, without "stability or uniqueness, the intrinsic interest of economic analysis based on the general equilibrium model was extremely limited" (Kirman 2006: 257). With respect to Keynesian economics the inflation and supply-side oil shocks of the 1970s were clearly empirical factors, and the rise of monetarism and the failure of the microfoundations project certainly contributed on the theoretical side.[28] It is not necessary to debate the details, or weight the relative significance, of any of these factors; for the purposes here all that is required is agreement that the Walrasian program has faltered during the last decade or so, the Keynesian program was seriously questioned by the 1980s, and that the things mentioned here on the theoretical and empirical side played some role in these negative developments. Given all this it seems quite clear that there are a few ways in which Keynesian economics – and the previous co-evolution of the two research programs – contributed to the decline of Walrasian microeconomics.

The main point of this section will be that Walrasian theory ran into trouble *at precisely the points where the Keynesian influence was most pronounced*. Consider stability first. Almost all of the serious theoretical problems associated with Walrasian microeconomics revolve around the *stability* of the tâtonnement adjustment mechanism (T). The problem is that the tâtonnement process is globally stable only when very restrictive additional assumptions are imposed on excess demand functions (and local stability is only slightly easier): these include gross substitutes, the Weak Axiom of revealed preference holding on aggregate excess demands, a dominant diagonal on the excess demand Jacobian matrix, and several others (see chapters 11 and 12 of Arrow and Hahn 1971). These assumptions are restrictive in at least four different senses. First, they are over and above what is implied by the standard assumptions on consumer and firm behavior (they are theoretically restrictive). Second, there is no obvious reason why the behavior they would require should actually be the behavior of consumers and firms in a competitive market economy (they are empirically restrictive). Third, they are much more restrictive than what is required for existence of competitive equilibrium (the main positive result of the research program). And fourth, they are only sufficient, not necessary, conditions. The goal of stability theory was to find out what stability implied – in the same way that Slutsky, Hicks, Allen, and others found out what income-constrained utility maximization implied – but all that could be found were a variety of different conditions that implied stability (not what stability implied). Of course, there were also problems with uniqueness, but in every special case where the tâtonnement process is globally stable the equilibrium price vector (p^*) is also unique (see chapter 9 of Arrow and Hahn 1971). And there were also problems with comparative statics, but again the problem is really about stability. The correspondence principle attempts to derive comparative statics *from* stability, but if the stability results are not available, or weak, or economically uninterpretable, then the comparative statics results inherit these same problems. As Arrow and Hahn explained:

> Thus what the "correspondence principle" amounts to is this: Most of the restrictions on the form of the excess-demand functions that are at present known to be sufficient to ensure global stability are also sufficient to allow certain exercises in comparing equilibria. It should be added that these same conditions also turn up in the discussion of the uniqueness of competitive equilibrium. All these restrictions share the characteristic that they are not

necessary for the task for which they were invented; they are only sufficient and this explains why the correspondence principle "isn't." (Arrow and Hahn 1971: 321)

As discussed in section 3.3, the stability of the system of differential equations (T) was not part of the original Walrasian model and by Pareto's *Manual* there was no discussion of multiple market stability at all. It was also not a part – and was considered one of the problems of the earlier theory – in the macro-Walrasian general equilibrium theory that came after the Keynesian fall from grace. As Robert Lucas (1981: 278–9) explains:

> Samuelson proposed a dynamic model of price adjustment in which the rates of change of prices offered in each market were related to the level of "excess demands" in all markets. Whatever the history or underlying objectives of this model of price dynamics ... this theory introduced sufficient additional (to those needed to describe tastes and technology) parameters to the equilibrium system so that, given an initial shock to the system, a wide variety of paths were consistent with its eventual return to equilibrium.
>   This introduction of additional ... free parameters held out the promise that one could construct a theoretical system the stationary point of which was a general equilibrium in the neoclassical sense but whose movements, out of equilibrium, might replicate the "Keynesian" behavior captured so well by the econometric models ... The objective of the enterprise was widely agreed to be "unification" of the two types of theories into which Keynesian ideas were translated in the 1930s and 1940s.[29]

The idea that the stability of the tâtonnement process should be one of the most important issues for Walrasian general equilibrium theory was a product of the neoclassical synthesis and the effort to unify Keynesian and Walrasian economics. It is clear from the contributions of those like Lange and Samuelson in the 1940s, and it is also clear from its rejection in the post-synthesis Walrasian macro literature of those like Lucas. The stability of the tâtonnement ultimately became a very serious problem for Walrasian economics, and it was a problem that developed right at the particular point in the theoretical edifice where the Keynesian co-evolution had left its greatest impact on Walrasian theory.

But this is not all there is to the story; there is yet another Keynesian aspect to the theoretical difficulties that developed within Walrasian general equilibrium theory. Not only was the stability of the neoclassical synthesis-inspired tâtonnement the main problem, "the stability problem" was itself a product of the *income terms* in the Hicks–Slutsky version of Walrasian demand theory. The effort to forge a seamless connection between Walrasian and Keynesian theory contributed to an emphasis on both tâtonnement dynamics and income effects; the income effects were the primary cause of instability in Walrasian models which in turn became the most important theoretical difficulty for the Walrasian program.

To see the problem, recall the discussion from section 3.4 above and the Slutsky expression given in (S). As noted there, the Slutsky matrix is negative semi-definite,[30] but consumer choice theory imposes no sign restrictions on the income effects (goods could be normal or inferior). As noted above, the standard way of proving global stability was to find a Liapunov function. Applying the Liapunov result from this period to the problem of Walrasian stability, we have that if there exists a function $V[p(t)]$ defined over the price path $p(t)$ generated by (T) with the following three properties (glossing over various mathematical complexities and assuming the numéraire good has been eliminated):[31]

a) $V[p(t)] > 0$ for all $p \neq p^*$,

b) $\dfrac{dV[p(t)]}{dt} < 0$ for all $p \neq p^*$,

c) $\dfrac{dV[p^*]}{dt} = V[p^*]$,

then the equilibrium price vector (p^*) is globally asymptotically stable. One popular Liapunov function was:[32]

$$V[p(t)] = \frac{1}{2}\sum_{i=1}^{n} z_i^2[p(t)].$$

Computing the time derivative of this Liapunov function we have:

$$\frac{dV[p(t)]}{dt} = z^T[p(t)]JZ[p(t)]z[p(t)] \text{ for all } p \neq p^*,$$

where the right-hand side is a quadratic form of the excess demand Jacobian matrix JZ. If the matrix JZ forms a negative definite quadratic form, then the expression on the right-hand side will be negative for all nonequilibrium prices and equal to zero at equilibrium, which in turn implies the tâtonnement is globally stable.

But the matrix JZ – remember it is the Jacobian of the excess demand function (demand minus supply) – will consist of three separate parts,

$$JZ = S - M - F,$$

where the S and M matrices are from the market demand functions – they are the market equivalents of the substitution and income effects in (S) respectively – and the F matrix is the supply function Jacobian (see Mukherji 1974: 247–8). We know the S matrix is negative definite from the standard Slutsky results on demand functions and we also know that the traditional assumptions on the production side of the Arrow–Debreu model guarantee that the matrix F is positive semi-definite (Arrow and Hahn 1971: 72). So both of these terms are signed the "right way" for stability. Neither the substitution effects on the demand side nor the supply side are a problem. The only problem – the only matrix that is not signed the "right way" by the standard assumptions – is the matrix of income effects (M above). This means that the full burden of all of the stability "problems" in general equilibrium systems rests with the income terms on the demand side of the market excess demand functions. The various conditions that have been demonstrated to be sufficient for global stability during the late 1950s and 1960s all amount in various ways to getting around these problematic income effects.

So it seems that Keynesian economics must bear some responsibility for the fall, or at least faltering, of Walrasian microeconomics during the last few decades. Any neoclassically-inspired theory that could get along with Keynesian economics well enough to form a stable partnership would need to be able to account for unemployment and disequilibrium in an otherwise general equilibrium world and it would need to have nominal income matter to consumer choice behavior: thus (T) and (S). And yet these two aspects of the Walrasian theory of the neoclassical synthesis are right at the heart of the Walrasian program's later technical difficulties. The features of Walrasian theory that were most influenced by its co-evolution with Keynesian economics during the middle of the twentieth century were precisely the features most responsible for its decline at the end of the century.

5. CONCLUSION

This chapter has tried to make a fairly simple point. What Keynesian and Walrasian economics evolved into – what they *became* – when they stabilized into textbook macro and (advanced) textbook micro during the 1950s and 1960s, was, at least in part, a result of the fact they were joined together in, and co-evolved within the context of, the neoclassical synthesis. Even if it is assumed they each contained certain core concepts identifiable across time, there were particular features of each in the later period that emerged because those particular aspects had survival value for the synthesis they were both a part of, and thus, because of the presence of the other theory. Many historians of economic thought readily accept that textbook Keynesian economics in its heyday was what it was at least in part because of its compact with Walrasian economics. My point was simply that the synthesis involved adaptations by both research programs and that influence flowed both ways. The neoclassical synthesis was made, not found.

In section 2, I listed four ways that Keynesian ideas contributed to the eventual success of Walrasian micro over its immediate theoretical competition and/or influenced the content of the theory in its final form. Frankly, taken in isolation, none of these points would be very significant, but I believe that taken together they provide a substantial amount of new insight into how the co-evolution of the two research programs manifested itself on the Walrasian side. One of the main arguments in this section was that the equilibrium within mid-twentieth century Walrasian economics – unlike the Walrasian tâtonnement – was highly path-dependent. In section 3, I tried to show how the main theoretical problems of Walrasian theory at the end of the century – primarily stability, but also related issues such as uniqueness and comparative statics – emerged at precisely the point within the Walrasian program where the Keynesian imprint was most visible.

Although I believe the story told here is an important explanation of both the rise and the fall (or faltering) of Walrasian microeconomics, I noted repeatedly in the chapter that I was in no way attempting to provide the only, or perhaps even the main, reason that Walrasian economics took the particular path that it did during the twentieth century. There are many other forces at work in the life-history of Walrasian economics – other forces that, at particular moments, may have mattered more than the Keynesian connection. My point was simply that Keynesian theory mattered – something not generally recognized – not that it was the only thing that mattered.[33]

NOTES

1. This chapter was initially presented at The First International Symposium on the History of Economic Thought "The Integration of Micro and Macroeconomics from a Historical Perspective," University of São Paulo, São Paulo, Brazil, August 3–5, 2009. Later versions were presented at the Center for the History of Political Economy at Duke University, October 2009; The Amsterdam–Cachan Workshop on the History and Methodology of Economics at the University of Amsterdam, December 2009; The American Economics Association Meetings in Atlanta, January 2010; and the Western Washington University Economics Department, February 2010. I received helpful comments from numerous people at these various venues.
2. Department of Economics, University of Puget Sound, Tacoma, WA, USA, hands@pugetsound.edu.

3. In addition to books of course, the history of general equilibrium theory, and mid-twentieth century microeconomics more generally, has received extensive discussion in history of economic thought journals, Handbooks and Companions, and to some extent journals in economic theory. A number of *History of Political Economy* annual conferences have also focused on aspects of the story.

4. As Coddington put it: "what Hicks was supposed to have done was to have taken the pristine work of Keynes's *General Theory* and, via a kind of Walrasian sleight of hand, transformed the profound and intellectually subversive message into something innocuous, insipid and even lifeless" (1983, xi).

5. I owe this way of thinking about "identity" – in terms of individuation and reidentification – to John Davis (2003).

6. This was primarily an Anglo-American phenomenon, but given the historical context of the immediate post World War II period, it came to characterize the discipline in general.

7. Note the "neoclassical synthesis" here and throughout refers to the original neoclassical synthesis and not the "new neoclassical synthesis" of dynamic stochastic general equilibrium (DSGE) models (Clarida, Galí, and Gertler 1999, Goodfriend and King 1997). See the Duarte chapter in this volume for a detailed discussion of DSGE models.

8. I will follow tradition and use the term "neoclassical synthesis," but in fact the term "synthesis" does not really capture the relationship very well. A synthesis suggests two things coming together to form a third that is unique and different from each of the things that entered into it: like the synthesis of water from hydrogen and oxygen. But the neoclassical synthesis was not like this. Microeconomics and macroeconomics remained identifiable and distinct fields; they did not disappear as separate entities upon the formation of the neoclassical synthesis. The main point of this chapter is that although Walrasian economics had certain core conceptions that were identifiable over time, it also evolved and changed in response to, and because of, its contact with Keynesian economics. This seems much more like *co-evolution* than synthesis. Each program remains distinct – it retains its own genetic material and some aspects of its earlier behavior – but also changes in various ways because it has formed a partnership with another research program. I will argue that what Walrasian economics was in the 1960s was in part because of its relationship with Keynesian economics – and the interaction of the partnership with the environment in which these two sets of ideas competed and survived – and yet it always maintained a separate identifiable existence.

9. As Luca Fiorito explains, focusing on the (first level) strife of radically different research programs blinds us "to the 'second level' of pluralism which characterized US interwar economics, i.e. not just variety *among* schools of thought but also variety *within* each school. This was true of that variegated universe that was pre-WW II American neoclassicism ..." (Fiorito 2000: 269). Also see Backhouse (2003) and Morgan and Rutherford (1998).

10. As historians of biology have noted about the Darwinian synthesis of experimental genetics and Darwinian evolutionary theory (during roughly the same time period as the neoclassical synthesis): "From the beginning, founders of the synthetic theory were concerned to make the modern synthesis appear as complete and coherent as possible" (Hull 1988: 204).

11. Including the other factors I have examined in previous research (for example, in Hands 1994, 2006, 2007, 2010a, 2010b; Hands and Mirowski 1998; or Mirowski and Hands 1998).

12. Only under very restrictive conditions can market demand be written as a function of the n prices and total income $M = \sum_h M^h$. This is one version of the notorious aggregation problem in demand theory. See the Hoover chapter in this volume for a discussion of the aggregation problem in macroeconomics.

13. See Hands (2011).

14. See Shafer and Sonnenschein (1982) for a survey and Rizvi (1998, 2003, 2006) for more historical discussion.

15. See Van Daal and Walker (1990) on the difference between Walras and Pareto on this matter.
16. My discussion of the tâtonnement of Walras (as opposed to the Walrasian tâtonnement) will focus primarily on his analysis of the pure exchange case. A detailed discussion of what Walras said about tâtonnement processes in general is not necessary for the task at hand. There were four (nested) models in the *Elements* – pure exchange, production, capital formation, and monetary theory – and the book went through five editions (counting the 4th definitive) and Walras offered different characterizations of the tâtonnement in different editions as well as for different models within various editions. In particular, the assumption of "no disequilibrium trading" or no trading at "false prices" was handled differently in various editions and models. The variation among editions is greatest in his analysis of production and capital formation, where his introduction of "tickets" ("*bons*") in the 4th edition provided a version of the "no trading at false prices" restriction for these models. Although there is some variation in his analysis of the pure exchange case, the core characterization offered in the 2nd edition remained basically intact in the later editions and that is the version of Walras's tâtonnement discussed here. Those interested in the details of how Walras's view of the tâtonnement changed across various editions and models can consult the various detailed discussions within the secondary literature (that is, Bridel and Huck 2002; Donzelli 2006, 2007; Jaffé 1967, 1980, 1981).
17. Uzawa (1960) noted that Walras's iterative process was a version of the Gauss–Seidel algorithm and proved that it converges under the assumption that all goods are gross substitutes.
18. Walras did not use the term "dynamic" for (any version of) his competitive price adjustment mechanism. For Walras, "dynamics" involved changes in the fundamentals of the analysis – tastes, technology, endowments, etc. – and the tâtonnement is not dynamic in this sense.
19. See Weintraub (1979, 1991) for more detail on these various economists (particularly Patinkin).
20. See Hands (2006, 2010a, 2011) for a more detailed discussion of, and evidence for, this argument and how it relates to various issues in the history of demand theory (integrability in particular) as well as to recent research in experimental and behavioral economics.
21. Consistent, that is, with respect to the symmetry of the behavior of the economic agent and the behavior of the competitive market. In other respects, Lucas's framework is much less consistent with Walras than Arrow and Hahn (1971) – his use of the representative agent being the most obvious inconsistency.
22. This was pointed out in Hands and Mirowski (1998: 366).
23. Symbolism follows (CCP), (ID) and (MD) above.
24. Note Friedman is only being quoted here to make the point about the Keynesian connection to the Slutsky equation and Friedman's criticism of it; it is not an endorsement of Friedman's interpretation of Marshall.
25. Consider for example recent developments in Walrasian general equilibrium theory such as the equilibrium manifold approach (e.g. Balasko 2009, Brown and Matzkin 1996, Brown and Shannon 2000, Chiappori and Ekeland 2004). See Rizvi (2006) for historical discussion of this literature.
26. See the various papers in De Vroey and Hoover (2004).
27. The literature here is quite extensive. See for example Ingrao and Israel (1990); Kirman (1989, 2006); Rivzi (1998, 2003, 2006); Scarf (1981).
28. See the Hoover chapter in this volume for a detailed discussion of the microfoundations literature.
29. Think of the k_is in (T') as Lucas's "free parameters."
30. And will be negative definite if the numéraire row and column is eliminated as it normally would be for stability analysis.
31. See Arrow and Hahn (1971, ch. 11).

32.   Arrow and Hurwicz (1958).
33.   As I indicated in note 11, I have discussed a number of other factors in previous research.

REFERENCES

Allen, R. G. D. (1936). Professor Slutsky's Theory of Consumer's Choice. *Review of Economic Studies*, 3 (2):120–29.
Amadae, Sonja M. (2003). *Rationalizing Capitalist Democracy: The Cold War Origins of Rational Choice Theory*. Chicago: University of Chicago Press.
Armstrong, W. E. (1939). The Determinateness of the Utility Function. *Economic Journal*, 49 (195):453–67.
Arrow, Kenneth J., H. David Block, and Leonid Hurwicz (1959). On the Stability of the Competitive Equilibrium II. *Econometrica*, 27 (1):82–109.
Arrow, Kenneth J., and Frank H. Hahn (1971). *General Competitive Analysis*. San Francisco: Holden-Day.
Arrow, Kenneth J., and Leonid Hurwicz (1958). On the Stability of the Competitive Equilibrium I. *Econometrica*, 26 (4):522–52.
Backhouse, Roger E. (2003). The Stabilization of Price Theory, 1920–1955. In *A Companion to the History of Economic Thought*. Edited by W. J. Samuels, J. E. Biddle, and J. B. Davis. Oxford: Wiley-Blackwell.
Backhouse, Roger E., and David Laidler (2004). What Was Lost with IS-LM? In *The IS-LM Model: Its Rise, Fall, and Strange Persistence. History of Political Economy* 36 supplement. Edited by M. De Vroey, and K. D. Hoover. Durham, NC: Duke University Press.
Balasko, Yves (2009). *The Equilibrium Manifold: Postmodern Developments in the Theory of General Equilibrium*. Cambridge, MA: MIT Press.
Barnett, Vincent (2004). E. E. Slutsky: Mathematical Statistician, Economist, and Political Economist. *Journal of the History of Economic Thought*, 26 (1):3–18.
Bernardelli, Harro (1952). A Rehabilitation of the Classical Theory of Marginal Utility. *Economica*, 19 (75):254–68.
Bowles, Samuel, and Herbert Gintis (2000). Walrasian Economics in Retrospect. *Quarterly Journal of Economics*, 115 (4):1411–39.
Bridel, Pascal, and Elisabeth Huck (2002). Yet Another Look at Leon Walras's Theory of Tâtonnement. *European Journal of the History of Economic Thought*, 9 (4):513–40.
Brown, Donald J., and Rosa L. Matzkin (1996). Testable Restrictions on the Equilibrium Manifold. *Econometrica*, 64 (6):1249–62.
Brown, Donald J., and Chris Shannon (2000). Uniqueness, Stability, and Comparative Statics in Rationalizable Walrasian Markets. *Econometrica*, 68 (6):1529–39.
Camerer, Colin F., and George Loewenstein (2004). Behavioral Economics: Past, Present, and Future. In *Advances in Behavioral Economics*. Edited by C. F. Camerer, G. Loewenstein, and M. Rabin. Princeton: Princeton University Press.
Chiappori, Pierre-Andre, and Ivair Ekeland (2004). Individual Excess Demand. *Journal of Mathematical Economics*, 40 (2004):41–57.
Chipman, John S. (2004) Slutsky's Praxeology and his Critique of Böhm-Bawerk. *Structural Change and Economic Dynamics*, 15 (3):345–56.

Chipman, John S., and Jean-Sebastien Lenfant (2002). Slutsky's 1915 Article: How it Came to be Found and Interpreted. *History of Political Economy*, 34 (3):553–97.

Clarida, Richard, Jordi Galí, and Mark Gertler (1999). The Scope of Monetary Policy: A New Keynesian Perspective. *Journal of Economic Literature*, 37 (4):1661–707.

Clower, Robert W. (1965). The Keynesian Counter-Revolution: A Theoretical Appraisal. In *The Theory of Interest Rates*. Edited by F. Hahn, and F. Brechling. London: Macmillan.

Coddington, Alan (1983). *Keynesian Economics: The Search for First Principles*. London: George Allen & Unwin.

Colander, David (2000). The Death of Neoclassical Economics. *Journal of the History of Economic Thought*, 22 (2):127–43.

Colander, David (ed.) (2006). *Post Walrasian Macroeconomics: Beyond the Dynamic Stochastic General Equilibrium Model*. Cambridge: Cambridge University Press.

Colander, David, Richard Holt, and Barkley Rosser (2004a). The Changing Face of Mainstream Economics. *Review of Political Economy*, 16 (4):485–99.

Colander, David, Richard Holt, and Barkley Rosser (2004b). *Changing Face of Economics: Conversations with Cutting Edge Economists*. Ann Arbor: University of Michigan Press.

Davis, John B. (2003). *The Theory of the Individual in Economics*. London: Routledge.

Davis, John B. (2006). The Turn in Economics: Neoclassical Dominance to Mainstream Pluralism. *Journal of Institutional Economics*, 2 (1):1–20.

Davis, John B. (2008). The Turn in Recent Economics and Return of Orthodoxy. *Cambridge Journal of Economics*, 32 (3):349–66.

Debreu, Gerard (1974). Excess Demand Functions. *Journal of Mathematical Economics*, 1 (1):15–21.

DellaVigna, Stafano (2009). Psychology and Economics: Evidence from the Field. *Journal of Economic Literature*, 47 (2):315–72.

De Vroey, Michel (2009). On the Right Side for the Wrong Reason: Friedman on the Marshall–Walras Divide. In *The Methodology of Positive Economics: Reflections on the Milton Friedman Legacy*. Edited by U. Mäki. Cambridge: Cambridge University Press.

De Vroey, Michel, and Kevin Hoover (eds) (2004). *The IS-LM Model. Its Rise, Fall and Strange Persistence*. History of Political Economy 36 supplement. Durham, NC: Duke University Press.

Donzelli, Franco (2006). Walras and Pareto on the Meaning of the Solution Concept in General Equilibrium Theory. University of Milano Economics, Business and Statistics Working Paper No. 2006-31. Available at SSRN: http://ssrn.com/abstract=939539.

Donzelli, Franco (2007). Equilibrium and Tâtonnement in Walras's Elements. *History of Economic Ideas*, 15 (3):85–138.

Evans, Griffith C. (1930). *Mathematical Introduction to Economics*. New York: McGraw-Hill.

Fiorito, Luca (2000). The Years of High Pluralism: U. S. Interwar Economics in Light of the Mitchell Correspondence. *Research in the History of Economic Thought and Methodology*, 18C:267–335.

Friedman, Milton (1953). The Marshallian Demand Curve. In *Essays in Positive Economics*. Edited by Milton Friedman. Chicago: The University of Chicago Press.

Friedman, Milton (1962). *Price Theory: A Provisional Text*, Revised Edition. Chicago: Aldine.

Frisch, Ragnar (1926). On A Problem in Pure Economics. *Norsk Matematisk Forenings Skrifter*. Translation by J. S. Chipman, published in *Preferences, Utility, and Demand*. Edited by John S. Chipman, Leonid Hurwicz, Marcel Richter, and Hugo Sonnenschein, 1971. New York: Harcourt Brace Jovanovich.

Gale, David (1963). A Note on Global Instability of Competitive Equilibrium. *Naval Research Logistics Quarterly*, 10 (1):81–7.

Georgescu-Roegen, Nicholas (1936). The Pure Theory of Consumer's Behaviour. *Quarterly Journal of Economics*, 50 (4):545–93.

Georgescu-Roegen, Nicholas (1950). The Theory of Choice and the Constancy of Economic Laws. *Quarterly Journal of Economics*, 64 (1):125–38.

Georgescu-Roegen, Nicholas (1968). Utility. In *International Encyclopedia of the Social Sciences*. Edited by D. L. Sills. New York: Macmillan, pp. 236–67.

Gilboy, Elizabeth Waterman (1930). Demand Curves in Theory and Practice. *Quarterly Journal of Economics*, 44 (4):601–20.

Giocoli, Nicola (2003). *Modeling Rational Agents: From Interwar Economics to Early Modern Game Theory*. Cheltenham, UK: Edward Elgar.

Goodfriend, Marvin, and Robert King (1997). The New Neoclassical Synthesis and the Role of Monetary Policy. *NBER Macroeconomics Annual 1997*, edited by B. S. Bernanke, and J. J. Rotemberg, 12:231–83.

Hands, D. Wade (1994). Restabilizing Dynamics: Construction and Constraint in the History of Walrasian Stability Theory. *Economics and Philosophy*, 10 (2):243–83.

Hands, D. Wade (2006). Integrability, Rationalizability, and Path-Dependency in the History of Demand Theory. In *Agreement on Demand: Consumer Theory in the Twentieth Century*. *History of Political Economy* 38 supplement. Edited by P. Mirowski, and D. W. Hands. Durham, NC: Duke University Press.

Hands, D. Wade (2007). 2006 HES Presidential Address: A Tale of Two Mainstreams: Economics and Philosophy of Natural Science in the mid-Twentieth Century. *Journal of the History of Economic Thought*, 29 (1):1–13.

Hands, D. Wade (2010a). Stabilizing Consumer Choice: The Role of "True Dynamic Stability" and Related Concepts in the History of Consumer Choice Theory. *European Journal of the History of Economic Thought*, 17 (2):313–43.

Hands, D. Wade (2010b). Economics, Psychology, and the History of Consumer Choice Theory. *Cambridge Journal of Economics*, 34 (4):633–48.

Hands, D. Wade (2011). Back to the Ordinal Revolution: Behavioral Economic Concerns in Early Modern Consumer Choice Theory. *Metroeconomica*, 62 (2), 386–410.

Hands, D. Wade, and Philip Mirowski (1998). Harold Hotelling and the Neoclassical Dream. In *Economics and Methodology: Crossing Boundaries*. Edited by R. Backhouse, D. Hausman, U. Mäki, and A. Salanti. London: Macmillan.

Hansen, Alvin (1949). *Monetary Theory and Fiscal Policy*. New York: McGraw-Hill.

Hicks, John R. (1937). Mr. Keynes and the 'Classics': A Suggested Interpretation. *Econometrica*, 5 (2):147–59.

Hicks, John R. ([1939] 1946). *Value and Capital: An Inquiry into Some Fundamental Principles of Economic Theory*. 2nd edn. Oxford: Clarendon Press.

Hicks, John R. (1980–81). IS-LM: An Explanation. *Journal of Post Keynesian Economics*, 3 (2):139–54.

Hicks, John R., and R. G. D. Allen (1934). A Reconsideration of the Theory of Value, Parts I and II. *Economica*, 1 (1–2):52–76, 196–219.

Hoover, Kevin D. (1988). *The New Classical Macroeconomics*. Oxford: Basil Blackwell.

Hotelling, Harold (1932). Edgeworth's Taxation Paradox and the Nature of Demand and Supply Functions. *Journal of Political Economy*, 40 (5):577–616.

Hull, David (1988). *Science as a Process*. Chicago: University of Chicago Press.

Ingrao, Bruna, and Giorgio Israel (1990). *The Invisible Hand: Economic Theory in the History of Science*. Cambridge, MA: MIT Press.

Jaffé, William (1967). Walras' Theory of Tâtonnement: A Critique of Recent Interpretations. *Journal of Political Economy*, 75 (1):1–19.

Jaffé, William (1980). Walras's Economics As Others See It. *Journal of Economic Literature*, 18 (2):528–49.

Jaffé, William (1981). Another Look at Léon Walras' Theory of Tâtonnement. *History of Political Economy*, 13 (2):313–36.

Kahneman, Daniel (2003). Maps of Bounded Rationality: A Perspective on Intuitive Judgment. *American Economic Review*, 93 (5):1449–75.

Kahneman, Daniel, Jack L. Knetsch, and Richard Thaler (1990). Experimental Tests of the Endowment Effect and the Coase Theorem. *Journal of Political Economy*, 98 (6):1325–48.

Keynes, John Maynard (1936). *The General Theory of Employment, Interest and Money*. London: Macmillan.

Kirman, Alan (1989). The Intrinsic Limits of Modern Equilibrium Theory: The Emperor Has No Clothes. *Economic Journal*, 99 (395):126–39.

Kirman, Alan (1992). Whom or What Does the Representative Individual Represent. *Journal of Economic Perspectives*, 6 (2):117–36.

Kirman, Alan (2006). Demand Theory and General Equilibrium: From Explanation to Introspection, A Journey Down the Wrong Road. In *Agreement on Demand: Consumer Theory in the Twentieth Century. History of Political Economy* 38 supplement. Edited by P. Mirowski, and D. W. Hands. Durham, NC: Duke University Press.

Knetsch, Jack L. (1989). The Endowment Effect and Evidence of Nonreversible Indifference Curves. *American Economic Review*, 79 (5):1277–84.

Knetsch, Jack L. (1992). Preferences and the Nonreversibility of Indifference Curves. *Journal of Economic Behavior and Organization*, 17 (1):131–9.

Knight, Frank H. (1944). Realism and Relevance in the Theory of Demand. *Journal of Political Economy*, 52 (4):289–318.

Lange, Oscar (1942). Say's Law: A Restatement and Criticism. In *Studies in Mathematical Economics and Econometrics: In Memory of Henry Schultz*. Edited by O. Lange, F. McIntyre, and T. O. Untema. Chicago: University of Chicago Press.

Lange, Oscar (1944). *Price Flexibility and Employment*. Bloomington, IN: The Principia Press.

Leijonhufvud, Axel (1968). *On Keynesian Economics and the Economics of Keynes: A Study in Monetary Theory*. Oxford: Oxford University Press.

Lerner, Abba P. (1944). *The Economics of Control: Principles of Welfare Economics*. New York: Macmillan.

Lucas, Robert E. Jr. (1981). *Studies in Business Cycle Theory*. Oxford: Basil Blackwell.

Mantel, Rolf R. (1974). On the Characterization of Aggregate Excess Demand. *Journal of Economic Theory*, 7 (3):348–53.

Mantel, Rolf R. (1977). Implications of Microeconomic Theory for Community Excess Demand Functions. In *Frontiers in Quantitative Economic IIIA*. Edited by M. D. Intriligator. Amsterdam: North-Holland.

Mayer, Thomas (2009). On the Right Side for the Wrong Reason: Friedman on the Marshall–Walras Divide. In *The Methodology of Positive Economics: Reflections on the Milton Friedman Legacy*. Edited by U. Mäki. Cambridge: Cambridge University Press.

Mirowski, Philip (2002). *Machine Dreams: Economics Becomes a Cyborg Science*. Cambridge: Cambridge University Press.

Mirowski, Philip, and Hands, D. Wade (1998). A Paradox of Budgets: The Postwar Stabilization of American Neoclassical Demand Theory. In *From Interwar Pluralism to Postwar Neoclassicism*. *History of Political Economy* 30 supplement. Edited by M. S. Morgan, and M. Rutherford. Durham, NC: Duke University Press.

Modigliani, Franco (1944). Liquidity Preference and the Theory of Interest and Money. *Econometrica*, 12 (1):45–88.

Moore, Henry Ludwell (1914). *Economic Cycles: Their Law and Cause*. New York: Macmillan.

Morgan, Mary S., and Rutherford, Malcolm (1998). *From Interwar Pluralism to Postwar Neoclassicism*. Durham, NC: Duke University Press.

Morgenstern, Oskar (1948). Demand Theory Reconsidered. *Quarterly Journal of Economics*, 62 (2):165–201.

Mukherji, Anjan (1974). Stability in an Economy with Production. In *Trade, Stability and Macroeconomics: Essays in Honor of Lloyd A. Metzler*. Edited by G. Horwich, and P. A. Samuelson. New York: Academic Press.

Pareto, Vilfredo (1971). *Manual of Political Economy*. New York: Augustus M. Kelley. Translated by Ann S. Schwier from the 1927 French edition.

Patinkin, Don ([1956] 1965). *Money, Interest, and Prices: An Integration of Monetary and Value Theory*. 2nd edn. New York: Harper & Row.

Pearce, Kerry A., and Kevin D. Hoover (1995). After the Revolution: Paul Samuelson and the Textbook Keynesian Model. In *New Perspectives on Keynes*. *History of Political Economy* 27 supplement. Edited by A. F. Cottrell, and M. S. Lawlor. Durham, NC: Duke University Press.

Rizvi, S. Abu Turab (1998). Responses to Arbitrariness in Contemporary Economics. In *New Economics and Its History*. *History of Political Economy* 29 supplement. Edited by John B. Davis. Durham, NC: Duke University Press.

Rizvi, S. Abu Turab (2003). The Stabilization of Price Theory, 1920–1955. In *A Companion to the History of Economic Thought*. Edited by W. J. Samuels, J. E. Biddle, and J. B. Davis. Oxford: Wiley-Blackwell.

Rizvi, S. Abu Turab (2006). The Sonnenschein–Mantel–Debreu Results After Thirty Years. In *Agreement on Demand: Consumer Theory in the Twentieth Century*. *History of Political Economy* 38 supplement. Edited by P. Mirowski, and D. W. Hands. Durham, NC: Duke University Press.

Robertson, Dennis H. (1952). *Utility and All That and Other Essays*. London: Allen & Unwin.

Samuelson, Paul A. (1938). A Note on the Pure Theory of Consumer's Behaviour. *Economica*, 5 (17):61–71.

Samuelson, Paul A. (1941). The Stability of Equilibrium: Comparative Statics and Dynamics. *Econometrica*, 9 (2):97–120.

Samuelson, Paul A. (1942). The Stability of Equilibrium: Linear and Non-Linear Systems. *Econometrica*, 10 (1):1–25.

Samuelson, Paul A. (1944). The Relation Between Hicksian Stability and True Dynamic Stability. *Econometrica*, 12 (3/4):256–7.

Samuelson, Paul A. (1947). *Foundations of Economic Analysis*. Cambridge, MA: Harvard University Press.

Samuelson, Paul A. (1955). *Economics*. 3rd edn. New York: McGraw-Hill.

Scarf, Herbert (1960). Some Examples of Global Instability of the Competitive Equilibrium. *International Economic Review*, 1 (3):157–72.

Scarf, Herbert (1981). Comment on: "On the Stability of Competitive Equilibrium and the Patterns of Initial Holdings: An Example". *International Economic Review*, 22 (2):469–70.

Schultz, Henry (1928). *Statistical Laws of Demand and Supply: with Special Application to Sugar*. Chicago: University of Chicago Press.

Schultz, Henry (1938). *The Theory and Measurement of Demand*. Chicago: University of Chicago Press.

Shafer, Wayne, and Hugo Sonnenschein (1982). Market Excess Demand Functions. In *Handbook of Mathematical Economics*, Vol. II. Edited by K. J. Arrow, and M. D. Intriligator. Amsterdam: North-Holland.

Slutsky, Eugene E. ([1915] 1952). Sulla Teoria del Bilancio del Consonatore. *Giornale degli Economisti*, 51, 1–26. Translated in Readings in *Price Theory*. Edited by G. J. Stigler, and K. E. Boulding. Homewood, IL: Richard D. Irwin.

Snowdon, Brian, and Howard R. Vane (2005). *Modern Macroeconomics: Its Origins, Development And Current State*. Cheltenham, UK; Edward Elgar.

Sonnenschein, Hugo (1972). Market Excess Demand Functions. *Econometrica*, 40 (3):549–63.

Sonnenschein, Hugo (1973). Do Walras' Identity and Continuity Characterize the Class of Community Excess Demand Functions? *Journal of Economic Theory*, 6 (4):345–54.

Thaler, Richard H. (1980). Toward a Positive Theory of Consumer Choice. *Journal of Economic Behavior and Organization*, 1 (1):39–60.

Tobin, James (1958). Liquidity Preference as Behavior Towards Risk. *Review of Economic Studies*, 25 (2):65–86.

Tobin, James (1969). A General Equilibrium Approach to Monetary Theory. *Journal of Money, Credit and Banking*, 1 (1):15–29.

Uzawa, Hirofumi (1960). Walras' Tâtonnement in the Theory of Exchange. *Review of Economic Studies*, 27 (3):182–94.

Van Daal, Jan, and Donald A. Walker (1990). The Problem of Aggregation in Walras's General Equilibrium Theory. *History of Political Economy*, 22 (3):489–505.

Walras, Leon (1954). *Elements of Pure Economics*. Translated by W. Jaffé from the 4th definitive edition 1926, Homewood, IL: Richard D. Irwin.

Weber, Christian E. (1999a). Slutsky and Additive Utility Functions. *History of Political Economy*, 31 (2):394–416.

Weber, Christian E. (1999b). More on Slutsky's Equation as Pareto's Solution. *History of Political Economy*, 31 (3):575–86

Weintraub, E. Roy (1979). *Microfoundations: The Compatibility of Microeconomics and Macroeconomics*. Cambridge: Cambridge University Press.

Weintraub, E. Roy (1985). *General Equilibrium Analysis: Studies in Appraisal*. Cambridge: Cambridge University Press.

Weintraub, E. Roy (1991). *Stabilizing Dynamics: Constructing Economic Knowledge*. Cambridge: Cambridge University Press.

Weintraub, E. Roy (2002). *How Economics Became a Mathematical Science*. Durham, NC: Duke University Press.

4. The Cowles Commission as an anti-Keynesian stronghold 1943–54

Philip E. Mirowski[1]

Today, it seems, just about anyone can get away with calling themselves a Keynesian, and they do, no matter what salmagundi of doctrinal positions they may hold dear, without fear of ridicule or reproach. Consequently, some of the most extraordinarily absurd things are now being attributed to Keynes and called "Keynesian theories". For instance, J. Bradford DeLong, a popular blogger and faculty member at Berkeley, has in a (2009) paper divided up the history of macroeconomics into what he identifies as a "Peel–Keynes–Friedman axis" and a "Marx–Hoover–Hayek" axis: clearly he has learned a trick or two from the neoliberals, who sow mass confusion by mixing together oil and water in their salad dressing versions of history. The self-appointed "New Keynesians" of the 1990s (including Gregory Mankiw, David Romer and Michael Woodford) took the name of Keynes in vain by unashamedly asserting a proposition that Keynes himself had repeatedly and expressly rejected, namely that market-clearing models cannot explain short-run economic fluctuations, and so proceeded to advocate models with "sticky" wages and prices (Mankiw, 2006). George Akerlof and Robert Shiller (2009) have taken three sentences from the *General Theory* out of context and spun it into some banal misrepresentation concerning what Keynes actually wrote about the notion of "animal spirits," not to mention his actual conception of macroeconomics.[2] And we observe contemporary journalists going gaga over Keynes, with almost no underlying substantive justification from the track record of the economics profession:

> More than three decades have passed since Richard Nixon, the Republican US president, declared: "We are all Keynesians now." The phrase rings truer today than at any time since, as governments seize on John Maynard Keynes's idea that fiscal stimulus – public spending and tax cuts – can help dig their economies out of recession. (Giles, 2008)

It is undeniably a Sisyphusian task to lean against this blustering tide of misrepresentation in the current Humpty Dumpty climate, with its gales of misinformation and gusts whipping about the turncoats, where economists harbor such easy contempt for history that words can be purported to mean anything that is convenient or politic for the selfish purposes of the writer. Indeed, in the current crisis, it may be a matter of urgency for the 'second-hand dealers in ideas' (as Hayek called them) to hastily rewrite history and their own previous pronunciamentos, if only to cover up the extensive complicity of modern economists in neutralizing financial deregulation, occupying governmental agencies and justifying the invention of the so-called 'toxic derivatives', hence contributing mightily to the contraction, not to mention their need to minimize their utter disarray when it comes to agreeing how to respond to the debilitating situation. Peter Hall (1989) has already demonstrated conclusively that the government policies pursued in the Great Depression across many nations had little or nothing to do with what Keynes wrote. "Roosevelt saw deficit spending more as a condition to be overcome ... than as a theoretical prescription to be followed" (Collins 1981: 4), which renders him a kissing cousin to the current Obama administration. Brad Bateman has pointed out that almost the entire stylized history concerning Keynes and Keynesianism has been refuted by one historian or another, essentially to no avail (Backhouse and Bateman 2006: 272). The ultimate irony for the historian is that Keynes after 1936 kept insisting there were limits to the state's ability to manage the economy (Bateman 1996: 146). So what could be the value-added contribution of one further attempt at clarification of the tortured relationship of Keynes and a small subset of the Keynesian pretenders, at this late hour?

I want to insist at the outset this is not another forlorn safari in search of the Real Keynes. Those who have read my other work know that I do not believe such Rocks of Ages really exist. I am here much more concerned to separate out those who seriously struggled with Keynes because they perceived some incompatibilities between his writing and their own theoretical commitments, and then to understand the ways they came to terms with their misgivings;[3] hence quarantining them from those for whom the adoption of a Keynesian label was nothing more than a temporary expedient mask they doffed to signal empathetic rapport with their audience (or quell their own political discombobulation). The latter are notoriously impervious to the charms of history, and indeed, have proven uninterested in real intellectual inquiry.

I want to begin with a proposition that can serve as a quick and dirty litmus test to separate out most of the economists who have taken Keynes seriously from the plethora of preening pretenders, particularly in the current climate. This proposition, hardly original in its inspiration, is that whatever Keynes' rhetoric may have done to blur the boundaries of his renunciation of his contemporary orthodoxy,[4] subsequent history demonstrates beyond a doubt that the Keynesian system is inherently incompatible with neoclassical microeconomic theory in its most rigorous manifestation, viz., the theory of Walrasian general equilibrium.[5] This case has been made time and again in the analytical mode, by figures as various as Robert Clower, Frank Hahn, John Hicks, Alan Kirman, Franklin Fisher, Paul Davidson, Hyman Minsky and a whole host of other illustrious figures.[6] Further, there is the oft-overlooked denunciation by Keynes himself, in a December 1934 letter to Nicholas Georgescu-Roegen: "All the same, I shall hope to convince you some day that Walras' theory and all the others along those lines are little better than nonsense!" (in Clower 1984; 190). So, if there has been any progress at all in macroeconomics since 1936, one might at least hope that everyone could come to agree that the economic theory of Keynes has proven conceptually antithetical to rigorous neoclassical microtheory, whichever of those traditions they wished to champion. If you fancied yourself a true believer in modern microeconomics, then you would graciously and prudently stop confusing and confounding it with Keynesianism, and vice versa. Reflex sneers about raddled 'microfoundations' would have to get checked at the door. The only substantive benefit from hewing to this proposition would be that the hapless non-economist might have some prayer of sorting through the allegiances of all those self-appointed saviors of the economy who clog the airwaves and blogs and what is left of the serious press.

But as I am sure my reader is aware, there has been no progress in macroeconomics in that respect. A few try to invent a third overlapping category by suggesting there is still a viable "Marshallian" economics that is both rooted in contemporary legitimate neoclassical microeconomics and at the same time respects the actual arguments one finds in Keynes' *General Theory*. This chapter does not have anything to say concerning that position.[7] Others, less nostalgic for those simpler Marshallian verities, simply assert that the only legitimate economics must start with the Walrasian model, or else something that bears a family resemblance to so-called dynamic general equilibrium, maximize this or that, and then go on to derive propositions which are loosely dubbed "Keynesian" with no further evidence or justification. This constitutes the vast bulk of what passes for research in economics journals these days, and indeed, the range of public discussion of the economic crisis seems almost entirely confined within the boundaries of this position. Sadly, it is literally gibberish. No wonder journalists are beginning to openly suggest that economists are as treacherous and slippery and dangerous as the bankers and hedge fund buccaneers who are conventionally indicted with causing the crisis (Coy 2009).

I have no illusions that mere historical research could somehow rectify this most unsatisfactory predicament. Every attempt in four decades to slay the Gorgon has resulted in the monster growing three new heads, meanwhile turning the pathetic Keynesian challenger to pumice. Charlatans will continue to hide behind the flimsy façade they call "Keynes" well into the foreseeable future. Nevertheless, I believe it would be a minor yet significant advance in the history of economic thought to make some effort to understand why the neoclassical yoke on the Keynesian donkey apparently can never be lifted. Once it becomes established that Keynesian economics will never be delivered from neoclassical corruption and misrepresentation, at least in this world, then perhaps a new set of options for the future of macroeconomics can be seriously put on the table; but that awaits a different future than the one we now face.

In the meantime, historians can demonstrate that Keynesian ideas were hobbled from birth, in the sense that two (and maybe even all three) of the postwar schools of American neoclassical economics were in a very palpable sense *hostile* to the theoretical content of the *General Theory*. The putative "Keynesian Revolution" of the 1940s in an interesting sense didn't really happen.[8] In other words, I want to counter the proposition that, "The radical approach identifies the problem as Walrasian theory" as Kevin Hoover (2006: 239) so clearly puts it. Here the role of historians is *not* to become embroiled in the old endless futile argument over "what Keynes really really meant"; and it is certainly not to "rescue" the shade of Keynes from his detractors. Rather, what historians should insist upon is that, if and when we get serious about what Keynes actually wrote, and how it was received in the immediate aftermath to 1936, then at least in America, it becomes clear that almost everyone responsible for the postwar neoclassical ascendancy in its first decade actually conceded in one way or another that Walras was indeed the problem, and that, were Keynesian ideas to be pursued, macrotheory must be revised and reconfigured to conform to Walras (or something very like it). If that meant lopping off some inconvenient appendages here or negating some doctrines there, then so much the worse for *The General Theory*. *There is nothing "radical" about this proposition*; it is simply historical fact.

1. THE KEYNESIAN REVOLUTION THAT WASN'T: AN OVERVIEW

The primary contention of this chapter is that far too many postwar neoclassical economists have been uncritically and misleadingly counted as 'Keynesians' in America; indeed, a more careful and thorough census would reveal that, in practice, they were actually much more scarce on the ground. The commonplace idea that there was some sort of grassroots groundswell 'Keynesian Revolution' in 1940s/50s America should itself then eventually come in for renewed skepticism and historiographic revision. Indeed, that particular storyline was first popularized by one of the major protagonists in the current chapter, Lawrence Klein (1947), whose own Keynesian credentials were curiously dodgy, as we shall soon discover. Instead, the predominant motivation seems to have been to render neoclassical theory safe *from* Keynes, whatever that safety was taken to mean in the various American precincts. This claim about the American economics profession – that it was overwhelmingly inclined in an anti-Keynesian direction – is rather broad, and would seem to require an impossibly large sample of representative agents to be done justice within a single chapter. Luckily, we can make reference to some previous literature in the history of economics to whittle the problem down to a manageable size.

We shall take as our point of departure a set of arguments made elsewhere[9] that there was no neoclassical orthodoxy in America prior to WWII; and thus when neoclassicism did rise to dominance, it did so in the format of three very different schools of thought – here identified for convenience's sake as the Chicago School, the MIT School, and the Cowles School. Everyone knows that one of the main tenets that united the Chicago School was hostility to everything they believed that Keynes stood for. Furthermore, this was a major consideration right out of the starting gate in 1946.[10] Hence we can save time by simply presuming that there is no problem recruiting the Chicago school to support our contention that neoclassical theory was incompatible with Keynes.[11] The challenge comes instead with the other two schools.

The cases of MIT and Cowles would at first glance appear more daunting. Paul Samuelson was a standard-bearer of the self-declared vanguard of the Keynesian Revolution in America, and undisputed leader of the MIT school; indeed he popularized "Keynes the economic theorist" through his successful introductory textbook, where he coined the later ubiquitous catchphrase "grand neoclassical synthesis". But historians have progressively become aware just how elusive and insubstantial the grand "synthesis" really was around MIT. Luckily, we can point to the work of the very same Kevin Hoover, who in (Pearce and Hoover 1995) indicates that:

> Samuelson's … analytic goal is to resolve the paradox between Keynes and the (neo)classics. This is accomplished through studious vagueness. There is no serious attempt to reconcile the macroeconomics of his first edition with microeconomics; resolution of the paradox is then mostly an avoidance of its implications. (1995: 200)

In the second edition of his textbook, Samuelson addressed the problem by simply wishing it away:

> In recent years, 90% of American economists have stopped being "Keynesian economists" or "anti-Keynesian economists." Instead they have worked toward a synthesis of whatever is valuable in older economics and modern theories of income determination. The result might be called neo-classical economics and is accepted in its broad outlines by all but about 5% of extreme left-wing and right-wing writers. (Samuelson 1951: 260)

This statement was a shameless whitewash when it was published, but does tend to capture the mindset of those postwar economists at MIT who struggled to reconcile their conflicting theoretical allegiances in the late 1940s. Samuelson revealed he was aware there might be some threat of incompatibility, but signaled he would proceed as if little things like logical contradictions could be easily evaded, if only one pursued the appropriate mathematics. What this meant in practice was strict adherence to a lowbrow version of price theory pitched somewhere between Marshall and Walras, plus promotion of a few "macroeconomic" models nowhere to be found in the *General Theory*. Of course, the infamous 45° diagram placed so prominently near the front of the textbook didn't represent the higher reaches of macroeconomics at MIT in the late 1940s: that tended to revolve instead around the IS-LM model, a subject of intense historical scrutiny in the interim.[12] Again, in this chapter we want to avoid the interminable and sterile arguments over whether or not IS-LM was 'really' legitimately Keynesian; rather, we simply want to endorse the literature which suggests that macroeconomic innovation at MIT happened almost entirely within the precincts of what was then deemed good neoclassical theory; whereas Keynes the author was treated at MIT more or less disparagingly as a bumbler who "did not really understand what he had written, and chose the wrong thing to publicize as his innovation" (Klein, 1947: 83); "Keynes seems never to have had any genuine interest in pure economic theory" (Samuelson 1946: 196); rather like a delirious prophet who spoke in tongues. By the way, it was not snarky critics that first drew that particular religious comparison; it was the Pope of MIT himself: "True, we find a Gospel, Scriptures, a Prophet, Disciples, Apostles, Epigoni, and even a Duality; and if there is no Apostolic Succession, there is at least an Apostolic Benediction" (Samuelson 1946: 189). Again quoting Pearce and Hoover (1995: 203), "Like the church, Samuelson's analytical framework had to adapt to modern conditions and confront the forces of schism and reformation." Along Mass Ave., testifying your fealty as "a Keynesian" was nearly as elastic an affiliation as avowing conversion as a born-again Christian,[13] which is perhaps why it has been so easy for Samuelson to write in retrospect, "The Keynesian Revolution was the most significant event in 20th-century economic science" (Samuelson 1988).

What would it mean for an historian to seriously assert that MIT was more anti-Keynesian than favorable to Keynes, on balance? It would start by scrutinizing the ways in which MIT bent over backward to insist that models having no perceptible basis in the *General Theory* (but obvious ancestry in neoclassical artifacts like utility functions and production functions) were in fact inspired by an imaginary personage they suggested should be called "Keynes". My own favorite would be MIT's most important contribution to macroeconomics in the first postwar decade, Robert Solow's version of growth theory. The theory had nothing whatsoever to do with Keynes, except possibly as a reprimand delivered to Harrod's growth model, which did exhibit a certain inspiration in Keynesian themes. Patently, Keynes did not believe in the intrinsic stability of capitalism (Backhouse and Bateman 2009), whereas Solow did. But there are a whole raft of similar exercises emanating out of MIT in the postwar decades, such as the Phillips curve, the overlapping generations model, Samuelson's early models of options pricing, the Modigliani–Miller theorem opening the floodgates to the proliferation of financial derivatives, and a host of others. This exercise would continue by showing how MIT was proudly in the vanguard of the quest to discipline and punish the actual followers of Keynes (Samuelson and Barnett 2007: 149) who had been maintaining personal loyalties in their Cambridge UK redoubt in the 1960s. Then it would explore how MIT just crudely suppressed all discussion of Keynes's rejection of Tinbergen's econometric models (Samuelson 1946: 197, fn11). It would conclude by taking seriously the admission – albeit in a Samuelsonian jocular tone – in the very midst of the events here documented that, "I am not myself a Keynesian, although some of my best friends are" (1946: 188).[14] This inability to face up to the consequences of their own theories has long been a hallmark of the MIT style: "I would guess that most MIT PhDs since 1980 might deem themselves not to be Keynesians" (Samuelson, in Samuelson and Barnett, 2007: 149).

Yet beyond MIT, the most dramatic historiographic re-evaluation would have to come with regard to the third school of postwar orthodoxy, the Cowles Commission in its Chicago years, especially the period 1943–54.[15] One of the most frequent mistakes in the literature on the history of macroeconomics is the simple presumption that because Cowles was politically identified with "the Left" in that period, its members must have been pro-Keynesian. It therefore may come as a shock to realize that many of the primary protagonists at Cowles were fairly hostile to Keynes; and further, to come to appreciate that an abiding reason for their disdain was because they knew that the *General Theory* was incompatible with Walrasian neoclassical economics. Since Cowles was the Trojan Horse responsible for the introduction of Walras into the USA, and its elevation to centerpiece of orthodoxy, it was a foregone conclusion that Keynes was viewed with skepticism by the opinion leaders at Cowles, at least during its most influential period, from the departure of Oskar Lange and before its move from Chicago to Yale in 1954. This period coincided with the research directorships of Jacob Marschak (1943–8) and Tjalling Koopmans (1948–54). It is the second contention of this chapter that a clearer understanding of the nature of the suspicions concerning Keynes at Cowles, and especially by Marschak and Koopmans, will result in a better understanding of why the Keynesian donkey would not slip out from under the neoclassical yoke in the later 20th century, thus further illuminating the predicament broached at the outset of this chapter.

Why haven't historians noticed the significance of Cowles as an anti-Keynesian stronghold in the first postwar decade? Curiously, part of reason can be attributed to the efforts of some members of the MIT School in retrospectively suppressing evidence that they were pretty much alone amongst their postwar neoclassical peers in trumpeting the virtues of Keynes, as we have already suggested in the citations from Samuelson's textbook. For whatever motivation, another MIT luminary has sought to rewrite history in the Orwellian mode in order to erase certain key events in the history of Cowles. Robert Solow has had the audacity to write in a retrospective on Cowles:

> It should be evident from the story so far that macroeconomics was not the chief glory of the Cowles Commission in its Chicago days. There emerged, as I mentioned early on, no Cowles Commission tradition in macroeconomics distinct from what was going on elsewhere ... The intellectually dominant senior figures at the Cowles Commission were Tjalling Koopmans and Jacob Marschak. Koopmans had no real interest in macroeconomics ... Marschak had much more interest in the subject ... Nevertheless, Marschak, for all his breadth of interest and sureness of taste, was not really 'into' macroeconomics either, in yesterday's cliché ... those senior people who were fundamentally involved in macroeconomics – Milton Friedman, Lloyd Mints, Henry Simons – were out of sympathy with the whole Cowles Commission enterprise of mathematical rigor and generality.[16] (Solow 1991)

It seems that if what happened at Cowles didn't fit one's preconceived notions of "macroeconomics" after the fact, then maybe it just didn't exist.

2. TINBERGERS, NOT KEYNESIANS

We have already suggested that Paul Samuelson's theoretical fealty to Keynes may have been less than reliable or comprehensive; but his treatment of the history of the period has been downright louche. Hard experience has dictated that one should not depend upon his published reminiscences for validation when it comes to other people's infatuations. In the following, another bold MIT move to rewrite history, he claimed to be paraphrasing something told to him by Hans Neisser:

> My friend, fellow immigrant Jacob Marschak, was right and I was wrong. When each new innovation came along – game theory, Keynes' notions of effective demand, econometric identifications – he embraced them all with enthusiasm, even overenthusiasm. (Samuelson 2004: xii)

Either Neisser was not as close to Marschak as he had believed, or else Samuelson is an unreliable *rapporteur*. Marschak was never an unalloyed enthusiast for game theory,[17] nor was he especially enamored of Keynes. If there was a hero to whom Jacob Marschak and those he hired at Cowles pledged their troth, a contemporary economist who embodied intellectual virtue in their eyes, it was unambiguously Jan Tinbergen. And since, at least in the 1940s, Keynes's *bête noire* was Tinbergen, it would seem unlikely that Cowles would just naturally become a bastion of Keynesian thought.

In order to understand the Cowles Commission at Chicago in the 1940s/50s as a nest of Tinbergers, it may be prudent to get straight on the timeline and cast of characters first. Cowles harbored a fair number of distinguished figures who helped shape macroeconomics in the immediate postwar period: Oskar Lange, Jacob Marschak, Lawrence Klein, Tjalling Koopmans, Don Patinkin, Franco Modigliani, and Karl Brunner. Oskar Lange was already a member of the Chicago economics department when Cowles moved there in September 1939, and for a short time was its most illustrious member. As early as 1938, Lange had already pioneered a trademark theme of macroeconomics at Cowles: "Thus both the Keynesian and the traditional theory of interest are but too limiting cases of what may be regarded as the general theory of interest. It is a feature of great historical interest that the essentials of this general theory are contained already in the work of Walras" (1938: 20).

However, dissatisfaction with events on the ground at the University of Chicago prompted him to serve as visiting professor at Columbia from 1942–44, "and it was uncertain whether he would return" (Cowles Commission 1952: 25). Since the existing research director, Theodore Yntema, had been diverted by war work, Lange suggested that Jacob Marschak be appointed research director in 1943. Marschak had briefly taught at the New School, after having been director of the Oxford Institute of Statistics 1935–9. While at Oxford, Roy Harrod wrote to Keynes, "We have a sort of minor Tinbergen here in the form of Marschak ... He himself is content with what you once called wisecracks, very good ones I think. But he happens to be a shrewd person." (Keynes 1973: 298). The war emptied out Cowles; but in compensation the war also deposited many refugees upon the doorstep of the Social Sciences Building at Chicago. Lange never did return, opting instead for joining the newly reinstated Polish government at the end of hostilities. In the meantime, Marschak set about putting his stamp on the research program and stabilizing the funding situation, which prior to that time had been supplied almost entirely at the pleasure of Alfred Cowles.[18] One way he did this was recruit people he perceived as fellow 'little Tinbergens' to invest economics with a bracing dose of scientific rigor.[19] Lawrence Klein reports on Marschak approaching him at the 1944 meetings of the Econometric Society: "Marschak prevailed on me to drop all other job search activities and develop what he said the country needed desperately – a new Tinbergen model of the US economy" (Klein 1991: 108).[20] Klein was employed as 'research associate at Cowles (*sans* faculty appointment) from November 1944 to July 1947; and then had to leave for reasons we shall shortly explore. Marschak also hired an actual direct protégé of Tinbergen in the person of Tjalling Koopmans in July 1944. Marschak brought on board one of his own protégés from his brief sojourn at the New School, Franco Modigliani, as research associate in 1947; but Modigliani rather rapidly decamped for the University of Illinois in November 1948. Another Marschak protégé was plucked from the graduate students at Chicago as a research assistant in May 1946; Don Patinkin was promoted to assistant professor and research associate in 1947, only to leave for Illinois in June 1948,[21] and Hebrew University in February 1949. Marschak brought Kenneth Arrow on board in April 1947, initially suggesting that he work on the Klein econometric model for his master's thesis. Finally, Karl Brunner had been a guest of the Commission from January 1950 to June 1951, supported by a Rockefeller grant.

On the face of it, with the possible exception of Karl Brunner, this roster might look like the Midwest farm team of the Keynesian Revolution in America; but appearances are often deceiving. Most of these individuals maintained an assured clear distance from what Keynes actually wrote during their careers, as explained below. But more dramatically, Marschak's Tinbergen project proved a roaring failure in sweet short order at Cowles, to such a stark degree that Koopmans brought all macroeconomic research to a screeching halt in the early 1950s, and effectively repudiated the prior empiricist orientation of Cowles in the 1940s; all econometric estimation was stopped cold. Hence, contrary to Solow, *Cowles at Chicago was not so much "uninterested" in macroeconomics as repelled by its internally-generated consequences.* By 1955, there was established but one God at Cowles, and his name was Walras; Arrow/Debreu became his newly anointed prophets. If (as the conventional wisdom has it) structural econometrics rode the back of the Keynesian Revolution to research dominance in the postwar American economics profession, then it didn't happen at Cowles.[22] There has only been one lone historian who has noted just how strange and abrupt the multiple renunciations, purges and repudiations were at Cowles in the late 1940s and early 1950s: Roy Epstein's sadly neglected *History of Econometrics* (1987). Epstein's clarity of vision derived from making use of the Cowles Commission archives, which we also access in this chapter. However, even Epstein did not see fit to explore the full extent to which the ambivalent critique of Keynes was part and parcel of the volte-face.

In hindsight, the recruitment of a platoon of Tinbergen clones to construct a mathematical macroeconomics conformable to the nouveau Walrasian ascendancy was a prescription for the disaster that actually occurred. As Marschak was well aware, Tinbergen had been commissioned by the League of Nations to test various business cycle theories; "but practically all of them proved to be too ambiguous to allow of such a test... Tinbergen took over all the relevant relationships suggested by the various authors and arranged them into a logically coherent system of equations."[23] Or, to put it in a less flattering light, the "model" of the business cycle in Tinbergen's *Statistical Testing of Business Cycle Theories* (1939) "eventually presented was not derived from any a priori economic theory, but rather defined his own theory" (Epstein 1987: 50). Tinbergen himself had never been especially partial to the Walrasian system; nor had he ever been a stickler for a dominant role for theory in empirical investigations. Rather, he displayed the rough-and-ready pragmatism of the bench physicist in those prewar days: you work with the flawed and incomplete data available, adjust the specifications of the equations according to data availability and statistical significance, and simply drop equations that don't "work" according to loose intuitive criteria. But, incongruously, Tinbergen also made sweeping claims for his chosen equations, suggesting that one might stabilize the business cycle by government changing the magnitudes of one or more of his estimated coefficients, much the way one might tune an antenna by turning a frequency dial. This could hardly constitute some sort of exemplary "mastery of the craft of model building" (Hendry and Morgan 1995: 52); nor was it a rigorous program of statistical theory testing according to the (then-)nouveau doctrines of Neyman and Pearson. Rather, not a few harbored suspicions that it bordered upon a glorified exercise in curve-fitting (Garrone and Marchionatti 2004), wedded to a misbegotten ambition to control the economy by altering some inexplicably manipulable behavioral parameters. (This had been one motivation for Keynes's scathing assessment of Tinbergen.) But, closer to the heart of the matter, in retrospect, the very notion that a Tinbergen-style approach would eventually lend credence to Walrasian "pure" economics as the foundation for the most rigorous option in the ongoing development of macroeconomics beggared belief.

Thus, if we can briefly imagine ourselves back into the 1940s, temporarily ignoring what has happened in the interim, perhaps we can begin to appreciate just how outlandish the ambitions of someone like Marschak may have appeared to his contemporaries. As Epstein (1987: 64) says, "It appears Marschak did not think a satisfactory theory existed in the textbooks that could offer causal explanations of macroeconomic phenomena." Pointedly, Keynes's *General Theory* was one of those textbooks.

3. JACOB MARSCHAK (AND LAWRENCE KLEIN)

Pace Solow, Jacob Marschak was concerned with macroeconomics from the very start of his career. Marschak's 1922 PhD at Heidelberg was on the quantity theory of money, and during his tenure at the Kiel Institute (1928–30) he engaged in numerous controversies about cures for the worsening depression in Germany. In 1931 he was running a seminar on Keynes's *Treatise on Money* at Heidelberg. Ejected by the Nazis in 1933, he was inducted as a member into the Oxford "trade cycle group" (Young 1989). As founding director of the Oxford Institute of Statistics, he attracted funds from the Rockefeller Foundation by promising a "multi-faceted attack on the problem of the business cycle". Marschak's OIS hosted the 1936 meetings of the Econometric Society where Harrod, Meade and Hicks presented their mathematical interpretations of the *General Theory*. Although he had written on Marxian theory in Germany in the 1920s, it appears by the early 1930s he had decided that many socialist precepts could be better expressed in the idiom of neoclassical theory.[24] While this was not an especially popular position in the Great Depression, neither was it altogether isolated; his insistence contra Mises that neoclassical theory revealed that calculation could take place under socialism allied him with Oskar Lange, the other famous neoclassical 'market socialist' of the era.

It is an interesting fact uncovered by Louçã (2007) that Marschak was instrumental in staging the famous session on the *General Theory* at the

1936 Oxford Econometric Society meetings. He reproduces a letter from Marschak to Ragnar Frisch:

> Incidentally, I had a few days ago a somewhat similar idea – that it would be good to ask one of Keynes' adherents to explain to us in a clear (i.e., mathematical) way the substance of his new book which now creates a sensation among English economists ... On pp.297–8 of his new book Keynes makes some nasty and unfounded remarks against mathematical economics. Owing to his enormous influence, that makes our task even more urgent.[25]

One observes from this letter that upon his first encounter, Marschak regarded the *General Theory* as murky and enigmatic, and potentially hostile to his own research program. But at this stage, subsisting as a vulnerable émigré in clubbish Oxbridge, he was not willing to go public with his doubts.

Further roiling this volatile situation, Keynes decided at that juncture that he would upbraid Jan Tinbergen's League of Nations volume *Statistical Testing of Business Cycle Theories* in the pages of the *Economic Journal.* The seeming incongruity of Keynes denouncing econometrics in its infancy, juxtaposed with the commonplace belief that Keynesian macroeconomics and econometrics mutually supported each other's rise to orthodoxy, has proven just too delicious a paradox to be passed up by historians; the result has been a massive secondary literature on the Keynes/Tinbergen imbroglio.[26] Because of this embarrassment of riches, I hope I need not summarize the content and early phases of the controversy here; nor do I need endorse or otherwise dispute the later Cowles/MIT view that Keynes was dodderingly inept when it came to technical topics in probability and statistics; instead, I merely direct our attention to how the critique had an impact upon Marschak and Cowles. Given his career up to that point, it is perhaps not surprising that Marschak interpreted Keynes's broadside as an oblique attack upon himself, at least as much as upon the hapless Tinbergen. Perhaps a little more unexpectedly, Oskar Lange equally took umbrage, and this prompted the duo to join forces to push back at Keynes (Louçã 2007). At that moment in time, Lange was at Cowles, while Marschak was still in New York.

These preliminaries set the stage for Marschak's first openly negative response to Keynes, in the format of a joint-authored attempt to defend Tinbergen from Keynes's critical review of his 1939 book. The 1940 manuscript was turned down by Keynes for the *Economic Journal,* and never appeared in Marschak's lifetime.[27] The tone, as befits the attempt to place it in the *EJ*, is respectful; both Marschak and Lange start off by pledging agreement with "the economic theories of Mr. Keynes"; but they are clearly distressed by Keynes's dismissal of Tinbergen's statistical methodology; and furthermore, they presume to lecture Keynes on what a "theory" should look like, which in their view should constitute a closed "system" of equations. In part, they attempt to respond to Keynes's critique that Tinbergen had no complete list of causal relations to hand by suggesting that a statistical test would still be valid if one could divide the world *a priori* into two subsets of "significant" versus minor causal factors, and then further tripped themselves up by insisting one could identify "significance" with substantial statistical correlation with the dependent variable. Here Marschak presaged a later tendency in his career of conflating statistical induction with "theory" *tout court*. Marschak and Lange ended up having to concede that changes in the parameters of the equations over time could wreak havoc with estimation, but as Louçã (2007) reveals, the worries expressed in their correspondence with each other were avoided in the final manuscript. At bottom, Marschak and Lange were attempting to make Tinbergen's model building process seem much more disciplined and constrained and systematic than it actually was, which is why their final retort ended up being so ineffectual. Keynes's main objection remained: "with a free hand to choose coefficients and time lag, once can ... always [be] cooking a formula to fit moderately well a limited range of past facts. But what does this prove?" (Keynes 1973: 286–7).

Lange personally lost interest in addressing this conundrum soon thereafter; but before he left the US, he brought Marschak to Cowles to keep hacking away at it. And that's what Marschak did, hitting the ground running, seeking to leverage his prior connections with the Rockefeller Foundation in order to fund his vision of an econometric program of macroeconomic research guided by "theory". But Marschak encountered stiff resistance at Rockefeller, in part due to some skepticism expressed behind the scenes by referees and expert informants located at the National Bureau for Economic Research. Joseph Willits, the foundation officer in charge, then approached Dean Robert Redfield at Chicago, with the complaint, "I can't quite understand what Marschak really has in mind" (Epstein 1987: 64). Willits forwarded some "questions" about the program back to Chicago, which were probably ghosted by Rockefeller referees Wesley Clair Mitchell and Arthur Burns.[28] Redfield then turned to Marschak, inquiring what exactly it was he conceived that Cowles should be doing. Marschak's response revealed his real opinions about Keynes in a way his more diplomatic publications might not:

> There is the important question as to whether the words "economic theory" were used to designate economic theory of the sort contained in our textbooks. The answer is "no" ... Yet there are notable attempts to make theory more precise.

For example, the essence of Keynes' theory of unemployment has been expressed by Hicks (*Econometrica* 1937), somewhat similarly by Lange (in *Economica* 1938) – as a system of three equations ... Although Keynes' theory thus formulated represents a great advance, it cannot be regarded but as a very rough approximation ... it answers the question how a given change in the exogenous variable (money) affects income, savings, and interest rate; but it is blind to any autonomous movement of these three variables in time ... In a sense, the systems of equations which Tinbergen attempted to test for U.S.A. 1919–32 ... can be regarded, in spite of their different historical origin, as such an expansion and "dynamization" of Keynes' system – but also of other systems ...

J.M. Keynes severely criticized Tinbergen before reading his decisive second volume. Thus, Keynes was not aware of Tinbergen's (and others') method of formulating logically clear and consistent theories by means of dynamic systems of equations. Keynes's criticism was, rather, concerned with the permissibility of traditional statistical correlation applied to economic data. However, although Tinbergen's statistical techniques are weak, his general approach, namely the setting up of theories in the form of equation systems, the statistical testing of such systems, and the subsequent measurement of the "destabilizing" effect of each single parameter, seems highly promising. As to concrete economic theories – that is, hypothetical systems of equations to be tested – there is a whole range between an over-simplified system like Keynes's (properly formulated and "dynamized") and the over-catholic and cumbersome one of Tinbergen's. Beyond that, any specification of "the" theory would, at present, mean merely setting one's mind on preconceived ideas often affected by emotional preference, as in the case of the role of wage rigidity, monopolies, income distribution and public spending.[29]

It is hard to know what the anthropologist Redfield made of all this. Certainly he would not have been aware that this litany of complaint represented the pent-up resentment dating from Keynes's rejection of the Lange/Marschak intervention of 1940. Perhaps Marschak had begun to frame his American opponents as being of a similar ilk: enemies were lurking everywhere. For a research group purportedly primarily devoted to the development of neutral technocratic statistical methods of empirical inquiry, an inordinate proportion of the grievances seemed to have to do with the protagonist "Keynes" and the disputed meaning of "theory". Because this became bound up with Rockefeller skepticism over the Cowles program, in 1947 the tensions broke out into the open as the infamous "Measurement without Theory" controversy.[30] For reasons having to do with immediate funding concerns, the explicit targets of the Cowles attack were American Institutionalists like Mitchell and Burns; but few realize that behind the scenes, a concurrent parallel target was also Keynes.[31] (Keynes's death in 1946 obviated any direct attack; thus barbs were often deflected onto surrogates.)

Marschak initially managed to press forward his ambitious program on three fronts: (1) the later infamous statistical work of Haavelmo, H.B. Mann and Abraham Wald on the maximum likelihood estimation of systems of equations, later celebrated as "simultaneous equation methods" or "structural econometrics"; (2) managing to winkle the measly sum of $7500 out of Rockefeller, and using it to hire Tjalling Koopmans in July 1944 (more on this below); and (3) from November 1944 Klein was explicitly engaged to begin building a Cowles macroeconomic model for purposes of postwar planning (also more anon). Marschak highlighted all three in his interim report to Willits in January 1945, suggesting that all three would synergistically interact:

> The most recent example is the impasse reached in the utterly important question of measuring separately the effect of incomes on consumers' savings and the effect of incomes (and other factors) on entrepreneurs' investment ... the size of national income, while affecting savings or borrowings is itself, in turn, determined by the actions of savers and borrowers. These simultaneous relationships cannot be measured by "classical" regression method ... In the last six months, Tjalling Koopmans of the Cowles Commission, assisted by Herman Rubin, has given the full solution of the statistical problem for an important class of cases, while Lawrence Klein and myself are supplying the specific economic questions and hypotheses.[32]

It seems that relations between the team members were not exactly the smooth well-oiled machine that Marschak made out in his reports to funders. Referring explicitly to 1945, Lawrence Klein hinted at the frictions in retrospect:

> Great faith was placed on the ability of sophisticated statistical methods, particularly those that involved advanced mathematics, to make significant increments to the power of economic analysis. I [Klein] personally, take more faith in the data base, economic analysis (institutional as well as theoretical), political insight, and attention to the steady flow of information. Some of the other members of the team showed disappointment that the results, when finally produced, were not sharper and more precise ... At the beginning of the project Marschak used to say, in public meetings, "just give us three years, and we shall deliver powerful new results for economic analysis." He always had at the back of his mind that we would be able to help decisively with postwar economic planning. (Klein 1991: 114)

But that didn't happen at Cowles, or at least not in the way Marschak had promised. First off, one must recall that fully-fledged digital computers were not yet available at Chicago to carry out econometric exercises. Cowles did manage to get intermittent use of the University's Card-programmed Electronic Sequence Analyzer, a sort of precursor to later mainframe computers (Klein, in Hymans 1982: 113), but elaborate calculations were slow, complex and awkward to carry out. Yet the Cowles statistical theorists were proposing elaborate maximum likelihood procedures for structural estimation that were so complicated that there was little hope of implementing them on anything larger than two or three equations with existing technology.[33] Yet that was only the tip of the iceberg.

It perhaps might have been worth slogging through the elaborate calculations if the new methods had demonstrably improved the quality of the estimated parameters; but alas, they did not. In the few instances in Klein's models where the new techniques of structural estimation were tried, parameter estimates and model diagnostics looked *worse* than those produced by the simpler but supposedly flawed ordinary least squares techniques.[34] It became apparent that Klein was more interested in building a model that made sense from many different (and potentially conflicting) evaluative perspectives – which meant constant tinkering with specifications and trying out different combinations – than the hard-nosed 'theory testing' being advocated by Marschak (and soon Koopmans). Klein's lack of fealty to any strict "Keynesianism" also played a role. The tinkering ruled out both repeated fancy maximum likelihood techniques due to computational limitations, and simplistic Neyman–Pearson ideas of "hypothesis testing." Hence it was noteworthy that, while he was searching for improved specifications, Klein kept reverting to simple OLS techniques – that is, methods which Cowles had taken to decrying in public. When Klein eventually found a specification he liked, he didn't even bother to test it for "identifiability"! Thus Klein was acting less and less like a team player from Marschak's perspective.

As if this were not bad enough, there was another source of dissention in the ranks. In his youth, Klein was as much or more inclined to embrace Marxism as he was to avow Keynesianism. He joined the Communist Party while in Chicago in 1945, soon after moving to Cowles. There were other Party members at Cowles at that juncture: Kenneth May, for one. At first, there seemed to be no reason for concern: after all, most Cowles members in the later 1940s were socialists of one stripe or another. In 1946, Klein wrote a paper favorably comparing Marxian to Keynesian theory; fissures began to be revealed when he proposed to have it included in the Cowles Discussion Paper series. Marschak, who had been a Menshevik in his radical youth, was doubly offended; Keynes may have been bad, but Marx was now situated beyond the pale. Marschak summarily refused to allow the paper to be linked to Cowles in any way. This did not auger well for Klein's future at Cowles. And then Klein's *Keynesian Revolution* appeared in 1947. Few people have read it today, but the first edition was an attempt to probe both the theoretical weaknesses and strengths of the *General*

Theory from an unapologetic Marxian viewpoint, or more accurately, a Lange-style neoclassical Marxism. Consider some of the following excerpts:

> Capital accumulation has long been stressed by Marxist writers but never adequately incorporated into the models of bourgeois economics ... Keynes' own treatment of the capital stock was exceedingly superficial. (1947: 68)

> The application of the Keynesian model to the working of a socialist economy is ironic because Keynes was quite outspoken in his distaste for socialism, especially the Soviet system ... Keynes, glorifier of bourgeois life, little knew that the arguments why the Russian economy has been and will continue to be one of interrupted full employment under socialism follow directly from his own simple model. (1947: 77-8)

> ... some of the modern Marxists who think seriously about economic affairs have supported Keynesian economics. What is there in Keynesian economics that would appeal to a Marxist? (1947: 130)

> In general, we can say that Marx analyzed the reasons why the capitalist system did not and could not function properly, while Keynes analyzed the reasons why the capitalist system did not but could function properly ... With these points in mind, it would seem that the principal relation between Keynes and Marx would be in their respective conceptions of the historical time paths of the marginal efficiency of capital and the rate of profit. (1947: 131)

> The Marxists do not oppose the Keynesian program ... They consider it to be in the interests of the common man and therefore support it, but the only smooth-working long-run solution for them is socialism ... Keynesian economics gives us a set of tools with which to work on the unemployment problem, but it does not deal at all with many other important socio-economic questions that also deserve a large share of our attention and study. (1947: 186)

It would be hard to settle on which aspect of this would have revulsed Marschak more: his discomfort with emotional enthusiasms in economics; the elevation of his *bête noir* Keynes into an epoch-making macroeconomic theorist; or the endorsement of a Marxism he felt he had outgrown and renounced long ago. Klein's inconvenient enthusiasms were not to be immediately stifled by his employer's disapproval, even after he was fired from Cowles in 1947. With the assistance of an SSRC fellowship, he repaired in 1948 to Ragnar Frisch's institute at the University of Oslo, where he produced such stridently market socialist manifestos as "Three Seminars on Econometric Tools for Planning" (1948a) and "The Case for Planning" (1948b). The former contained elaborations upon his earlier macroeconomic model work with nary a reference to Keynes, but instead planting the entire theoretical scaffolding upon neoclassical supply and demand equations. The latter was an implicit reprimand to Marschak, arguing that the justification of a planned economy on the basis of market imperfections in a Walrasian/Paretian model was insufficiently compelling, and that "Complete planning leads generally to a higher level of welfare than perfect competition even in the case where wealth redistribution is permitted in the latter system" (1948b: 24). There Klein explicitly propounded his belief that, "Full-employment planning (functional finance or compensatory fiscal policy) is not enough" (1948b: 3).

In any event, a confluence of forces soon rendered any such expressions of socialist fervor moot for American economics. Three things dictated that Cowles attend to its political proprieties starting in 1947: first, the Red Scare started to really heat up, particularly in Illinois, with ominous threats of loyalty oaths being imposed upon the university; second, Cowles began to get access to serious military funding through its nascent connections developed at RAND (Mirowski 2002a: 219–21); and third, Cowles got its chance at informing high-level policy in a way that Marschak had been insisting all along was the ultimate objective of everything done at Cowles, and it had failed miserably.

None of these events has drawn adequate notice from historians of economics; but I believe the third debacle was crucial for dashing Marschak's previous ambitions for economics. The Cowles members had enjoyed close relations with some members of the Committee for Economic Development, and one of them, Albert Hart, approached Marschak and Klein in 1945 for assistance in its quest to argue for expansive postwar economic policies.[35] Hart suggested that the Klein model be used to project the effects of demobilization upon national income and employment after the war under different policy scenarios; the CED would then use them in its lobbying campaign (Klein 1991: 114). Klein generated some projections in 1946, and presented them both to various government agencies in Washington and to the CED, where they were roundly rejected. The lesson drawn from this flash in the pan at Cowles was that the political classes did not seem to want what Klein was purveying, and this proved the final straw. Klein and May were summarily ejected from Cowles in 1947; and macroeconomic model-building was demoted at Cowles to a remote minor region of the research agenda.[36] With the accession of Koopmans to the research directorship, all concern with Keynes was effectively banished for the rest of Cowles' tenure at Chicago.

One side effect of these developments was that Marschak's notion of the subordination of econometric modeling to the service of social engineering of political change rather shriveled after 1947, and it was this, and not some Solovian unexplained ineffable "disinterest" in macroeconomics that accounts for the dramatic turn taken at Cowles, and indeed, in his own research agenda. Thenceforth, Marschak became ever more rigidly Walrasian, insisting that each and every single question be driven back to its "fundamental" determinants in neoclassical tastes, technologies and endowments. The purpose of econometrics itself was transformed, from something that the economic scientist engages in to discipline empirical inquiry, to something that the *economic agent* does implicitly, in order to dynamize and operationalize the Walrasian equations in conditions of change and uncertainty. Marschak had already admitted as much in a letter to Joseph Schumpeter in November 1946:

> The great difficulty in deriving a macrodynamic system from the postulates of rational behavior consists (apart from the aggregation question) in the fact that the equations of rational behavior relate optimal (ie., profit-maximizing) values of certain measurable variables to certain variables that are the expectations of individuals. These expectations may be related to the measurable quantities by psychological equations. In the choice among these equations, one might look for help from the principle of rational behavior in the following way: one assumes the individuals to handle their, and their predecessors', past experience, in a way the rational inductive investigator, i.e., a statistician would handle it.[37]

This practice of treating the agent as a little intuitive econometrician whose cognitive makeup is then conflated with a neoclassical model of rational choice blown up to the level of the nation has become so ubiquitous in what is now deemed "macroeconomics" that it may have escaped notice that it appears Marschak was the earliest progenitor of what eventually became the main anti-Keynesian tradition in macroeconomic theory, the one that supposedly was only conceived in the 1970s as the brainchild of the "rational expectations" school. Indeed, Kevin Hoover has asserted repeatedly that most of what is currently known as the "Lucas critique" of econometric models can be found in Marschak's (1953) paper "Economic Measurement for Policy and Prescription".[38] But this should not be read as a garden-variety exercise in the history of economics that searches for unsung "precursors" to raise the profile of the conventional wisdom. It is rather to point out that the "Keynesian Counter-revolution" began early in America – well before any supposed Revolution had actually acceded to power; it just took a few decades for the profession to come to admit it.

It may seem odd that one of the stalwart pillars of Cowles would have sought to undermine the credibility of econometric macromodels, until one comes to understand the extent to which Cowles by 1948 came to accept that their preferred Walrasian framework was incompatible with Keynesian theory. Marschak, for one, interpreted this as a warrant for a new-found political quietism: "To experiment with the institution [of the economy] would require too much trial and error" (1953: 25). After all, Cowles after

1947 was happy to describe macroeconomic fluctuations as attributable to unanticipated shocks to the system, rather than simple harmonic motion arising from a fixed economic structure (Marschak 1953: 12). As Marschak told the Cowles advisory committee in 1947, "we do not believe in past or future stability of structure" (Epstein, 1987: 70). Marschak's 1948/9 Chicago lectures on macroeconomics, published as *Income, Employment and the Price Level* (Marschak 1951), were amazingly neutral with regard to the validity of Keynesian theory; but his lecture 19 therein innovated the subsequent practice of organizing the entire model around an aggregate supply/aggregate demand framework, and blamed unemployment on sticky wages (sound familiar?). By 1950, Marschak was admitting in print that he, at least, had given up on the whole idea of an empirical Keynesian macroeconomics:

> Like the rest of macro-economics, [Keynes's liquidity preference] equation is still in need of being related to assumptions of rational behavior. Should the liquidity preference equation and other Keynesian equations have purely empirical claims, *these would be hard to establish* [my italics]: the observed time series of relevant variables (quantity of money, interest rate, price level, consumption, national income and, possibly, its distribution) are no doubt consistent with a large number of equations systems other than the Keynesian one. (1974: 96)

There is a bit of apocryphal history which states that Milton Friedman was the wily culprit who killed Keynesianism in America, with a little help from the stagflation of the early 1970s, and that the *coup de grace* was delivered by Robert Lucas. In this, the neoliberals have once again managed to inflate their prowess and efficacy all out of proportion by wildly overstating their role in the intellectual ecology of the era. Keynesianism in America was killed off slowly, by degrees, by its purported promoters; its opponents needed only to give it a little nudge to finish it off.

4. TJALLING KOOPMANS

In a sense, the accession of Tjalling Koopmans to the research directorship of Cowles in 1948 merely ratified trends which had already become apparent the previous year: Cowles was pulling out of econometric empiricism, leaving behind structural estimation, and divesting itself of macroeconomics. Koopmans proved to be the ideal helmsman to negotiate these abrupt reversals, although there would have been no way of predicting his efficacy even just a few years prior to the changing of the guard. For Koopmans had been hired by Marschak first and foremost because he was a direct Dutch protégé of Tinbergen, carrying on the Tinbergen legacy in building econometric business cycle models at the behest of the League of Nations in Geneva, until he left Europe in 1940. Koopmans's training was in quantum physics, and in the late 1930s to the early 1940s Koopmans actually knew very little economics; he followed in his mentor's footsteps by selling himself as a specialist in mathematical statistics. Koopmans's career in economics had been extremely tenuous until Marschak plucked him from obscurity. In the mid-1930s, he had gone to Oslo Institute of Economics in order to sit at the feet of Ragnar Frisch, only to discover to his dismay that the titan of the Econometric Society rejected his own sampling approach to business cycle models (Louçã 2007: 232–6). Tinbergen then got him the job at the League of Nations, to demonstrate the efficacy of his approach. The model building at Geneva had not gone well; his two years there produced little of note. Subsequently as a foreign refugee in wartime America, he bounced from one temporary position to another: part-time lecturer in night school at NYU; statistician at Penn Mutual Life Company; and statistician at the Combined Shipping Adjustment Board. Were it not for Marschak, one can very easily imagine that this dissatisfied chap bouncing from one brief job to another, never really fitting in anywhere, might have left no mark whatsoever on the history of economics.

It didn't hurt that Tinbergen would vouch for his protégé, but two things in particular recommended him to Marschak: in the midst of his exodus, he had managed (where Marschak had failed) to get a defense of Tinbergen vis-à-vis Keynes published in the *Journal of Political Economy* (Koopmans 1941); and in another publication had revealed a predisposition to entertain a kind of non-Keynesian macroeconomics (Koopmans 1942). In other words, *pace* Solow, he was hired (at least in part) as a particularly congenial species of macroeconomist for Marschak's Cowles. Although that intellectual identity didn't last for long, it may clarify matters to revisit just what kind of macroeconomist the tyro Koopmans once was.

Koopmans's defense of Tinbergen in the 1941 JPE was a very curious performance, even more so when we realize that he had shown previous drafts to Tinbergen for comments.[39] While it starts off suggesting it will respond point by point to Keynes' critique, in practice it is prosecuted at a very rarified abstract level where an unspecified "business cycle theorist" confronts a "mathematical statistician" of uncertain provenance. In this disembodied ideal posited by Koopmans, the statistician attends to data problems while the theorist supervises "outside" variables exercising their causal discipline over "inside" variables. In Tinbergen's actual practice, there had been no separation; and at first, the paper seems to suggest that a better division of labor and separation of analytic roles might lead to better quality models. In the paper, Koopmans barely mentions many of Keynes's actual substantive objections, a number of which had to do with technical points of statistical inference (Garrone and Marchionatti 2004). The two he does cite, having to do with strained assumptions of linearity of equations and constancy of coefficients, he dismisses as being subject to statistical test. Koopmans never said very much about the specific methods deployed by the "theorist", probably because he rapidly would have found himself out of his depth there. After endorsing the newly proposed Neyman–Pearson approach to hypothesis testing (concerning which Tinbergen had been necessarily unaware at the time), the paper then takes a vertiginous turn, essentially rejecting the practical possibility of the division of labor he had previously broached:

> [N]o single clear-cut answer can be given to our initial question: to what extent the results of econometric business-cycle research depend on the data and to what extent on additional information and hypotheses. The relative importance of data and additional information varies from one case to another. Their combination is a complicated process, the result of a continuous dialogue, of a game of give and take, between economist and statistician. (1941: 178)

Perhaps Koopmans was correct that the quarantine between the concerns of the theorist and the statistician was impractical in the real world; but that did little to help motivate his original thesis. Somehow, this observation was supposed to justify the scientific legitimacy of Tinbergen's own repeated iteration between estimation, model re-specification, and subsequent estimation as against Keynes' skepticism; although by most accounts this was precisely the sort of behavior Neyman–Pearson methods were supposed to restrain and banish. Koopmans had defended his mentor by essentially ignoring the gist of the statistical objections which Keynes had broached in 1939. When Koopmans sent a copy to Keynes, the latter politely and patiently reiterated one of his primary objections, which remains as true today as it was in May 1941:

> There is one point, to which in practice I attach great importance, you do not allude to. In many of these statistical researches, in order to get enough observations they have to be scattered over a lengthy period of time; and for a lengthy period of time it very seldom remains true that the environment is sufficiently stable. That is the dilemma of many of these enquiries, which they do not seem to me to face. Either they are dependent on too few observations, or they cannot rely on the stability of the environment.[40]

This objection undoubtedly helped set the stage for Koopmans' later embrace of the Gospel of Structure at Cowles.

Koopmans's 1942 maiden foray into theoretical macroeconomics was, if possible, even more incongruous. The only economics text cited therein is Keynes's *How to Pay for the War*, which he praises as "an admirably clear and concise statement of the essential characteristics of inflationary war finance" (1970: 50), but then proceeds to write down some algebraic expressions that have nary a whit to do with Keynesian macroeconomics, but are rather based on some tendentious manipulations of simple definitions, starting with the identity that the percentages of output going to labor, "entrepreneurs" and government must sum to one. He then posits that time-lags in expenditures can unhinge the identity, which is then maintained by a change in the price level. A simple fraction is driven to bedlam by the superimposition of further time-lags and something he calls "the marginal propensity to consume", but the consumption function is nowhere to be seen; indeed, there are no behavioral equations whatsoever. It seems plausible Koopmans had little idea of what a Keynesian model looked like, even though he had been occupied modeling business cycles in Geneva for two years prior to then. Further, there is no evidence that Koopmans was aware of neoclassical economics at this stage, and thus a glaring absence of price theory suffused a paper nominally concerned with inflation. Amazingly, the entire discussion was carried on absent any mention of money or monetary theory whatsoever, probably a symptom of the holes in Koopmans's own economic education. There was no data to speak of, with Koopmans arbitrarily plugging parameter values plucked from the air into his overgrown fraction (for there were no functional equations in the conventional sense). Furthermore, for most of the paper it is simply assumed that production cannot be expanded in the face of government deficits, so it follows near tautologically that government expenditures cause inflation. It is difficult to see how the editors of the *Review of Economics and Statistics* were persuaded to deem the paper warranting publication.

Nonetheless, Koopmans privately harbored a high opinion of his two sallies contra Keynes. We know this from letters he sent back to Tinbergen during the war. In a pre-Cowles note sent in August 1941, he states:

> I believe I haven't told you that I had quite some response to my article on the logic of econometric business cycle research ... This response came in particular from the main person towards whom the article was critical [i.e., J.M. Keynes-P.M.]. I received a very nice and appreciative letter, and on top of that, I had the honor to sit at the right hand of this person during an informal lunch, apparently to accede to the wish of the visitor and to the surprise of the big shots at Princeton. The matter became more comical because, at the same time, I was looking to them for a job. By the way, nothing materialized...[41]

As we have already pointed out, Keynes had used his charm to gently upbraid Koopmans about the 1941 critique; but the exiled and partially unemployed Koopmans misinterpreted this as encouragement. He also took the opportunity of the encounter at Princeton to press the second paper upon Keynes, which was met with even less in the way of encouragement. It is interesting to observe the skill with which Keynes dismembers the 1942 paper in his response:

> The main criticism I should be inclined to make is that the changes in the propensity to consume arising as the result of the inflationary process need more detailed consideration than you have given them. The only reference to the propensity to consume, which I have found, is on page 12, and that is incidental ...

> There are four other basic assumptions to your argument, if I understand it rightly, which perhaps deserve to be made explicit and emphasized: (1) You assume that prices are the element of freedom in the system. Historically this has predominantly been the case. But it is rapidly falling out of fashion ... (2) You assume that there are no stocks of consumable commodities. If there are, this clearly decelerates the process. (3) You assume the sellers always exact the highest possible price and are not significantly influenced by any reasons (there are a variety of them) which might dictate a contrary policy. (4) You do not allow for a time lag in price raising which leads to shop shortages.[42]

This turned out to be the last contact between Keynes and Koopmans. Keynes did not devote much time to Koopmans; after all, he had much bigger fish to fry. But it is hard to miss that Koopmans's combative stance towards Keynes probably rendered him an epsilon more attractive to Marschak. In any event, Marschak used his Rockefeller subvention to pluck Koopmans from obscurity; and Koopmans discovered his métier in the process. His reports back to Tinbergen describe his delight:

> I got an opportunity I couldn't refuse. I have never been so happy in my work as here in Chicago. We have a small group under the supervision of Marschak which is working on a system of equations for the US 1920–40. But we are not in a hurry, although we are working hard. I am mainly busy reworking the statistical adjustment methods making it possible to estimate all equations simultaneously through an iterative method ... Our work is based on a division of labor, where the different parts are highly complementary. Marschak is the general manager, and participates actively in all matters except pure mathematics. In particular, he works on the theoretical economics side. Lawrence Klein drafts the equations, tries different assumptions and because of the tempo by which he moves through the different subsets of the system of equations, he gives the others no opportunity to lose themselves in theoretical or methodological details. Leonid Hurwicz is our critic, a role which fits his sharp and nimble spirit.[43]

Yet soon thereafter, Koopmans rapidly soured on the Klein model, in the course of the events described in the previous section. By 1947 he realized all his high-tech armamentarium of simultaneous equations estimation

procedures and identification tests were not getting Cowles much of anywhere. Yet, in the interim, Koopmans had picked up a fair knowledge and
enthusiasm for Walrasian economics, as well as a shared determination to
ground his models in their fundamental triad of tastes, technologies and
endowments. Furthermore, in 1947 Milton Friedman had taken to attending the Cowles seminars and ridiculing the Klein model mercilessly to their
faces. Friedman seemed to reserve special venom for Koopmans.[44] In this
maelstrom, rather than blame the econometric techniques, it seems that
Koopmans came round to the opinion that it was Keynesian macroeconomics itself which had frustrated the hopes at Cowles. By 1947, he
basically concurred with Marschak that the time had come to "move
gradually into the field of long run economics, while bringing to comple-
tion our attempts in the field of business cycle theory"[45]

Koopmans's accession to research directorship at Cowles in 1948 was the
occasion to sweep out the old order and the attendant fascination with
macro models. Klein was summarily ejected; although Koopmans did not
make this clear to the Rockefeller Foundation for a few years.[46] He did hire
Carl Christ to clean up the Klein model, re-estimate it for the period
1921–47, and "do it right" from the Cowles perspective; but unfortunately,
the consumption function and other key equations did not pass muster
with regard to serial correlation and characteristic root tests, and worse,
predictions made for 1948 were no better than those made by crude trend
extrapolation (Christ, in NBER 1951: 87). The conference on business
cycles held at NBER in November 1949 was the donnybrook for the
remnants of the Cowles program in macroeconomics. Milton Friedman
was scathing in his commentary at the conference where Christ's results
were presented: "the construction of a model for the economy as a whole is
bound to be almost a complete groping in the dark. The probability that
such a process will yield a meaningful result seems to me almost negligible"
(Friedman, in NBER 1951: 113). Klein himself at the same conference
washed his hands "for anything that Christ has done. I participated to a
negligible extent in this work" (Klein, in NBER 1951: 115). No one wanted
to claim ownership of the failed research.

The notes on the post mortem on the conference back at Cowles revealed
the depths of dissatisfaction with the entire program of building macroeconometric models:

> Koopmans: Noted that conference showed differences in expectation regarding
> possible results of our work ...

> Leontief: Many data, don't need hyper-refined methods ...

Metzler: "theory" in Klein's work not sufficiently systematic ...

Marschak: Clarification: behavior rather than mechanical relationships ...

Hildreth: Traditional theoretical model not always the most useful to interpret data with (e.g., production function) ...

Marschak: Education of profession in use of simple models

Koopmans: Not fight too much

Christ: Need to show some results

Hildreth: How anxious should we be to convince everyone?[47]

It is one thing to have to "convince everyone" when your funding and institutional situation was precarious, as it was when Marschak took over at Cowles in 1943. It was quite another thing if instead you had just discovered a new patron with deep pockets, one avid to buy whatever you were selling, and indeed, one who had just become a major supporter of the University where you happened to be located. From the time when the atomic pile first went critical under Stagg field, the University of Chicago became a major outpost of military research. The Cold War, which in 1947 had seemed to be threatening the equanimity of Cowles, unexpectedly turned into the best thing that could have happened to Koopmans, Marschak, Hurwicz, and the rest blessed under the new research agenda.

Although initially the situation seemed dire, Koopmans already had an ace up his sleeve. From 1948 onwards, he cultivated close connections, first at RAND, and later elsewhere in the military, to fund an entirely different sort of research. The report to Rockefeller in early 1951, after briefly mentioning the work on the Klein model, launches into a litany of new departures: "Under a contract for RAND corporation, for example, they are working on a theory of resource allocation for the Department of Defense ... They are also working on the formulation of theory for the measurement of technological changes resulting from specified innovations. The study of the impact of atomic energy done under an earlier RF grant was one aspect of this work; another is a study for RAND on how to determine the ramifications in the defense program of technological changes. They are negotiating with the Office of Naval Research for a grant to carry forward their work on the general theory of organization."[48] This reorientation led to such landmarks in the history of Walrasian theory as the Arrow–Debreu model, Koopmans's "activity analysis", linear programming, the CES production function, the Nash equilibrium in game theory, and a host of lesser innovations.

The New Order under Koopmans turned out to be such a success that thenceforth, macroeconomics was essentially banished from Cowles at Chicago. Perhaps this is why Solow could even think that Cowles had no macroeconomic footprint at Chicago. What tends to get overlooked is that, at least for Koopmans, it was the banishment of *Keynesian* economics that was the logical outcome of his directorship. It was simultaneously a capitulation to the growing influence of Milton Friedman within the Chicago economics department. Rather than contemplate that the failure of the efforts toward macro model-building in which he participated in the period from his hiring to 1948 was due to the choices made at Cowles, such as, say, the dead end of structural identification and estimation, the Tinbergen ideal of snap-together models for policy, or his insistence on reliance upon Walras or nothing else, he would instead lay the blame at the feet of the literary economist Keynes and his ramshackle notion of aggregate economic theory. Koopmans felt sufficiently confident in his gravitas as an economist (even while in residence at a very different Cowles now situated in New Haven) to commit his opinion to print in 1959:

> In general the state of macroeconomic theory is unsatisfactory. There are too many reasonable alternatives which presently available observations of aggregate economic time series cannot easily discriminate. A greater stock of relevant observations could be collected and brought to bear if the basic assumptions of dynamic economics were made about the behavior of individual firms and consumers, and the implications traced through to the aggregates. (Koopmans 1970: 375–6).

5. HANDS ON THE "KEYNESIAN EFFECT"

It should be apparent that this chapter was composed before I had read Wade Hands' contribution to this volume on the "Keynesian Effect" on the evolution of Walrasian theory in the postwar period. More than one auditor of both chapters has reasonably asked: don't the theses of Mirowski and Hands contradict one another? My reaction, upon extended contemplation, is no, they need not negate one another in the least. It is true that Hands sometimes writes as though most people working on problems of uniqueness and stability of the Walrasian model in some sense "wanted" to be Keynesians, but when one realizes that in most of those instances he in fact refers to some version of the "neoclassical synthesis", then much of the seeming contradiction melts away. Indeed, he spends much more time citing Samuelson and Hicks than anyone specifically resident at Cowles in the period covered in this chapter. The fascination with the income terms in demand theory, the presumptive separation of the existence of equilibrium from dynamics, the pitching of analysis at the level of market demand – these were all unabashed preoccupations of Marschak just as much as Samuelson, and were hallmarks of mathematical neoclassicism in the 1950s. If I could suggest a minor amendment to his thesis: most mathematical economists in that decade more or less presumed that Walrasian general equilibrium provided a *macroeconomics* as much as it underpinned a microeconomics; they didn't really care one way or the other whether it captured whatever one might conceivably find in that confusing, wordy text, *The General Theory*. The economics of Keynes and the content of macroeconomics could easily be elided without too much concern for purity from either side of the analytical divide. Thus, I can wholeheartedly endorse Hands's thesis that a concern with what they considered to be "macroeconomics" shaped their formal approaches to attempting to "solve" problems of uniqueness and stability in the Walrasian system, even while continuing to point out that most of the denizens of Cowles were leery of Keynes the economic theorist. The fact that their project failed miserably, as Hands insists, simply reinforces the observation that it was Walras they were attempting to defend, and that, in some important sense, the incompatibility of Keynes and Walras lay at the heart of this failure.

6. DEPARTING IN MID-STREAM, BY WAY OF A CONCLUSION

The story did not end there, although here is where we must conclude. For instance, a serious history of the disdain held towards Keynes at Cowles would have to take into account a raft of other important figures, each of whose tenure at Cowles was too brief to justify fully-fledged individual narratives here, such as Franco Modigliani, Don Patinkin, Evsey Domar, Andrew Marshall, and a whole host of others. It would also have to devote some close attention to someone rarely understood as a skeptic concerning Keynesian economics, the iconic figure Kenneth Arrow.[49] And then there is the even stranger coda to our story: Cowles was uprooted lock, stock and barrel and transported to New Haven in 1954/5, where it was put under the leadership of someone whom many consider the archetypical neoclassical Keynesian of the postwar era, James Tobin. Why would our anti-Keynesians so readily acquiesce in devolution of their bustling thriving unit to someone whose entire intellectual identity seemed so wrapped up with Keynes?

These are questions I leave to other historians, perhaps more concerned with the fine points of Keynes's legacy and the way it became stunted in America.[50] Rather, I want to briefly consider the writing of the one protagonist of our Cowles drama who did avail himself of a retrospective on the events we recount here. Don Patinkin later in life notoriously struggled with the impact of Keynes on economics, on his own career and that of others. In his "On the Differing Interpretations of the *General Theory*" (1990), he confronts the vexed historiographic problem of why Keynesian exegesis has persisted in being so multifarious and contentious. Not unexpectedly, he starts off his answer with the line which had become established at Cowles and MIT by the mid-1940s: Keynes knew not what he had done; he was a prophet babbling in tongues; the *General Theory* "never pulled together various analytical components into an explicit and complete model." So, says Patinkin, it was a hodgepodge where everyone could see in it what they wanted. Nevertheless, he insists that prior to 1960, there were "no significant differences among the various interpretations of the *General Theory*." Only afterwards did comity and decorum break down, with Joan Robinson starting to disparage opponents as "bastard Keynesians" around 1962 or thereabouts (Parker 2005: 699). Before then, everyone who mattered was united in concord, as if part of a single invisible college, in attempting to divine the true meaning and import of Keynesian macroeconomics. In other words, in his version of events, no one in Patinkin's inner circle was ever openly hostile to Keynesian macroeconomics.

I find this retrospective utterly implausible, historically misleading, and a symptom of the intellectual debility that we conjured at the start of this chapter.[51] It is based upon what one might call the Cowles Creed: everyone who is said to count as a real economist necessarily believes what our crowd believes, viz., that Walrasian general equilibrium theory is the only game in town. If we then think someone has said something economically interesting, then they must submit to our recasting of it into our own favored mathematical idiom, and further, anything that doesn't fit must be jettisoned. Any objections to our procedures on the part of the originator are due to some lapse in moral fibre or congenital weakness. Since our Walrasian idiom is intrinsically neutral, we would never entertain the possibility that some of our orthodox peers petulantly dislike the doctrine under scrutiny, regard it as nonsense on stilts, and went out of their way to undermine and destroy it. There is only one Science, and it is Our Science. There is but one God, its name is Walras, and Arrow–Debreu is his prophet. In this Passion Play, Keynes was just a minor Simeon Stylites. Journalists who proclaim "we are all Keynesians now" are barking up the wrong pillar.

The evidence presented herein reveals the Creed has a few serious lacunae.

ARCHIVE ABBREVIATIONS

CFAY   Cowles Foundation Archives, Yale University
CRAN   Cowles Papers, Rockefeller Archives, Sleepy Hollow New York
JMUC   Jacob Marschak Papers, Young Library, Univ. California–LA
JTEH   Jan Tinbergen Papers, Erasmus University, Holland
TKSY   Koopmans Papers, Sterling Library, Yale University
UOFA   University of Oslo Frisch Archives, Dept. of Economics

NOTES

1. I would like to thank Perry Mehrling, Wade Hands, Pedro Duarte, and the participants of the ASSA session on the history of macroeconomics in Atlanta, and the audience at the São Paulo conference on microfoundations of macro for their comments, and the assistance of Lars Mjoset and Olav Bjerkholt in gaining access to the Lawrence Klein papers held at the University of Oslo.
2. Keynes was not some "behavioral economist" *avant la lettre* proposing minor amendments and nudges to utility theory; he rejected it (Backhouse and Bateman 2009: 666). In a delicious turnabout, the neoliberal Richard Posner has pointed this out: "Akerlof and Shiller think that by 'animal spirits' Keynes meant noneconomic motives and irrational behaviors, and they imply that he wanted government to countervail the excesses that occur because of our animal spirits. This is a misreading. The passage in the *General Theory* is not about excesses, and it does not argue that 'animal spirits' should be dampened" (Posner 2009) at http://www.tnr.com. At least the neoliberals do their enemies the courtesy of reading Keynes, unlike some of our modern self-styled "Keynesians".
3. This has special relevance to the thesis of D. Wade Hands (Chapter 3 in this volume); I will return to the ways in which our respective theses may not be at such cross-purposes as it may first appear.
4. The standard quote from the *General Theory* is: "But if our central controls succeed in establishing an aggregate volume of output corresponding to full employment as nearly as is practicable, the classical theory comes into its own from this point onwards" (Keynes 1936: 379). It may not be amiss even here to insist Keynes never referred to Walras as "classical theory". However, as Bleaney (1985: 17 et seq) points out, he did avoid the appearance of obvious departures from (Marshallian) orthodoxy in his assumptions.
5. In this respect, I want to signal my sympathy with various contemporary right wing economists who feel that they have been wronged by the jeremiads of people like Paul Krugman (2009). We don't have to share political positions to realize that they have a legitimate point.
6. For modern restatements see Colander et al. 2008; Colander 2006; Clower 1984; De Vroey 2009. A nice summary of the state of play circa 1985 was *The Rise and Fall of Keynesian Economics* (Bleaney 1985).
7. See Chapter 5 in this volume, by Michel De Vroey. That does not mean I don't think the position is crucially flawed, not because it is easy to argue that Keynes retained many Marshallian methodological moves (which he did), but rather because one cannot bridge the yawning conceptual gap between Marshallian practice and Walrasian theory. The most astute advocate of this position, Axel Leijonhufvud, has been one of the most indefatigable advocates of using history to maintain a Third Way between Walras and Keynes. But his interpretation is explicitly rejected by establishment figures like Paul Samuelson (in Samuelson and Barnett 2007: 148).

8. Many similar arguments have previously been supplied for the European case – see Young 1985; Bleaney 1985; Hall 1989; Louçã 2007). Clearly I omit rival schools to neoclassical theory in this virtual census. When it comes to the contemporary scene, I want to be clear that current self-described pro-Keynesians do not perform any better than anti-Keynesians in this regard. When Paul Krugman, the darling of the sanctioned contemporary left, is quoted (in Coy 2009) as saying, "This is really shameful, that we should be wasting precious months as an [economics] profession retracing debates that were settled 70 years ago", or calls the era 1970–2008 the "Dark Ages of Macroeconomics," Krugman blog, http://krugman.blogs.nytimes.com/2009/01/27/a-dark-age-of-macroeconomics-wonkish, it is evidence that *nothing* Krugman writes about the history of economics should be taken at face value, Nobel or no Nobel.

9. See Mirowski and Hands 1998; Mirowski 2002a; Mirowski 2006.

10. This statement is documented in Mirowski and Plehwe 2009; Mirowski and Hands 1998. The article by Mirowski and van Horn (in Mirowski and Plehwe 2009) explains why the birthdate of the Chicago school should be 1946. An anonymous referee suggested that Friedman partook of "Keynesian methods", even if he rejected the politics. I am not persuaded by this distinction, but here is not the place to deal with the subtleties of Chicago's neoliberal strategies.

11. Of course, most of the early Chicago members were also eventually hostile to Walras – but that is a complication which we need not explore here.

12. See Young 1985; Darity and Young 1995; De Vroey and Hoover 2004. For an example of how this manifested itself, witness Lawrence Klein's PhD thesis (1947: 87–8). IS-LM first made its appearance in Samuelson's third edition of his textbook, but only as an appendix (Pearce and Hoover 1995: 210).

13. "To brand or label someone as a Keynesian economist ... is not very constructive, from my point of view" (Klein 2006: 165). "In [the *General Theory*] the Keynesian system stands out indistinctly, as if the author were hardly aware of its existence or cognizant of its properties ... Flashes of insight and intuition intersperse tedious algebra. An awkward definition gives way to an unforgettable cadenza. When it is finally mastered, we find its analysis to be obvious and at the same time new" (Samuelson 1946: 190).

14. Serious historical re-examination of the actual history of the MIT school must await the promised delivery of Samuelson's personal papers to the Perkins Library archive at Duke.

15. This reconsideration would extend to retraction of a sentence I had once penned: "Sometime between the first flush of enthusiasm in 1944 and 1947, structural econometrics at [Cowles] stopped being about price theory and switched allegiance to Keynesianism" (Mirowski and Hands 1998: 280). While this is a reasonable representation of what happened to econometrics within the American profession, the situation at Cowles was more baroque, as this chapter explains.

16. This bit of apocrypha then got repeated elsewhere, for example: "[Cowles] largely stood apart from the Keynesian Revolution, focusing more on developing estimation techniques than on solving the riddle of macroeconomic failure" (Parker 2005: 195).

17. He was rather enthusiastic about the appendix to *The Theory of Games and Economic Behavior* which sketched what became known as von Neumann–Morgenstern expected utility theory; in other words, he was a decision theorist, *not* a game theorist. This is discussed in Mirowski 2002a: 289–92.

18. For data on the funding situation at Cowles during the war, see Mirowski 2002a: 217–18.

19. It has not gone unnoticed that Marschak believed training in the natural sciences was the best way to achieve this. Tinbergen himself had started out as a PhD physicist. Marschak had an advanced degree in engineering, while Koopmans was a PhD physicist, Leonid Hurwicz and Kenneth Arrow had backgrounds in meteorology, and Carl Christ held a physics degree.

20. Note well: Marschak did not say a *Keynesian* model, even though Klein's thesis had been on Keynes.

21. The debacle at Illinois is described in Solberg and Tomilson 1. We briefly return to the case of Patinkin at the conclusion of this chapter.
22. The story gets muddied when Cowles moved to Yale in 1955, with James Tobin as the new research director. That story lies beyond the scope of the current chapter. See, however, Mirowski 2002a, chap.5.
23. Marschak to Robert Redfield, Feb 15, 1944; CFAY.
24. "I knew that Marschak is a Socialist, but I have a very strong impression that in the matters of the Econometric society he is guided by uniquely scientific motives." (Ragnar Frisch to Joseph Schumpeter, 12 November 1932, quoted in Louçã 2007: 347).
25. Marschak to Ragnar Frisch, Feb. 8, 1936; quoted in Louçã (2007: 192).
26. I will just point to some of the high points in this effusion of commentaries: Keuzen-kamp 2000; Epstein 1987; Pesaran and Smith 1985; Louçã 2007; Garrone and Marchion-atti 2004; Dostaler 2007.
27. The manuscript was first published in *Foundations of Econometric Analysis* (Hendry and Morgan 1995), along with a reproduction of Keynes's original review. Keynes was not impressed with the quality of the performance, and wrote to Pigou that he had "a very poor opinion of Marschak and only a moderately good one of Lange" (letter Keynes to Pigou, March 29, 1940, quoted in O'Donnell 1997: 154-5).
28. "there seems to be a difference of opinions and sympathies between our approach here and that used by Mitchell and Kuznetz [sic] at the National Bureau ... It seems that Willits has been advised by representatives of the 'other school', hence this difficulty in understanding some of our terms." Marschak to Louis Wirth, 8 February 1944, CFAY.
29. Marschak to Robert Redfield, February 15, 1944. CFAY
30. The key texts are reprinted in *Scientific Papers of Tjalling Koopmans* (Koopmans 1970: 112–61). For commentary on the controversy, see Mirowski 1989. It is interesting to note that Marschak had already laid out the characterizations of the opposing sides as early as 1944, even though Koopmans was to be credited with the argument in 1947: "the approach of Mitchell and Kuznetz [sic] is to manipulate on [sic] economic figures in a purely descriptive way. They fit a trend and describe the cycle of each economic activity without trying to find the causation by going down to assumptions of economic behavior. In other words, they treat the material on men as if it were physical bodies; they do not take advantage of the fact that we know something about men from our own knowledge and experience. The combination of economic theorists and statisticians in Chicago is interested in a closer connection between statistics and theory." Marschak to Louis Wirth, 8 February 1944, CFAY.
31. The third leg of this hermeneutic macroeconomic triangle, namely the relationship between the Institutionalists and the Keynesians, was also fraught with suspicions and misunderstandings. While we cannot discuss them here, consult Rutherford and Desroches 2008.
32. Marschak to Joseph Willits, January 12, 1945; CFAY. This letter also expresses Mar-schak's disdain for interviews and surveys as a source of economic data, in the context of his wrapping-up of the Rockefeller-funded project on Price Controls run by George Katona. Marschak summarily terminated Katona as part of his new clean sweep of the Cowles stables.
33. "An early version of the methods had been presented at the 1945 Chicago conference and it was recognized that they were generally very burdensome, frequently prohibitive" (Hildreth 1986: 50).
34. See the discussions of Klein's Models I, II and III in Christ in NBER 1951; Epstein 1987: 104–13; Basmann in Colander 2006. Andrew Marshall was assigned the task of re-estimating Klein's model III in 1947 and extending its purview, only to find discourag-ing results (Cowles Commission 1952: 49).
35. For some history of the Committee on Economic Development in the early postwar era and its tepid relationship to Keynesian doctrine, consult Collins 1981, chaps. 4–6).

36. As Klein (1991, 115) puts it delicately in his retrospective, "senior researchers at the Commission were not satisfied with the performance of models that had been constructed during the expansionary phase of the research program and there was relatively little carry-on activity in empirical model building ... Macro model building continued on a smaller scale after 1947, but it ceased to be the central thrust in the same way that it was during 1944–47". Klein was once again ejected for his leftist beliefs, from the University of Michigan in 1953/4 (Hymans 1982: 221–2). Epstein (1987, 110–13) calls this period at Cowles "The Retreat from Structure."
37. Marschak to Joseph Schumpeter, 23 November 1946; transcribed copy, CFAY.
38. See, for instance, Hoover 2006; 2009. As usual, Epstein (1987: 194) got there first, noting that the rational expectations model of the 1980s was "surprisingly similar to the general program that the Cowles researchers initially contemplated".
39. See, for instance, Koopmans to Jan Tinbergen, 18 December 1940; JTEH.
40. Keynes to Tjalling Koopmans, 29 May 1941; quoted in Garrone and Marchionatti 2004.
41. Koopmans to Jan Tinbergen, 22 August 1941; JTEH. I wish to thank Albert Jolink for this translation from the Dutch original.
42. J.M. Keynes to Koopmans, 2 June 1941; TKSY Box 17, folder 311.
43. Koopmans to Jan Tinbergen, 18 July 1945; JTEH, Jolink translation from the Dutch.
44. "Koopmans was just foolish ... I thought that Koopmans' was a very sophomoric attack and had no effective content – he didn't tell you where you went from here. And of course you realize that I had been involved in very long arguments with the Cowles Commission people when they were in Chicago ... So I was very unsympathetic to Koopmans from the beginning – before he wrote that [1947] article." (Milton Friedman in Hammond 1992: 231).
45. Marschak to Evsey Domar, 11 April 1947; quoted in Epstein 1987: 110.
46. See the interview of LCD with Koopmans and Marschak dated 21 March 1951 concerning the Cowles research agenda; CRAN.
47. "Discussion to Size-up Results of Business Cycle Conference, December 1949" CFAY
48. Excerpt from interview of LCD with Koopmans and Marschak dated 21 March 1951 concerning the Cowles research agenda; CRAN. The story of the new research at Cowles is related in Mirowski (2002b).
49. See Arrow (1983: 201), where in his Nobel lecture he treats "the great Keynes" as a critic of Walrasian general equilibrium. He also leaves no doubt whom he deems the weaker theorist: "The fundamental question remains: how does an overall total quantity, say demand, as in the Keynesian model, get transformed into a set of signals and incentives for individual sellers?" Arrow (2006: xiii) dismisses Keynes as a theorist altogether.
50. One example of the sort of work I have in mind is "Patinkin's Interpretation of Keynesian Economics: A Genetic Approach" by Rubin (2008), who demonstrates admirably that early versions of Patinkin's PhD thesis attempted a disequilibrium interpretation of Keynes based upon institutional bargaining power, but under pressure from Marschak's and Koopmans's harsh critique, was pushed in the direction of the infamous "Pigou effect".
51. Not to mention covering up the history of his own personal road to Keynes. See Rubin 2008.

REFERENCES

Akerlof, George, and Robert Shiller (2009). *Animal Spirits: How Human Psychology Drives the Economy.* Princeton: Princeton University Press.

Arrow, Kenneth (1983). *Collected Economic Papers, Vol.2 General Equilibrium.* Cambridge, MA: Harvard University Press.

Arrow, Kenneth (2006). Foreword. In *Samuelsonian Economics and the 21st Century.* Edited by Michael Szenberg et al. Oxford: Oxford University Press.

Backhouse, Roger, and Bradley Bateman (eds) (2006). *The Cambridge Companion to Keynes.* New York: Cambridge University Press.

Backhouse, Roger, and Bradley Bateman (2009). Keynes and Capitalism. *History of Political Economy*, 41 (4):645–72.

Bateman, Bradley (1996). *Keynes' Uncertain Revolution.* Ann Arbor: University of Michigan Press.

Bleaney, Michael (1985). *The Rise and Fall of Keynesian Economics.* London: Macmillan.

Clower, Robert (1984). *Money and Markets. Essays by Robert Clower.* Edited by Donald Walker. New York: Cambridge University Press.

Colander, David (ed.) (2006). *Post Walrasian Macroeconomics.* New York: Cambridge University Press.

Colander, David, Peter Howitt, Perry Mehrling, and Axel Leijonhufvud (2008). Beyond DSGE Models. *American Economic Review Papers and Proceedings*, 98 (2):236–40.

Collins, Robert (1981). *The Business Response to Keynes.* New York: Columbia University Press.

Cowles Commission (1952). *Economic Theory and Measurement: A 20 Year Research Report.* Chicago: Cowles.

Coy, Peter (2009). What Good are Economists Anyway? *Business Week*, April 19.

Darity, William, and Warren Young (1995). IS-LM: An Inquest. *History of Political Economy*, 27 (1):1–41.

DeLong, J. B. (2009). What Has Happened to Milton Friedman's Chicago School? available at http://delong.typepad.com.

De Vroey, Michel (2009). Getting Rid of Keynes? In *Keynes General Theory after 70 Years.* Edited by Robert Dimand, Robert Mundell, and Andrea Vercelli. London: Palgrave.

De Vroey, Michel, and Kevin Hoover (eds) (2004). *The IS-LM Model: Its Rise, Fall and Strange Persistence. History of Political Economy* 36 supplement. Durham: Duke University Press.

Dostaler, Giles (2007). *Keynes and his Battles.* Cheltenham: Edward Elgar.

Epstein, Roy (1987). *A History of Econometrics.* Berlin: Springer.

Garrone, Giovanna, and Roberto Marchionatti (2004). Keynes on Econometric Method: A Reassessment of his Debate with Tinbergen. University of Torino Working Paper No. 01/2004.

Giles, Chris (2008). The Undeniable Shift to Keynes. *Financial Times*, Dec 30, available at: http://www.ft.com/cms/s/0/c4cf37f4-d611-11dd-a9cc-000077b076 58.html?nclick_check=1.

Hall, Peter (ed.) (1989). *The Political Power of Ideas.* Princeton: Princeton University Press.

Hammond, J. Daniel (1992). An Interview with Milton Friedman on Methodology. *Research in the History of Economic Thought and Methodology*, vol. X.

Hendry, David, and Mary Morgan (eds) (1995). *Foundations of Econometric Analysis.* Cambridge: Cambridge University Press.

Hildreth, Clifford (1986). *The Cowles Commission in Chicago.* Berlin: Springer-Verlag.

Hoover, Kevin (2006). The Past as Future. In *Post Walrasian Macroeconomics.* Edited by David Colander. New York: Cambridge University Press.

Hoover, Kevin (2009). Microfoundations and the Ontology of Macroeconomics. In *Oxford Handbook of Philosophy of Economics*. Edited by Harold Kincaid, and Don Ross. New York: Oxford University Press.

Hymans, Saul (ed.) (1982). *Economics and the World Around It*. Ann Arbor: University of Michigan Press.

Keuzenkamp, Hugo (2000). *Probability, Econometrics and Truth*. Cambridge: Cambridge University Press.

Keynes, John Maynard (1936). *The General Theory of Employment, Interest and Money*. London: Macmillan.

Keynes, John Maynard (1973). *The General Theory and After: The Collected Writings of John Maynard Keynes, v.14*. Edited by Donald Moggridge. London: Macmillan.

Klein, Lawrence (1947). *The Keynesian Revolution*. New York: Macmillan.

Klein, Lawrence (1948a). Three Seminars on Econometric Tools for Planning. Unpub memo, Socialokonomiske Institutt, Jan. 15: UOFA.

Klein, Lawrence (1948b). The Case for Planning. Unpub memo, Socialokonomiske Institutt, April 26: UOFA.

Klein, Lawrence (1991). Econometric Contributions of the Cowles Commission, 1944–7. *Banca Nazionale del Lavoro Quarterly Review*, (177):107–17.

Klein, Lawrence (2006). Paul Samuelson as a "Keynesian" Economist. In *Samuelsonian Economics in the 21st Century*. Edited by Michael Szenberg, Lall Ramrattan, and Aaron Gottesman. Oxford: Oxford University Press.

Koopmans, Tjalling (1941). The Logic of Econometric Business-Cycle Research. *Journal of Political Economy*, 49 (2):157–81.

Koopmans, Tjalling (1942). The Dynamics of Inflation. *Review of Economic Statistics*, 24 (2):53–65.

Koopmans, Tjalling (1970). *Scientific Papers of Tjalling Koopmans*. Berlin: Springer.

Krugman, Paul (2009). How Did Economists Get it so Wrong? *New York Times Magazine*, Sept. 6.

Lange, Oskar (1938). The Rate of Interest and the Optimum Propensity to Consume. *Economica*, 5 (17):12–32.

Louçã, Francisco (2007). *The Years of High Econometrics*. London: Routledge.

Mankiw, Gregory (2006). The Macroeconomist as Scientist and Engineer. *Journal of Economic Perspectives*, 20 (4):29–46.

Marschak, Jacob (1951). *Income, Employment and the Price Level*. New York: Augustus Kelley.

Marschak, Jacob (1953). Economic Measurement for Policy and Prediction. In *Studies in Econometric Method*. Cowles Monograph 14. Edited by William Hood, and Tjalling Koopmans. New Haven: Yale University Press.

Marschak, Jacob (1974). *Economic Information, Decision and Prediction. Selected Essays, vol. III*. Dordrecht: Reidel.

Marschak, Jacob, and Helen Makower (1938). Assets, Prices and Monetary Theory. *Economica*, 5 (19):261–88.

Mirowski, Philip (1989). The Measurement without Theory Controversy. *Economies et Societes*, no. 11 (June):65–87.

Mirowski, Philip (2002a). *Machine Dreams: Economics Becomes a Cyborg Science*. New York: Cambridge University Press.

Mirowski, Philip (2002b). Cowles Changes Allegiance. *Journal of the History of Economic Thought*, 24 (2):165–93.

Mirowski, Philip (2006). Twelve Theses Concerning the History of Postwar Neo-classical Price Theory. In *Agreement on Demand. History of Political Economy* 38 supplement. Edited by Philip Mirowski, and D.W. Hands. Durham: Duke University Press.

Mirowski, Philip, and D.W. Hands (1998). A Paradox of Budgets. In *From Interwar Pluralism to Postwar Neoclassicism. History of Political Economy* 30 supplement. Edited by M. Morgan, and M. Rutherford. Durham: Duke University Press.

Mirowski, Philip, and Dieter Plehwe (2009). *The Road from Mont Pèlerin*. Cambridge, MA: Harvard University Press.

NBER (National Bureau of Economic Research) (1951). *Conference on Business Cycles*. New York: NBER.

O'Donnell, Rod (1997). Keynes and Formalism. In *A Second Edition of the General Theory*. Vol. 2. Edited by G. Harcourt, and P. Riach. London: Routledge.

Parker, Richard (2005). *John Kenneth Galbraith: His Life, His Politics, His Economics*. New York: Farrar, Strauss, Giroux.

Patinkin, Don (1990). On the Differing Interpretations of the *General Theory*. *Journal of Monetary Economics*, 26 (2):205–43.

Pearce, Kerry, and Kevin Hoover (1995). After the Revolution: Paul Samuelson and the Textbook Keynesian Model. In *New Perspectives on Keynes. History of Political Economy* 27 supplement. Edited by Allin Cottrell, and Michael Lawlor. Durham: Duke University Press.

Pesaran, Hashem, and R. Smith (1985). Keynes on Econometrics. In *Keynes' Economics: Methodological Issues*. Edited by Hashem Pesaran, and Tony Lawson. London: Croom Helm.

Posner, Richard (2009). Shorting Reason. *The New Republic*, April 14.

Rubin, Goulven (2008). Patinkin's Interpretation of Keynesian Economics: A Genetic Approach. In *The Anti-Keynesian Tradition*. Edited by Robert Leeson. London: Palgrave.

Rutherford, Malcolm, and Tyler Desroches (2008). The Institutionalist Reaction to Keynesian Economics. *Journal of the History of Economic Thought*, 30 (1):29–48.

Samuelson, Paul (1946). Lord Keynes and the *General Theory*. *Econometrica*, 14 (3):187–200.

Samuelson, Paul (1951). *Economics*. 2nd edn. New York: McGraw-Hill.

Samuelson, Paul (1988). Keynesian Economics and Harvard. *Challenge*, July/August, (31):32–4.

Samuelson, Paul (2004). Foreword: Eavesdropping on the Future? In *New Frontiers in Economics*. Edited by Michael Szenberg, and Lall Ramrattan. New York: Cambridge University Press.

Samuelson, Paul, and William Barnett (eds) (2007). *Inside the Economist's Mind*. Oxford: Basil Blackwell.

Solberg, Winton, and Robert Tomilson (1997). Academic McCarthyism and Keynesian Economics. *History of Political Economy*, 29 (1):55–81.

Solow, Robert (1991). Cowles and the Tradition of Macroeconomics. In *Cowles 50th Anniversary*. New Haven: Cowles Foundation.

Tinbergen, Jan (1939). *Statistical Testing of Business Cycle Theories*. 2 vols. Geneva: League of Nations.

Young, Warren (1985). *Interpreting Mr. Keynes*. Boulder: Westview.

Young, Warren (1989). *Harrod and his Trace Cycle Group*. New York: NYU Press.

5. Microfoundations: a decisive dividing line between Keynesian and new classical macroeconomics?

Michel De Vroey

INTRODUCTION

The transition from Keynesian IS-LM macroeconomics to dynamic stochastic macroeconomics deserves to be labeled as a scientific revolution *à la* Kuhn. This expression refers to an episode in the history of a discipline where a period of normal science is disturbed by the persistent existence of apparently insoluble puzzles and a drive to push the agenda and the research methods in new directions. This is accompanied by thundering declarations of war (for example, Keynesian theory is dead), a confrontation between the young and the old generation, the rise of new stars in the profession and the eclipse of old ones. The relevance of the scientific revolution hinges on the existence of a 'before' and an 'after', with a well-delineated series of events in between, so that the type of work members of the community are engaged in after the revolution bears little resemblance to earlier practices.

The revolution in macroeconomics resulted from a sequence of episodes related both to the intricacies of the internal development of the discipline and to outside events. Friedman (1968) and Lucas ([1972] 1981) recounted the story of the real effects of monetary expansion in a non-Keynesian way, thereby disqualifying the policy-menu idea associated with the Phillips curve. The emergence of stagflation in the 1970s was proclaimed to be a real-time experiment that confirmed Friedman's predictions about the inability of monetary policy to have a long-lasting effect on employment (Friedman 1968). Lucas and Rapping's work (1969) extending the sphere of equilibrium analysis began the downfall of the neoclassical synthesis – why try to graft disequilibrium onto an equilibrium theory if the equilibrium category is all-inclusive? The blending of rational expectations and time inconsistency led to the dismissal of state interventions in the economy that were previously believed to be effective in increasing social welfare. Last but not least, Lucas's critique ([1976] 1981) questioned the ability of traditional macroeconomic models to serve the purpose of choosing between alternative policy options. All these factors brought the traditional Keynesian approach to its knees. As stated by Samuelson, this process had a ring of revenge: "The new classical economics of rational expectationists is a return with a vengeance to the pre-Keynesian verities" (Samuelson 1983: 212).

This revolution – at present often viewed as having led to the rise of DSGE (dynamic-stochastic general equilibrium) macroeconomics – occurred in two stages. In a nutshell, Lucas did the job of attacking the Keynesian paradigm and of introducing a series of new concepts and principles. Kydland and Prescott (1991) transformed Lucas's qualitative modeling into a quantitative research program – as Greenwood ([1994] 2005: 1) put it, they took macroeconomics to the computer.

This chapter is concerned with one particular aspect of the revolution, namely the claim that the introduction of the microfoundations requirement was one of its distinctive features.[1] Is this account valid, or are things more complicated? The purpose of this chapter is to answer this question. Not surprisingly, since I felt the need to write the chapter, I am of the second opinion. I shall make two claims. The first is that the way in which Lucas and others posit the problem is unsatisfactory. An alternative, less demanding, conception of the microfoundations requirement, which I shall call the Hayek–Patinkin conception, ought to be considered. When this is taken into account, the new classical/real business revolution can be viewed as a narrowing of the content of the microfoundations requirement from its Hayek–Patinkin to its Lucasian version, rather than the replacement of a non-microfounded macroeconomics with a microfounded one. My second claim is that, while it is true that Keynes's theory and Keynesian macroeconomics are defective with respect to the Lucasian criterion for microfoundations (with some ironic exceptions), it is nonetheless mistaken to conclude that they lack microfoundations. In particular, Keynes's *General Theory* (1936) abides by the Hayek–Patinkin criterion, to me the most appropriate one.

The chapter comprises five sections. In the first, I discuss Lucas's conception of the microfoundations requirement, and in the second his indictment of Keynesian macroeconomics. Section 3 discusses the justification for Lucas's standpoint. In section 4, I introduce the alternative Hayek–Patinkin view of the microfoundations requirement and assess the Lucasian conception. In section 5, I assess Keynesian macroeconomics against the two criteria.[2]

1. THE MICROFOUNDATIONS REQUIREMENT AS EXPRESSED BY LUCAS

From the 1970s onwards, a new methodological principle came to prominence in macroeconomics: the microfoundations requirement. This principle became the *sine qua non* of valid theoretical practice. The condition for a macroeconomic model to be microfounded is that it starts with a description of how agents make their choices, it being supposed that these are made in an optimizing way. That is, an objective function has to be maximized or minimized under given constraints. For all its generality, this condition is deemed sufficient to identify models that do not accord with it, and so ought to be rejected.

The same requirement has also been expressed differently by Lucas and Sargent (and Lucas on his own) under the name of 'equilibrium discipline'.[3] It states that, to be valid, economic models should rest on two postulates: (a) that agents act in their own self-interest and their behavior is optimal; and (b) that markets clear (Lucas and Sargent, [1979] 1994: 15).[4] Here market clearing is the central notion. It refers to a situation where all agents' optimizing plans are compatible. Either they participate in trade or they prefer not to do so in view of the prevailing prices. These two postulates are deemed to constitute a universal requirement rather than being linked to particular models in view of their specific purpose. In the expression 'equilibrium discipline', the 'discipline' term refers not to agents but to economists. It is a rule that economists impose upon themselves and which stamps their specific way of looking at social reality. Accepting such a standpoint results in proclaiming that the notion of disequilibrium, which was widely used before, should be banned from the economic lexicon. The underlying reason is that it lacks microfoundations (Lucas [1977] 1981: 221) or refers to 'unintelligent behavior' (p. 225).

In the same vein, Kydland and Prescott (1991) have repeatedly identified the notions of neoclassical theory and the microfoundations requirements. To them, a model is neoclassical when it is constructed from "agents maximizing subject to constraints and market clearing" (Kydland and Prescott 1991: 164). Any model lacking microfoundations is not neoclassical. So, Kydland and Prescott view themselves as having transformed the initial Solow model, which was not neoclassical, into a neoclassical model by providing it with microfoundations.

One result of such a standpoint is the disappearance of the frontier between microeconomics and macroeconomics. As Lucas said:

> The most interesting recent developments in macroeconomic theory seem to me describable as the reincorporation of aggregative problems such as inflation and

the business cycle within the general framework of 'microeconomic' theory. If these developments succeed, the term 'macroeconomic' will simply disappear from use and the modifier 'micro' will become superfluous. We will simply speak, as did Smith, Ricardo, Marshall and Walras of *economic* theory. (Lucas 1987: 107–108)

Two additional remarks are worth making. First, it is sometimes claimed that new classicists invented market clearing.[5] For my part, I disagree with such an assessment. Although the expression is new, the idea of market clearing is of long standing in economics. Its presence in Walrasian theory is beyond dispute. But the same is true for Marshallian theory (with the additional complication that market clearing and disequilibrium can coexist – see De Vroey, 2007).[6] By challenging this consensus in the profession, Keynes was clearly thinking out of the box. Thus, rather than having invented market clearing, new classicists have just restored it at a higher level, signaling the end of the Keynesian recess.

2. LUCAS'S INDICTMENT OF KEYNES'S *GENERAL THEORY* AND KEYNESIAN MACROECONOMICS

The gist of Lucas's criticism of Keynesian theory is that it does not abide by the equilibrium discipline. His attack develops at two levels. The first pertains to the general way in which Keynes addressed the issue of unemployment in his *General Theory*. In Lucas's ([1977] 1981) eyes, the mere intention to produce a theory of involuntary unemployment constitutes an infringement of the equilibrium discipline. As Lucas and Sargent ([1979] 1994) put it:

> After freeing himself of the straightjacket (or discipline) imposed by the classical postulates, Keynes described a model in which rules of thumb, such as the consumption function and liquidity preference schedule, took the place of decision functions that a classical economist would insist be derived from the theory of choice. And rather than require that wages and prices be determined by the postulate that markets clear – which for the labor market seemed patently contradicted by the severity of business depressions – Keynes took as an unexamined postulate that money wages are sticky, meaning that they are set at a level or by a process that could be taken as uninfluenced by the macroeconomic forces he proposed to analyze. (p. 15)

Keynes's lapse from the equilibrium discipline, Lucas is ready to admit, was understandable in view of the apparent contradiction between cyclical phenomena and economic equilibrium in the context of the Great Depression. Still, *ex post* it ought to be interpreted as having prompted a long detour in the progress of economic theory. It is an example of 'bad social science: an attempt to explain important aspects of human behavior without reference either to what people like or what they are capable of doing' (Lucas, 1981: 4). And what is true for Keynes is also true for Keynesian macroeconomics, Lucas declared in an interview published in a University of Colorado magazine, *The Margin*:

> I think a lot of the work in Keynesian economics has gotten too far away from thinking about individuals and their decisions at all. Keynesians don't often worry about what actual individuals are doing. They look at mechanical statistical relationships that have no connection with what real individuals are actually doing. (Lucas undated, Box 27, Correspondence 1989 folder)

The second level of criticism is the well-known 'Lucas critique' ([1976] 1981). Here, his target is the macroeconometric models of the time, all of which had a Keynesian inspiration. Lucas's claim is that, although they do a fairly good job of forecasting, these models are a failure as far as the assessment of alternative policies is concerned. Their main flaw is their lack of microfoundations. This leads to endogenous variables, sensitive to variations in economic policy, being transformed into exogenous ones. As a result, a model of the economy estimated at a period during which a particular institutional regime holds sway will provide inadequate information for assessing what might occur under a different regime. According to Lucas, to avoid this defect, the parameters of the model need to be 'deeply structural' – that is, they must be derived from the fundamentals of the economy, agents' preferences, and technological constraints.

3. LUCAS'S JUSTIFICATION OF THE MICROFOUNDATIONS REQUIREMENT

To paraphrase Keynes, the microfoundations requirement conquered macroeconomics as quickly and as thoroughly as the Holy Inquisition conquered Spain. More curiously, this conquest occurred without any justification being provided, as if the case was so obvious that none was needed. In view of the central character of this methodological principle, such a lack looks odd. In this section, I ponder on why this is the case and reconstruct how Lucas might justify his standpoint.

To make sense of the microfoundations requirement, it is necessary to view it in the broader context of Lucas's methodological world view. Two points have to be brought out. The first is that, to him, a theory and a model (that is, a mathematical model) are the same thing. A theory/model is concerned with fictive imaginary constructions, and is necessarily unrealistic. This conception, it should be noted, Lucas inherited from Walras.

> On this general view of the nature of economic theory, then a 'theory' is not a collection of assertions about the behavior of the actual economy but rather an explicit set of instructions for building a parallel or analogue system – a mechanical, imitation economy. (Lucas [1980] 1981: 271–2)

The second point is that, to Lucas, equilibrium is a characteristic of the way in which economists look at reality, rather than a characteristic of reality. Let me expand on this.

The traditional view, from Smith onwards, is that equilibrium forces are at work in reality. While there is a low probability that equilibrium is realized at any given moment, the very fact that the economy is out of equilibrium triggers feed-back effects which bring it closer to equilibrium. In other words, it is asserted that equilibrium and disequilibrium, viewed as part and parcel of the same notion, are features of reality. As a rough approximation, such a statement has common sense going for it. The originality of Lucas's standpoint is the way in which he distances himself from common sense by arguing that the issue of whether equilibrium or disequilibrium prevails in reality cannot be solved. There is no way to ascertain whether a market is in equilibrium – and neither can we ever delineate a market, which would be a prerequisite to deciding whether the market were in equilibrium. The conclusion to be drawn is not that we should forego the notion of equilibrium, but that we should use it differently. The following quotations make the point.

> Cleared markets is simply a principle, not verifiable by direct observation, which may or may not be useful in constructing successful hypotheses about the behavior of these series. Alternative principles, such as the postulate of the existence of a third-party auctioneer inducing wage rigidity and uncleared markets, are similarly 'unrealistic', in the not especially important sense of not offering a good description of observed labor market institutions. (Lucas and Sargent [1979] 1994: 21)

> I think general discussions, especially by non-economists, of whether the system is in equilibrium or not are almost entirely nonsense. You can't look out of this window and ask whether New Orleans is in equilibrium. What does that mean? Equilibrium is a property of the way we look at things, not a property of reality. (Lucas's interview with Snowdon and Vane, 1998: 127)[7]

Thus, Lucas's adoption of market clearing is made without any claim as to its real-world realization. It is simply a postulate. The validity of adopting it hinges on how 'productive' the models based on it are, and what can be done using such models (for example, can models of the business cycle be constructed on such premises?). So, Lucas claims, the equilibrium discipline is justified by 'the proof of the pudding is in the eating' type arguments. The fact that he and others have been able to construct an equilibrium theory of the business cycle is one such proof.

While Lucas's standpoint will look odd to Marshallian macroeconomists who insist on the need for models to be realistic, it will be congenial to those who define themselves as Walrasians. Optimizing behavior and market clearing are the hallmarks of Walras's theory and of neo-Walrasian models. This may explain why Lucas and his associates felt they hardly needed to justify the equilibrium discipline: it is a mere by-product of having made macroeconomics Walrasian (De Vroey, 2004a).

Does the new conception of equilibrium amount to attributing a greater or a lesser role to the notion of equilibrium? Removing disequilibrium from the picture suggests a greater role for equilibrium. But the fact that equilibrium has become a postulate, and that it is no longer claimed that equilibrium and disequilibrium are characteristics of reality, amounts to shrinking the scope of the new conception of equilibrium as compared to the earlier one. Moreover, when every outcome is by construction an equilibrium, the normative connotation that was previously associated with equilibrium vanishes. Welfare considerations now need to bear on the comparison of alternative equilibrium positions.

Defending the microfoundations requirement also involves answering the objections that can be leveled against it. The first objection to be considered is that the market-clearing assumption is blatantly false. This is certainly the most widespread criticism of the Lucasian standpoint. Here are two examples, from amongst many other possible ones.

I have probably to remind you that an important school of thought in modern economics chooses to deny everything. Its members argue that supply and demand actually do balance in the labor market as they do in the fish market. (Solow 1990: 28)

For twenty years or so, economics has taught that markets 'clear' continuously. (Skidelsky 2009: xiii)

Lucas's reaction to this criticism is that it is based on a total misunderstanding of his standpoint. Since he made it clear from the outset that to him market clearing is a trait of the model economy, and not of reality, any criticism of its lack of reality is ineffective.[8] As a retort, he could ask his opponents how they propose to assess the presence of market non-clearing. The real difference lies deeper: it concerns the acceptance or rejection of the neo-Walrasian paradigm. While Lucas is an avowed neo-Walrasian, his critics are against this approach,[9] and stand on the Marshallian side.

Instead of viewing a theory and a model as identical, they hold that a theory and a model are two separate entities, the model being subservient to the theory.[10]

A second objection to market clearing is that it is outrageous to apply the optimizing behavior assumption to people who live in poor conditions or are even on the verge of starvation. Lucas's retort is that depicting agents as behaving in an optimizing way should not be equated with stating that they are blissfully happy. Frustration, on the one hand, and optimizing behavior and market clearing, on the other, can co-exist. In an interview with Klamer, Lucas calls John Steinbeck, a left-leaning author, to his rescue to make the point:

> Did you ever look at Steinbeck's book *The Grapes of Wrath*? It's a kind of protest pamphlet from the '30s about migrant farmers in California. There's one passage in there that is a better anecdote that I could have written for the kind of models I like. It illustrates the auction characteristic of the labor market for migrant farm workers. He writes about a hundred guys who show up at a farm where there are only ten jobs available. The farmer will let the wage fall until ten people are willing to work for that wage and ninety people say 'the hell with it', and just go on down the road. (Klamer, 1984: 46)

Finally, Lucas, going on the offensive, argues that many of the critics of the market clearing assumption are inconsistent, revealing split intellectual personalities. They may well defend the market non-clearing cause in meta-theoretical discussions, but when it comes to constructing models they fall back on the market-clearing assumption. Tobin is one example. The following passage from a draft version of his review of Tobin's Yrjö Jahnson lectures (Lucas 1981), a passage that is absent from the published version, makes the point. It also shows Lucas's awareness of the difficulty of defending market clearing because it runs so deeply counter to common sense.

> One [loose end] is 'cleared markets'. Tobin heaps scorn on the idea that any sane person would approach a macroeconomic problem with this particular simplifying assumption in hand. I see Tobin use it in *all* the substantive analysis in the present volume and in all of his most valuable earlier work, and I see my colleagues in every applied field in economics put it to good use on a wide variety of problems, without apologies and without philosophizing. Yet, at the same time I *know* that if a plebiscite were taken among macroeconomists Tobin's view (when he philosophizes, I mean, not when he is actually producing economics) would win over mine hands down. Well, so much the worse for science by plebiscite. I will work my side of the street, and let others work theirs, and if mine be less crowded, perhaps I shouldn't complain. (Lucas Archives, undated, Box 23, Tobin folder)

4. AN ASSESSMENT OF LUCAS'S STANDPOINT

The equilibrium notion has played a central role in political economy since its inception. So the idea of the equilibrium discipline as the hallmark of economics makes sense. However, I am unconvinced by the way in which Lucas and Sargent conceive it. Despite what they say, it actually contains only one criterion. Optimal behavior and market clearing are two sides of the same coin. They consider the same object at two distinct levels: optimal behavior refers to individual or personal equilibrium, while market clearing relates to what could be called 'interactive equilibrium', a state where all individuals' optimal plans have been made compatible. Moreover, their conception sweeps under the rug a distinction that I, for one, find crucial. It was expressed long ago by Hayek ([1937] 1948), but subsequently felt into disuse.

> I have long felt that the concept of equilibrium itself and the methods which we employ in pure analysis have a clear meaning only when confined to the analysis of the action of a single person and that we are really passing into a different sphere and silently introducing a new element of altogether different character when we apply it to the explanation of the interactions of a number of different individuals. (p. 35)

A similar insight is to be found under Patinkin's name when he draws a distinction between individual and market experiments (1965: 11–12, 387–92). Yeager aptly commented on this distinction:

> An individual experiment involves discovering, at least conceptually, the desired behavior of an individual person, of a small or large group of individuals, or even of all individuals in the community, acting in certain capacities, under certain specified circumstances. Whether these circumstances are compatible with other economic conditions and whether they can in fact prevail (whether they are genuinely or even conceptually attainable, to use the Chicago terminology) is beside the point: it is not the purpose of an individual experiment, by itself, to describe the economic equilibrium that will tend to emerge. ... This other type of analysis, which pulls together the results of various individual experiments, examines the conditions under which the plans of various persons would and would not mesh, describes the processes at work when plans fail to mesh, and describes the equilibrium position, is what Patinkin means by market experiments. (Yeager 1960: 59)

It follows from Hayek's and Patinkin's standpoints that the notions of the *optimizing plan* and *optimizing behavior* designate different realities. Optimizing plans refers to agents' intentions before the opening of trading, the solution to the choice-theoretical problem with which they are faced.[11] Optimizing behavior refers to what is observable after trading has started.

Thus, optimal behavior implies that the optimal plan has been realized. The gist of the above quotations is that optimizing plans and optimizing behavior need to be logically separated – there is a difference between finding a solution to a choice problem and implementing this solution. In contrast, whenever optimizing behavior is the sole concept used, the possibility of there being a difference between them is discarded by definition. This is the standpoint taken by Lucas and Sargent. Once it is adopted, it becomes misleading to claim, as they do, that the microfoundations requirement is based on two criteria, optimizing behavior and market clearing. A single criterion is needed, and it is irrelevant whether this is called generalized optimizing behavior or market clearing.

This difference can also be expressed with reference to the notions of equilibrium and disequilibrium. Individual equilibrium is a state where an agent is able to achieve one element of his or her optimal plan. Individual disequilibrium refers to the opposite case, the inability of some agents to have any element of their optimal plan transformed into optimal behavior. As stated by Solow in his interview with Klamer, it refers to 'situations in which people did not contemplate being at the start of the game' (Klamer 1984: 140). 'Equilibrium' here refers to what I labeled 'interactive equilibrium' above. 'The general equilibrium implies that all subsets of agents are in equilibrium and in particular that all individual agents are in equilibrium' (McKenzie 1987: 498). That is, equilibrium requires individual equilibrium. This quotation confirms my view that optimizing behavior and market clearing are one and the same thing. Symmetrically, in the conception that I defend, optimizing plans and market clearing are distinct, while market non-clearing and individual disequilibrium go hand in hand.

Thus, we have two definitions of microfoundations. The Hayek–Patinkin conception requires that economic analysis is grounded on the assumption that agents formulate optimizing *plans*. The issue of whether all optimizing plans come through – that is, whether market clearing prevails – is not considered as an element of the microfoundations requirement. The Lucasian conception is grounded on the stronger requirement of generalized optimizing behavior – that is, market clearing. In the same vein, there also exist two ways of understanding the 'neoclassical' label. According to Lucas, and Kydland and Prescott, the granting of the neoclassical label ought to be conditional on the presence of the generalized-optimizing-behavior/market-clearing result. According to the Hayek–Patinkin conception, it suffices that the economic discourse is based on an explicit formulation of optimizing plans.

Which of these interpretations of microfoundations is preferable? They have in common the optimizing plan criterion, the adoption of which raises no serious objections.[12] So the answer hinges on the need for the market-clearing postulate.

Market clearing is the consequence of some prior assumptions related to 'trade technology' – that is, the institutional set-up that is needed to make the realization of equilibrium possible. Like other Walrasian models, Lucas's models are based on the *tâtonnement* or auctioneer hypothesis. This is a theoretical scenario explaining how the equilibrium values calculated by the economist when studying the logical existence of a general equilibrium could come into existence in the artificial economy described by the model. As soon as this hypothesis is adopted, the matter is decided: market clearing always occurs. But then market clearing is the direct consequence of the auctioneer hypothesis rather than a consequence of self-interest and rationality. The problem with the auctioneer hypothesis is that it runs counter to the essential nature of the theory's theoretical *explanandum*, because it amounts to picturing a decentralized system as a centralized organization of trade.[13]

So, at the level of principle, there is no reason to adopt the market clearing postulate. On the contrary, states of individual disequilibrium seem to be a normal feature of the market system. In effect, in a system where decisions are taken separately in anticipation of future demand, it would be a miracle if no decision were ever proven wrong and coordination failures never occurred. The presence of these features is not synonymous with the system's lack of viability. Hence such states should be part of the theoretical representation of the economy. Because the Hayek–Patinkin conception of microfoundations allows their incorporation while the Lucasian does not, the Hayek–Patinkin interpretation appears to be more satisfactory than the Lucasian.

This being stated, it must be admitted that to date the incorporation of disequilibrim into economic theory has proven to be an almost insuperable task. From Adam Smith onwards, economists have neglected to address it in earnest. Keynes was the exception. He ought to be credited for having attempted the task, even though he failed in this enterprise. Subsequent Keynesian economists did not do much better.[14] So, to date, no robust general theory of individual disequilibrium is available. As a result, keeping the market-clearing premise can be justified on the Wittgensteinian grounds that 'whereof one cannot speak, thereof one must be silent'. This justification is grounded on expediency – the admission that there is no alternative to the auctioneer scenario for arriving at equilibrium. But expediency should not be transformed into methodological virtue. Nor can it be claimed that the aim of constructing a disequilibrium theory must be rejected as a matter of first principle. Had Lucas contented himself with pointing out that Keynes had failed to achieve his disequilibrium project, I would have no complaints. My disagreement is with his further claim that the mere desire to engage in such a project is a sufficient reason for exclusion from the neoclassical economics community.

5. ASSESSING KEYNESIAN THEORY AGAINST THE MICROFOUNDATIONS CRITERION

Let me finally address the issue of whether Keynesian theory abides by the microfoundations requirement. This issue can be broken down into three sub-questions. First, is there an adhesion to this principle? Second, if yes, to which of its two versions, the Lucasian or the Hayek–Patinkin version, does it adhere? And third, is the microfoundations requirement crucial to the theory or is it dealt with off-handedly? As Keynes was a Marshallian economist, I start my investigation by considering how Marshall fared on this requirement.

5.1 Marshall

In Walras's *Elements*, the presence of the microfoundations perspective strikes the reader at once, as a result of Walras assuming that theory and model are identical. With Marshall, things are more complicated. The presence of the microfoundations requirement can certainly be detected in many passages of the *Principles* (Marshall 1920). Marshall's manifold references to the substitution principle are a testimony to this. But these passages belong to what can be considered the meta-theoretical part of Marshall's text, the purpose of which is to motivate or qualify his more substantive results. Chapter II of Book V of the *Principles*, introducing the corn model, provides a fine illustration of this. In its introductory paragraph, Marshall evokes the case of a young boy weighing the marginal utility of eating blackberries against the marginal disutility of picking them (without even mentioning these notions). The boy stops picking when these factors become equal. Marshall then jumps to a discussion in terms of market supply and demand. He proceeds in the same way in the other chapters of Book V of the *Principles*, the most theoretical part of the book. While frequently referring to agents' decision-making processes, especially firms', he is concerned with market supply and demand analysis. Hence the impression that Marshall deals with microfoundations in an off-hand way. However, one should not stop at this impression. Looking at the Mathematical Appendix to the *Principles*, a different impression emerges: here the microfoundations perspective comes fully into play.

As to the question of whether the microfoundations requirement as conceived by Marshall is of the Lucas or the Hayek–Patinkin type, the answer has already been given at the beginning of the article. In Marshall's models market clearing is always present (De Vroey 2007). Hence in this respect, Marshall anticipates Lucas's understanding of the microfoundations requirement.

5.2 Keynes's *General Theory*

Considering the *General Theory* (Keynes 1936) rather than Keynesian macroeconomics in general, it is clear that Keynes does not abide by the microfoundations requirement *à la* Lucas since his main purpose was to overthrow it (as it stood in his day). In other words, the move that Lucas interprets as an effect of the demanding character of the equilibrium discipline was to Keynes a deliberate attempt to break away from it for the very reason that it excluded involuntary outcomes, while everything indicated that the contrary was true in reality.

As to the question of whether Keynes's *General Theory* abides by the softer Hayek–Patinkin requirement, my answer is yes.[15] There are no signs that Keynes wanted to depart from depicting agents as making optimizing plans. He certainly wanted his theory of effective demand, actually an extension of Marshall's analysis of firms' short-period production decisions, to be based on entrepreneurs' profit maximization (Keynes 1936: 23). Another testimony to Keynes's commitment to microfoundations is his introduction of involuntary unemployment in Chapter 2 of the *General Theory* . Its presentation as an infringement on the second fundamental 'postulate' of classical economics amounts to constructing it in a microfounded way.[16] Translated into modern terminology, the second postulate consists of stating (a) that agents will participate in the labor market only if the market wage exceeds their reservation wage, and (b) that in a divisible labor context they will participate up to the point where the marginal rate of substitution between consumption and leisure equals the real wage rate. To me, this is a strong sign that Keynes (unwittingly of course) reasoned in terms of the Hayek–Patinkin conception of microfoundations – that is, starting the analysis from agents' optimizing plans without pre-empting the issue of whether these plans would be achieved. Keynes, of course, made the explicit claim that optimizing plans were not always transformed into optimizing behavior, but this does not invalidate the point: as soon as an optimizing plan is the starting point, the Hayek–Patinkin microfoundations requirement is satisfied.

I can now answer the question of whether Keynes's *General Theory* should be characterized as neoclassical. If the Hayek–Patinkin understanding of the microfoundations requirement is adopted, the answer is 'Yes', while if Lucas's definition is taken, it is 'No'. This being said, if Keynes was in favor of a microfounded analysis, he contented himself with expressing this necessity without doing the job of providing such microfoundations. He was in too much of a hurry to try to do it (and, had he tried, he would not have succeeded, the task being too difficult).

Additional evidence for my claim can be found in Keynes's criticism of Tinbergen's work. Keynes was sent proof copies of Tinbergen's two books, *A Method and its Application to Investment Activity* and *Business Cycles in the United Nations of America* (which became the two volumes of Tinbergen's *Statistical Testing of Business Cycle Theories* (Tinbergen 1939)), in order that he might comment on and approve them for publication. This led to an exchange of letters, first, with R. Tyler, his correspondent at the League of Nations, and, second, with Harrod. Eventually, Keynes wrote a review, which appeared in the September 1939 issue of the *Economic Journal*. Tinbergen's reaction to Keynes's criticism was published in the March 1940 issue. Keynes added a reply in the same issue. Here, I focus only on the passages that are relevant to my inquiry. In a letter to Tyler, dated 23 August 1938 (Moggridge 1973: 285–6), Keynes expresses his dissatisfaction with Tinbergen's approach in a way that Lucas could easily endorse. One of his criticisms was that the coefficients of Tinbergen's model were calculated arbitrarily (Moggridge 1973: 286) – the equivalent of Lucas's statement that they lack microfoundations. Keynes also complained about the absence of expectations in Tinbergen's estimations: "Is it assumed that the future is a determinate function of past statistics? What place is left for expectations and the state of confidence relating to the future?" (p. 287). This should be music to Lucas's ears. Finally, in a letter to Harrod, dated 16 July 1938, Keynes wrote:

> I also want to emphasize strongly the point about economics being a moral science. I mentioned before that it deals with introspection and with values. I might have added that it deals with motives, expectations, psychological uncertainties. One has to be constantly on guard against treating the material as constant and homogeneous. It is as though the fall of the apple to the ground depended on the apple's motives, on whether the ground wanted the apple to fall, and on mistaken calculations on the part of the apple as to how far it was from the centre of the earth. (Moggridge, 1973: 300)

The difference between Keynes and Lucas, it turns out, is that Keynes makes an anticipatory criticism of what was to become macroeconometric modeling, while Lucas criticized it *ex post*. But they both based their criticism on the argument that microfoundations were lacking.

5.3 Keynesian Macroeconomics: Theoretical Models

Keynesian macroeconomics is too wide a field to be fully covered here. Moreover, it contains several different standpoints about microfoundations. To show this, I will consider two works that shaped the course of Keynesian macroeconomics, Modigliani's 1944 article and Klein's 1947 book, *The Keynesian Revolution*.

Modgliani's article played a decisive role in the development of macroeconomics by recasting Hicks's original model into its now standard textbook version.[17] The result, which Modigliani hails as a case of involuntary unemployment, follows from a labor supply schedule exhibiting a perfectly elastic section up to a kink, above which it becomes vertical. The employment level corresponding to the kink is called 'full employment'. And, 'unless there is "full employment", the wage rate is not really a variable of the system but a datum, a result of "history" or of "economic policy" or of both' (Modigliani 1944: 47). Whenever the demand for labor intersects the supply schedule on its horizontal section, involuntary unemployment is declared to exist. This model has been widely popular but with hindsight it is surprising that its flaws have remained undetected. For all the claim that it is Keynesian, this model has a market clearing outcome.[18] Moreover, as I have shown elsewhere (De Vroey, 2004b: Chapter 8), what Modigliani calls full employment, the maximum level of employment, does not dominate lower levels as far as welfare is concerned. This is due to the fact that in order to have an inverse-L supply schedule, it must be assumed that hours supplied to the labor market and hours of leisure are perfect substitutes. The conclusion to be drawn is that, semantics to the contrary notwithstanding, the Modigliani model and the myriad of models based on it satisfy the microfoundations requirement as understood by Lucas: they feature market clearing and optimizing behavior!

In one sense, Klein's *Keynesian Revolution* was more Marshallian than *The General Theory* because it contained a mathematical appendix.[19] However, in this appendix, Klein took a Walrasian viewpoint emphasizing the need to give macroeconomics strong microfoundations. He derived aggregate consumption and liquidity preference functions from constrained individual utility maximization, considering 'an individual household trying to maximize its utility function, which depends on the consumption of present and future commodities, and its structure of assets in the form of money and various types of securities' (Klein 1947: 192).

Likewise, Klein derived the firms' investment function from a maximization of profit program. 'The entrepreneur will be assumed to behave, with regard to the purchase of capital assets, according to the principles of profit maximization over the anticipated future life of the assets in question' (Klein 1947: 196). At the time, this was an advanced way of positing agents' programs. After a few, more or less *ad hoc* manipulations, Klein's reasoning ended up with the standard aggregate functions of the IS-LM model. His ultimate aim was to get to a market non-clearing result. To this end, he argued that the model lacked a full-employment solution, the effect of making the assumption, which he claimed was empirically verified, of a low interest-elasticity of the investment function. As a result, the saving and investment functions failed to intersect at any positive rate of interest. However, their matching was conceivable at a less-than-full-employment level of output, and Klein took the further step of assuming that such a shift in output would occur. In turn, this decrease in output, he claimed, would have an impact on the labor market, generating excess labor supply and trade away from the supply curve. This was involuntary unemployment in Keynes's sense.[20]

It would be unreasonable to expect an economist writing in the 1940s, with the aim of defending the Keynesian cause, to provide a waterproof demonstration of his claim. But in spite of its shortcomings, Klein's contribution was remarkable. With respect to the purpose of this chapter, it shows that Klein wanted Keynesian theory to be firmly embedded in the neoclassical framework, at least in so far as this embodies the Hayek–Patinkin understanding of the microfoundations requirement.

Klein's project of firmly anchoring Keynesian analysis in a micro-founded perspective was later taken up by Patinkin in his *Money, Interest and Prices* (1965). In turn, Patinkin's work, in conjunction with Clower's ([1965] 1984), served as a springboard for the so-called disequilibrium approach in macroeconomics associated with the names of Barro and Grossman (1971), Benassy (1975), Drèze (1975) and Malinvaud (1977). All these authors had a microeconomics background and they set themselves the task of improving Keynesian theory by giving it more rigorous micro-foundations (in the Hayek–Patinkin sense).

5.4 Keynesian Macroeconomics: Econometric Models

Klein did more than reconstruct Keynes's theory theoretically. To him, the conceptual apparatus set up by Keynes in the *General Theory* 'cried out for empirical verification (or refutation)' (Bodkin, Klein and Marwah 1991: 19). Undertaking this empirical extension became his life's work. Success came as Klein's joint work with Goldberger, *An Econometric Model of the*

United States (1955) blazed the way for a new field of research: macro-econometric modeling.

The path to the econometric study of the economy as a whole had been opened almost two decades earlier by Tinbergen in his 1939 book, discussed above. In this book, Tinbergen expressed a view of micro-foundations that was to be adopted by most of the members of the profession until Lucas launched his critique:

> Economic analysis may be applied to the behavior of individual persons or firms; or to the behavior of 'industries', defined in some more or less arbitrary manner; or, again, to the behavior of whole groups of industries, such as those producing consumption and investment goods respectively, and of whole categories of economic persons, such as those engaged in the credit markets, or the labor market, as a whole. It is this last type of economic approach (sometimes spoken of as a 'macro-economic' approach) which will be employed. ... For it is this type of approach which seems most relevant to cyclical fluctuation, and which alone makes it possible to limit the number of variables considered to a figure which permits of their being effectively handled. It goes without saying that, in this approach, the coefficients found do not give any indications of the behavior of individual entrepreneurs, consumers, etc., but only to the average reactions of many individuals. (Tinbergen, 1939: 14)

This is a polite way of saying that, to all intents and purposes, microfoundations can be the object of benign neglect. Klein is the finest illustration of this standpoint. In his early writings, which were purely theoretical, he insisted on the need to base the analysis on the study of individual optimizing planning. However, when he began to do empirical work, he quickly realized that it was too difficult to deliver on this need.[21]

This remark brings me back to Lucas's criticism of Keynesian theory. I have argued that this criticism put the bar too high in that there is no solid reason for arguing that the Lucasian understanding of microfoundations is superior to the Hayek–Patinkin conception. However, when it comes to the second part of Lucas's criticism, the 'Lucas critique' proper, I have no complaints to make. The rational-expectations assumption accepted, Lucas is right in claiming that agents should be depicted as changing their optimal plans whenever the policy regime is modified. Actually, his criticism remains valid even when the Hayek–Patinkin definition is adopted since it bears on agents devising their optimal plans. In other words, although they cannot be blamed in view of the difficulty of the task, traditional Keynesian macroeconometric models fail to abide by the Hayek–Patinkin conception of the microfoundations requirement, let alone the Lucasian conception.

6. CONCLUDING REMARKS

This chapter has attempted to assess whether the microfoundations requirement is a decisive criterion for separating Keynesian macro-economics from new classical macroeconomics. My conclusion is that, phrased in this way, the question is unanswerable. In effect, two different views of the requirement have to be distinguished. The Hayek–Patinkin view is based on a separation between optimizing plans and optimizing behavior, and implies that any model that starts from the agents' optimizing plan satisfies the microfoundations requirement. The Lucasian view puts the bar higher. To all intents and purposes, it conceives of the microfoundations requirement as being based on a single criterion, market clearing. That is, any model of market non-clearing fails this requirement. To my mind, there is no reason for adopting such a narrow definition as a question of principle. Its adoption as a modeling expediency is, however, defensible, in view of the difficulty of constructing market non-clearing models.

This chapter has also assessed Keynes's work and Keynesian macro-economics against the two understandings of the requirement. To limit myself here to a single result pertaining to Keynes's own work, the chapter made two points. First, Keynes's theory should not be depicted as a failure to abide by the equilibrium discipline, since Keynes's aim was in fact to breach it. Second, when *The General Theory* is gauged against the Hayek–Patinkin conception of microfoundations, it passes the test hands down.

NOTES

1. While scientific revolutions are always a collective enterprise, it is nonetheless widely accepted that one person, Robert Lucas, played a pivotal role in the transformation of macroeconomics. As I result, I shall take him as the spokesperson for the wider group of economists who developed the new paradigm.
2. My concern in this chapter is limited to traditional Keynesian macroeconomics since there is no dispute about the fact that new Keynesian macroeconomics is solidly microfounded. Duarte (Chapter 6 in this volume) discusses the differences between new classical/real business cycle models, on the one hand, and new Keynesian models, on the other.
3. Henceforth the terms 'microfoundations' and 'equilibrium discipline' will be used interchangeably.
4. Two implicit assumptions underpinning the equilibrium discipline are: (a) that people do not leave perceived gains from trade unexploited; and (b) that agents have learned everything there was to be learned.
5. For example, 'New classical economics introduced two new and radical theoretical doctrines: ... Second, the notion of market clearing required that such models should assume that supply and demand were kept continuously equal to one another in all markets' (Laidler, 2006: 56).

6. Earlier economists' justification for the presence of market clearing were different from Lucas's. Take for example Marshall. He might have claimed that a proper domain, other than value analysis, was available for the market non-clearing phenomenon, namely business cycle and monetary theory. He might also have stated that that there was little harm in postulating market clearing, since the only important equilibrium concept was normal equilibrium. Discarding the possibility of disequilibrium as a departure from normal equilibrium would have been inadmissible, but discarding the possibility of departures from market-day equilibrium (the lower equilibrium concept) would be a matter of benign neglect.
7. The same point was made earlier by Weintraub: 'This symposium provided additional examples of such argumentations: the discussions generated by McCallum's paper, and Grandmont's, contained various appeals to the "Principle" that the world either was or was not in equilibrium. The commentators in this audience seemed to think that they had a way of discussing the truth of the idea that observed states were equilibria without committing themselves to any particular theory of macroeconomics. This is, of course, an illusion: equilibrium states, or disequilibria are characteristics of our theories, and are thus imposed on the world" (1990: 273).
8. The same holds for the rational-expectations assumption. Lucas holds that it ought to be viewed as a technical model-building principle rather than a proposition about reality. 'One can ask for example, whether expectations are rational in the Klein–Goldberger model of the United States economy; one cannot ask whether people in the United States have rational expectations' (Lucas Archives, undated, Box 23, Barro Folder).
9. Hoover, this volume, minimizes the importance of Lucas's Walrasian affiliation.
10. Leijonhufvud aptly characterized this viewpoint as follows: 'I propose to conceive of economic "theories" as a set of beliefs about the economy and how it functions. They refer to the "real world". ... "Models" are formal but partial representations of theories. A model never encompasses the entire theory to which it refers' (1997: 193). The wider contrasts between the Marshallian and the Walrasian approaches are discussed in De Vroey (2012).
11. In Patinkin's words: 'We can consider the individual – with his given indifference map and initial endowment – to be a "utility-computer" into whom we "feed" a sequence of market prices and from whom we obtain a corresponding sequence of "solutions" in the form of specified optimum positions' (1965: 7).
12. The optimizing plan criterion amounts to assuming that agents have the ability to optimally solve any decision problem they encounter (with the ensuing correlates of rationality, information and rational expectations). This assumption is certainly an exaggeration, yet it is nonetheless acceptable as it is probably better, and certainly more tractable, than alternative assumptions.
13. See De Vroey (1998) for further discussion of this point.
14. See De Vroey (2004b).
15. Hoover (in Chapter 1 of this volume) makes the same claim using different arguments.
16. 'The utility of the wage when a given volume of labor is employed is equal to the marginal disutility of that amount of employment' (Keynes 1936: 5).
17. See De Vroey (2000).
18. Lucas and Rapping characterized their 1969 model as Keynesian in spite of its market clearing result on the grounds that Modigliani's model, which was viewed as an emblematic Keynesian model, also featured market clearing (Lucas and Rapping, 1969).
19. Mirowski (in Chapter 4 of this volume) provides an unorthodox study of the relation between Klein and his Cowles Commission colleagues.
20. For a criticism of Klein's reasoning, see De Vroey (2004b).
21. The main reason for this, he stated, was the lack of data. With hindsight, it should be added that a lack of appropriate concepts was another effective barrier. For a study of Klein's intellectual progression from theory to econometrics, see De Vroey and Malgrange (2012). Hoover (Chapter 1 of this volume) discusses Klein's aggregation methods.

REFERENCES

Barro, Robert J., and Herschel I. Grossman (1971). A General Disequilibrium Model of Income and Employment. *American Economic Review,* 61 (1):82–93.

Benassy, Jean-Pascal (1975). Neo-Keynesian Disequilibrium Theory in a Monetary Economy. *Review of Economic Studies,* 42 (4):503–23.

Bodkin, Ronald, Lawrence R. Klein, and Kanta Marwah (eds) (1991). *A History of Macroeconometric Model-Building.* Aldershot: Edward Elgar.

Clower, Robert ([1965] 1984). The Keynesian Counterrevolution: A Theoretical Appraisal. In *Money and Markets. Essays by Robert Clower.* Edited by Donald Walker. Cambridge University Press: Cambridge.

De Vroey, Michel (1998). Is the Tâtonnement Hypothesis a Good Caricature of Market Forces? *Journal of Economic Methodology,* 5 (2):201–21.

De Vroey, Michel (2000). IS-LM '*à la* Hicks' versus IS-LM '*à la* Modigliani'. *History of Political Economy,* 32 (2):293–316.

De Vroey, Michel (2004a). *Involuntary Unemployment: The Elusive Quest for a Theory.* London: Routledge.

De Vroey, Michel (2004b). The History of Macroeconomics Viewed Against the Background of the Marshall–Walras Divide. In *The IS-LM Model. Its Rise, Fall and Strange Persistence. History of Political Economy* 36 supplement. Edited by Michel De Vroey, and Kevin D. Hoover. Durham, NC: Duke University Press.

De Vroey, Michel (2007). Did the Market-clearing Postulate Pre-exist New Classical Economics? The Case of Marshallian Theory. *The Manchester School,* 75 (3):328–48.

De Vroey, Michel (2012). Marshall and Walras: Incompatible Bedfellows? *European Journal of the History of Economic Thought* (forthcoming).

De Vroey, Michel, and Pierre Malgrange (2010). From *The Keynesian Revolution* to the Klein–Goldberger Model: Klein and the Dynamization of Keynesian Theory. *History of Economic Ideas* (forthcoming).

Drèze, Jacques H. (1975). Existence of Equilibrium under Price Rigidities. *International Economic Review,* 16 (2):301–20.

Friedman, Milton (1968). The Role of Monetary Policy. *American Economic Review,* 58 (1):1–17.

Greenwood, Jeremy ([1994] 2005). Modern Business Cycle Analysis. Rochester Center for Economic Research, Working Paper, No. 520.

Hayek, Friedrich ([1937] 1948). Economics and Knowledge. In *Individualism and Economic Order.* Chicago: The University of Chicago Press.

Keynes, John Maynard (1936). *The General Theory of Employment, Interest, and Money.* London: Macmillan.

Klamer, Arjo (1984). *The New Classical Macroeconomics. Conversations with the New Classical Economists and their Opponents.* Brighton: Wheatsheaf Books.

Klein, Lawrence (1947). *The Keynesian Revolution.* New York: Macmillan.

Klein, Lawrence, and Arthur Goldberger (1955). *An Econometric Model of the United States, 1922–1952.* Amsterdam: North Holland.

Kydland, Finn, and Edward Prescott (1991). The Econometrics of the General Equilibrium Approach to Business Cycles. *Scandinavian Journal of Economics,* 93 (2):161–78.

Laidler, David (2006). Keynes and the Birth of Modern Macroeconomics. In *The Cambridge Companion to Keynes*. Edited by Bradley Bateman, and Roger Backhouse. Cambridge: Cambridge University Press.

Leijonhufvud, Axel (1997). Models and Theories. *Journal of Economic Methodology*, 4 (2):193–8.

Lucas, Robert E., Jr. ([1972] 1981). Expectations and the Neutrality of Money. In Lucas (1981), pp. 65–89.

Lucas, Robert E., Jr. ([1976] 1981). Econometric Policy Evaluation: A Critique. In Lucas (1981), pp. 104–30.

Lucas, Robert E., Jr. ([1977] 1981). Understanding Business Cycles. In Lucas (1981), pp. 215–39.

Lucas, Robert E., Jr. ([1980] 1981). Methods and Problems in Business Cycle Theory. In Lucas (1981), pp. 271–96.

Lucas, Robert E., Jr. (1981). *Studies in Business Cycle Theory*. Cambridge, MA: The MIT Press.

Lucas, Robert E., Jr. (1987). *Models of Business Cycles*. Oxford: Basil Blackwell.

Lucas, Robert E., Jr. (undated). Robert E. Lucas, Jr. Papers. Rare Book, Manuscript, and Special Collections Library, Duke University.

Lucas, Robert E. Jr., and Leonard A. Rapping (1969). Real Wages, Employment, and Inflation. *Journal of Political Economy*, 77 (5):721–54.

Lucas, Robert E., Jr., and Thomas Sargent ([1979] 1994). After Keynesian Macroeconomics. In *The Rational Expectations Revolution – Readings from the Front Line*. Edited by Preston J. Miller. Cambridge, MA: The MIT Press.

Malinvaud, Edmond (1977). *The Theory of Unemployment Reconsidered*. Oxford: Basil Blackwell.

Marshall, Alfred (1920). *Principles of Economics*. 8th edn. London: Macmillan.

McKenzie, Lionel (1987). General Equilibrium. In *The New Palgrave. A Dictionary of Economics*. Edited by John Eatwell, Murray Milgate, and Peter Newman. London: Macmillan, pp. 498–512.

Modigliani, Franco (1944). Liquidity Preference and the Theory of Interest and Money. *Econometrica*, 12 (1):45–88.

Moggridge, Donald (ed.) (1973). *The Collected Writings of John Maynard Keynes.* Vol. XIV: The General Theory and After, Part II Defence and Development. London: Macmillan.

Patinkin, Don (1965). *Money, Interest and Prices*. 2nd edn. New York: Harper and Row.

Samuelson, Paul (1983). Comment on Leijonhufvud. In *Keynes and the Modern World*. Edited by George D. N. Worswick, and James A. Trevithick. Cambridge: Cambridge University Press.

Skidelsky, Robert (2009). *Keynes: The Return of the Master*. London: Public Affairs.

Snowdon, Brian, and Howard R. Vane (1998). Transforming Macroeconomics: An Interview with Robert E Lucas Jr. *Journal of Economic Methodology*, 5 (1):115–45.

Solow, Robert (1990). *The Labour Market as a Social Institution*. Cambridge: Blackwell.

Tinbergen, Jan (1939). *Statistical Testing of Business Cycle Theories*. Geneva: League of Nations.

Walras, L. (1954). *Elements of Pure Economics*. Translated by W. Jaffé. London: Allen and Unwin.

Weintraub, E. Roy (1990). Methodology does not Matter, but the History of Thought Might. In *The State of Macroeconomics – Proceedings of the Symposium, Whiter Macroeconomics?* Edited by Seppo Honkapohja. Oxford: Oxford University Press.

Yeager, Leland (1960). Methodenstreit Over Demand Curves. *Journal of Political Economy*, 68 (1):53–64.

6. Not going away? Microfoundations in the making of a new consensus in macroeconomics

Pedro Garcia Duarte[1]

Macroeconomics is now, as it has always been, the subject of intense controversy.
(Robert Solow 1979: 340)

When the outside world tells us that no two economists ever agree on anything, it is talking about macroeconomics.
(Stanley Fischer 1983: 275)

While macroeconomics is often thought as a deeply divided field, with less of a shared core and correspondingly less cumulative progress than in other areas of economics, in fact, there are fewer fundamental disagreements among macroeconomists now than in the past decades. This is due to important progress in resolving seemingly intractable debates.
(Michael Woodford 2009: 267)

1. INTRODUCTION

Macroeconomics here, according to the economists discussed in this chapter, refers to "the branch of economics concerned with fluctuations in the overall level of business activity, with the determinants of inflation, interest rates, and exchange rates, and with the effects of government policies ... that are considered mainly with regard to their effects upon the economy as a whole" (Woodford 2000: 1). Therefore, the focus is on business cycle and the theory of economic stabilization (with greater emphasis on monetary economics) rather than on growth.

In the last decade a growing number of macroeconomists have advertised their field as a steadily progressing enterprise because they now work on a common theoretical framework. Clearly, these economists have an understanding of the current consensus that is indissociable from their view that in the past macroeconomics could not progress much because competing schools fought never-ending theoretical battles. My goal in this chapter is to discuss how modern macroeconomists see this consensus that emerged in their field. Because they view this consensus as the last step in a historical ladder, its characterization is intimately related to how they see the history of their sub-discipline.[2] In particular, I shall stress how a particular understanding of the microfoundations that macroeconomics needs formed a common ground on which economists could agree and reach a consensus.

In contrast to economists working in other areas of economics, macroeconomists perceive their field to be not only composed of competing schools of thought but also characterized by a somewhat recurrent state of disarray.[3] For instance, in the 1970s Robert Hall, "as a gross oversimplification," divided the macroeconomic thought in the US of the time into two opposing schools: the freshwater school refers to the new classical (and later the real business cycle) economists located in universities near lakes or rivers such as the University of Chicago, Carnegie-Mellon, Rochester and Minnesota; and the saltwater school composed of the Keynesians at universities near either coast like Harvard, Berkeley, MIT, Princeton, Stanford and UCLA. Hall (1976: 1) explains:

> The fresh water view holds that fluctuations are largely attributable to supply shifts and the government is essentially incapable of affecting the level of economic activity. The salt water view holds shifts in demand responsible for fluctuations and thinks government policies (at least monetary policy) is capable of affecting demand. Needless to say, individual contributors vary across a spectrum of salinity.

Although Hall's (1976) dichotomy, as Robert Gordon (1989: 177) puts it, "has dominated the coffee-break oral tradition of American macroeconomic conferences" for decades, he was not alone in using the idea of a school of thought. Axel Leijonhufvud (1976), among others, explored more systematically how economics and its schools of thought could be interpreted according to the ideas of Thomas Kuhn ([1962] 1970) – which became very popular in economics in the late 1960s and 1970s (Weintraub 2002, 263)[4] – and of Imre Lakatos (1970). Given Kuhn's and Lakatos's notoriety among economists from the 1970s onward, and given that the view economists have about how science is done shape the history they (and historians of economics) write, it is not surprising to see macroeconomists increasingly using concepts as schools of thought, normal science, revolutions, research programs and paradigms, and talking about accumulation of knowledge and progress in their field.[5]

Given that a school of economic thought is a loose concept that can be associated either to a Kuhnian paradigm or to Lakatosian research program, its strong survival in economics from the 1970s until nowadays is not accidental.[6] For example, Edmund Phelps (1990) identified seven schools of macroeconomic thought: the macroeconomics of Keynes; monetarism; the new classical school; the new Keynesians; supply-side macroeconomists; neoclassical and neo-neoclassical real business cycle theory (RBC); and the structuralist school. Brian Snowdon, Robert Vane, and Peter Wynarczyk (1994) identified the same number of schools (or paradigms).[7] Perhaps some would add the post-Keynesian school to this list.[8] What becomes clear is that macroeconomists have a loose understanding of what a school is and ultimately identifies anyone with a particular idea to a school of thought. As an emblematic example of such loose use of schools in macroeconomics, Snowdon asked Leijonhufvud in an interview: "Do you attach any school of thought label to yourself? Do you see yourself as some kind of Leijonhufvudian Keynesian?" To which Leijonhufvud (2004: 127) answered: "In one sense the groupings have disappeared because not many economists are interested anymore. One of my weaknesses is that I am psychologically averse to running with some herd, or even breeding a herd of my own."

As for the understanding that the history of macroeconomics, in contrast to that of other areas of economics, is not a steady progress within an unchanged explanatory framework, here I quote at length Michael Woodford's (2000: 2) account of the evolution of the fields of macro and microeconomics, an understanding shared by N. Gregory Mankiw (see Snowdon and Vane 1995: 50–51):[9]

> A discussion of the century's progress in general economic theory – with primary emphasis upon what is taught in courses on "microeconomic theory", which emphasize the decisions of individual households and firms – would surely be more suitable if my aim were to boost the prestige of my own field among the many distinguished representatives of other disciplines present here. But the story would be one with little suspense. For it would not be too much of an oversimplification to present the field as having progressed smoothly and steadily, developing theories of ever greater power and broader scope within an essentially unchanged explanatory framework, based on the concepts of optimizing individual behavior and market equilibrium, that were already central to economic thought in the previous century. Macroeconomics instead has been famously controversial ... Discussions of twentieth-century developments in macroeconomics make frequent references to "revolutions" and "counter-revolutions", and the question of whether there has been progress at all (or which broad developments should count as progress) is a more lively topic of debate among economists than one might believe would be possible in the case of a topic with such a canonical status in the curriculum.[10]

We then come to another central element of the macroeconomists' comprehension about the nature and evolution of their field: macroeconomics has not only several competing schools and from time to time is in a state of disarray, but it also has moments of consensus when knowledge seems to progress at a faster rate.[11] These economists identify two consensuses in the history of their sub-discipline: the neoclassical synthesis of the 1950s and 1960s and the recent new consensus (from the late 1990s to the present day),[12] labeled as the new neoclassical synthesis by Marvin Goodfriend and Robert King (1997).[13] Macroeconomists tend to characterize and to tout such periods of synthesis as moments when the intellectual disarray and the untamed competition among schools – both with respect to macro-economic theories and to policies to be prescribed – are replaced by balanced conversations, points of convergence, better policymaking and scientific progress.[14]

Macroeconomists emphasize progress and secure knowledge at times of consensus as a way of stressing that the science of the consensus is good and strong.[15] The flip-side of this argument used by macroeconomists in the ivory tower of academia is to say that having schools competing in a state of disarray is a synonym for weak science: Stiglitz (1992: 40) pondered whether the fact that macroeconomists' views were so divergent indicates that they are "simply ideologues looking for justifications for [their] politi-cal biases, or (no less worse) technicians, taking the assumptions provided to [them] by [their] ideologue brethren and exploring their consequences." Returning to Kuhn ([1962] 1970), when there is no dominant paradigm, there is no normal science: macroeconomists have an epistemological fear that the scientific foundations of their studies are weak or absent if they are always in a state of intellectual disorder.[16] Additionally, their scientific and academic prestige among both economists in general and other scientists could be boosted if they had a story of steady progress and secure knowledge to tell (see Woodford's quotation above and Mankiw's welcom-ing words to the emerging consensus in Snowdon and Vane 1995: 60). In this respect, macroeconomists working within a unified framework is what one needs. Alan Blinder's (1989: vii) words could not be more emphatic about this perception among macroeconomists:

> ... macroeconomic debates during my professional career have been distressingly unrelenting, acrimonious, and even ideological. The constant state of intense disputation takes a personal toll and, more importantly, inhibits scientific progress. Too much of our time, it seems to me, is spent defending obvious positions against preposterous challenges, too little doing what T. S. Kuhn called normal science. Sometimes I wonder if we are doing science at all.[17]

On the other hand, policymakers keep asking macroeconomists what theory they should use to guide policy, and intellectual disarray is not a good sign here either. Macroeconomists can give a convincing answer as long as they are able to show that there is a core of usable macroeconomics that they all believe in (to use the theme of a session at the AEA meetings of

1997).[18] In this sense, it is symptomatic that Frederic Mishkin (2007), who was a member of the Board of Governors of the Federal Reserve System from 2006 to 2008, argued that the major advances in monetary economics have made monetary policy become more of a science.[19] Mishkin's opinion was earlier a hope with which Goodfriend and King (1997) closed their article, and it is also shared to some degree by V. V. Chari and Patrick Kehoe (2006), by Goodfriend (2007), and by Jordi Galí and Mark Gertler (2007).[20]

In the new wave of consensus in macroeconomics (the new neoclassical synthesis), mainstream macroeconomists are emphasizing greatly the progress achieved nowadays. For them, in essence, there is no Kuhnian substitution of one paradigm by another via revolutions, but rather a merging of previously rival paradigms and a "steady accumulation of knowledge" (Blanchard 2000: 1375). How is that possible? "Largely because facts have a way of not going away" (Blanchard 2009: 210, paraphrasing his earlier statement that "the force of facts is hard to avoid" (Blanchard 1997a: 245)). Put another way, "to some extent, this is because positions that were vigorously defended in the past have had to be conceded in the face of further argument and experience" (Woodford 2009: 268). Therefore, facts and arguments made economists from different camps develop "a largely shared vision both of fluctuations and of methodology" (Blanchard 2009: 210).[21]

In a nutshell, both in theory and practice, advertising a consensus means that mainstream macroeconomists now agree on the right way of doing macroeconomics – and it is right because it is generally accepted, after facts and arguments have refuted wrong theories and conventions have become uniform.[22] Knowing how to do it is the prerequisite for doing it right and thus for increasing the stock of knowledge.

In order to proceed with the analysis of the new consensus, I shall first point out briefly that macroeconomists understand that disagreements still exist nowadays. Following this point I shall explore how these economists picture the period of wide disagreements after the breakdown of the first neoclassical synthesis (roughly from the 1970s to the early 1990s). Having this picture clearly in mind is important because the progress associated with the new consensus is identified by comparing the current macroeconomics with the preceding disarray. I will then discuss how mainstream macroeconomists saw the emergence of the new synthesis: the construction of a theoretical ground on which different schools could negotiate models and empirical evidence and thus tame disagreements to reach a consensus.[23] Identifying macroeconomics with this area implies that macroeconomists who are not willing to play this game are outsiders and do not count for the consensus. I shall stress how such an area was built by imposing a particular understanding of the microfoundations that macroeconomics thus understood needs.

2. A NEW CONSENSUS IN MACROECONOMICS

For many followers of the new neoclassical synthesis, the existence of a consensus in their field does not mean that room for disagreement no longer exists (Goodfriend 2007: 3; Blanchard 2009: 210; Woodford 2009: section III; Chari, Kehoe, and McGrattan 2009). After all, as Solow (1983: 279) pointed out, there is always (some degree of) disagreement at the frontier. Nonetheless, they all agree that modern macroeconomics, in theory and in practice, has changed substantially when compared with the 1970s, and for the better:

> Over the last three decades, macroeconomic theory and the practice of macro-
> economics by economists have changed significantly – for the better. Macro-
> economics is now firmly grounded in the principles of economic theory. These
> advances have not been restricted to the ivory tower. Over the last several
> decades, the United States and other countries have undertaken a variety of
> policy changes that are precisely what macroeconomic theory of the last 30 years
> suggests. (Chari and Kehoe 2006: 3)[24]

In the 1970s and the 1980s, continue those economists, macroeconomics "looked like a battlefield" with "researchers split in different directions, mostly ignoring each other, or else engaging in bitter fights and controversies" (Blanchard 2009: 210): the neoclassical synthesis had broken down and over time monetarists, new classical and real business cycle (freshwater) economists, and new Keynesian (saltwater) economists fought against one another and disagreed on many issues. Mainstream macroeconomists see the new synthesis as a bridge between two broad fields: the classical (which incorporates monetarist ideas and is composed of the new classical and real business cycle theorists) and the Keynesian (basically the new Keynesians and the Keynesians of the 1970s associated with the large-scale econometric models).[25] As Woodford (2009: 268) argues, while in the 1970s and 1980s there were "fundamental disagreements among leading macroeconomists about what kind of questions one might reasonably seek to answer or what kinds of theoretical analyses or empirical studies should even be admitted as contributions to knowledge," nowadays these deep disagreements and questionings no longer exist.

Before discussing how macroeconomists characterize the new synthesis, I would like to stress briefly the differences between the new classical and RBC research programs on the one hand, and the new Keynesian on the other.

3. BATTLING MACROECONOMICS

The Keynesian orthodoxy of the 1950s and 1960s, with the then ubiquitous IS-LM model, was shattered in the 1970s – to use Hoover's (1988: 3) words.[26] On the theoretical side, weak microfoundations increasingly made professional economists unhappy with this Keynesianism. On the practical side, the stagflation of the 1970s made economists question the ability of the Keynesian device to incorporate inflation into their IS-LM framework: the Phillips curve (Hoover 1988: chap. 1).[27] Milton Friedman (1968) and Edmund Phelps (1967) criticized the Phillips curve for ignoring the long-run neutrality of money and for not incorporating expectations (De Vroey and Hoover 2004: 7).[28] New classical macroeconomists like Robert Lucas and Thomas Sargent wanted to bury Keynesian theorizing (as in their famous 1979 article) and to propose a market-clearing approach to economic fluctuations – or "to see whether the 'expectations view' can be pushed far enough to yield something like a full business cycle theory."[29]

Lucas (1976) criticized the use of reduced-form econometric models for policy evaluation (that is, simulating and comparing paths of endogenous variables under alternative economic policies): the parameters of estimated aggregate relationships are themselves functions of deeper preference and technology parameters and such functions change when the government adopts a new policy. New classical, RBC and new Keynesian economists all worked in a similar fashion to address the Lucas critique, by providing the kind of microfoundations that nowadays characterizes not only their research programs but also the models of the new consensus macro-economics.[30] It is important to add that these economists used the conceptual tool of a representative agent as part of their answer to the Lucas critique, without providing clear justification (as already pointed out by Hoover in Chapter 1 of this volume).

During the 1970s, the 1980s and early 1990s new classical, real business cycle and new Keynesian economists were in a battlefield. They had important points of disagreement, but they also shared some methodological and theoretical elements. To some degree, mostly with respect to policy implications of their models, the new classical and real business cycle macroeconomists on the one hand, and the new Keynesians on the other, seemed to criticize each other from the ground up – to repeat Solow's (1983) words. Or, to use Paul Krugman's words, there was a great schism in macroeconomics in the 1980s, with on the one hand the RBC economists arguing that, according to Krugman (2000: 39), "because [they] have not managed to find a micro-foundation for non-neutrality of money, money must be neutral after all," and, on the other, the new Keynesians arguing that "[they] need some other explanation of apparent non-neutrality, resting in something like menu costs or bounded rationality."

Even macroeconomists not connected to either of those two approaches understood that these groups differed by a sort of faith in alternative sets of tenets. For instance, David Cass, a student of Hirofumi Uzawa and an economist who made seminal contributions to the optimal growth literature – the model that is the benchmark in the RBC literature – stated in an interview in 1998:[31]

> But the thing about real business-cycle theory I suppose is that it is almost like a religion. I have talked quite a bit with Victor [Rios-Rull], whom I have a lot of respect for, who has this view, this view that he is convinced quite strongly about, that this is the only way to look at the world, to look at economics.[32] When anybody tells me it's the only thing, I'm skeptical. I don't believe that using general equilibrium theory is the only way of looking at the world. ... But I also think that the general equilibrium model itself has a role, that it is still an important benchmark, and that there are still a lot of interesting things that can be done with that theory.

What, then, are the core elements of each of the two groups, the new classical/RBC and new Keynesian macroeconomics? The new classical and RBC followers both worked in a framework with three basic tenets that Hoover (1988: 13–14) used to describe the new classicism. First, agents (in fact, a representative agent) choose real variables based solely on real, instead of nominal or monetary, factors. Second, agents are continuously in equilibrium because, "to the limits of their information," they are "consistent and successful optimizers" (p. 14). Third, agents have rational expectations – that is, they "make no *systematic* errors in evaluating the economic environment" (p. 14). I add to this set of assumptions the economic environment that they commonly assume: an economy working in perfect competition with prices that are flexible to adjust and clear all markets. Moreover, the new classical/RBC intertemporal equilibrium model of the business cycle that emerged from these hypotheses identifies either real shocks (including both aggregate demand and aggregate supply shocks, like fiscal policy and technology shocks) or errors in expectations as the sources of fluctuations.

Over time, several of the models in this new classical/RBC tradition generated five neutrality results, as George Akerlof (2007: 6) concisely discussed: (a) the independence of consumption and current income through the life-cycle permanent income hypothesis (that is, a denial of the consumption function used in the IS-LM model); (b) the irrelevance of current profits to investment spending through the Modigliani–Miller theorem; (c) the natural rate theory of unemployment that states that long-run inflation and unemployment are independent (that is, the long-run Phillips curve is vertical);[33] (d) the inability of monetary policy to stabilize output as a consequence of the rational expectations hypothesis (economic policies cannot systematically affect real output, a result known as the policy irrelevance; therefore, actual output is systematically equal to its potential level); and (e) the irrelevance to consumption of taxes and debt as ways of financing budget deficits (Ricardian equivalence). These neutrality results went against many results associated either with the Keynesian orthodoxy of the postwar period or, more importantly, with the new Keynesian camp that I shall discuss later.

3.1   Differences Among Siblings: The New Classical and the Real Business Cycle Macroeconomics

Although it is sometimes convenient to group together the new classical and the real business cycle macroeconomists[34] – a group to be contrasted with the new Keynesians in the present narrative – there are three important differences between these two approaches. First, at their origins these groups had different methods of bringing their models to the data. New classical economists developed not only solution methods to their model but also estimated them.[35] In contrast, RBC theorists became known mostly for their calibration method, as clearly defended by Kydland and Prescott (1991a), and for their disapproval of econometrics.[36] They generally calibrate the parameters of their models based on equations evaluated at steady-state so that the business cycle models replicate "stylized facts" of long-run growth theory: the steady-state variables are substituted by their sample means (or other moments) in the data, and the equations are solved for the unknown parameters: Kydland and Prescott (1982: 1346) referred to this procedure as estimating parameters "using steady-state considerations," while Kydland (1992: 477) put it as determining "parameter values on the basis of non-business-cycle measurements." To this end, microeconomic empirical evidence can also be used to calibrate some parameters of the model. After calibrating the parameters, these authors test the model's ability to reproduce short-run facts as co-movements, variances and means of aggregate variables in the data (real output, consumption, hours worked, and so on).[37] Kydland and Prescott (1991a) claim to be the heirs of a tradition that dates back to Ragnar Frisch in the 1930s. However, contrary to the models calibrated by Frisch and to those calibrated by other economists in the 1960s and 1970s, the RBC theorists of the 1980s and the 1990s choose calibration as their empirical method not because they "lacked the time series needed to estimate" the equations and thus calibration was the only option available (p. 169), but because they believe that their method is the best for measuring the parameters "that characterize preferences, technology, information structure, and institutional arrangements" assumed in their general equilibrium model (p. 168). Kydland and Prescott (1991a: 169) summarize their empirical method as follows:

> The key econometric problem is to use statistical observations to select the parameters for an experimental economy. Once these parameters have been selected, the central part of the econometrics of the general equilibrium approach to business cycles is the computational experiment. This is the vehicle by which theory is made quantitative. ... The main steps in econometric analyses are as follows: defining the question; setting up the model; calibrating the model; and reporting the findings.

It is important to stress that the opposition between calibration and the use of statistical regressions in macroeconomic models was really not minor. Kydland (1992: 477) implicitly makes the case that calibration is better than estimation because "the parameters should not be chosen so as to produce the best fit of the model to the business cycle data. The goal is to provide the clearest possible answer to the question [at hand]. In some cases, deviations of the theory from the data even provide independent verification of the answer." As late as the early 2000s, after looking closely at models used in several central banks, Sims (2004) argued that the probability approach to macroeconomic models has not yet disappeared but it "is under siege" (p. 170). He then mentions the existing "dispute today between econometricians and 'extreme calibrationists'" (p. 171) explaining that:

> By the latter I mean economists who would claim that calibration, i.e. inference without formal appeal to probability-based statistical methods, is not just an occasionally, arguably, necessary expedient when probability-based inference is too complicated, but instead an improved replacement for probability-based inference.

A second distinction between new classical and RBC theorists is the nonexistence of money in most RBC models and, thus, their focus on the real sources of fluctuations: among these sources Kydland and Prescott (1991b) estimate that technological shocks (summarized in the Solow residual) explain about seventy percent of US business cycle fluctuations in the period after the Korean War. For instance, Lucas (1998: 129), when asked about the differences between Friedman, Tobin and himself on the one hand, who thought (according to Snowdon and Vane, the interviewers) of the economy as fluctuating around a long-run smooth trend, and RBC economists like Prescott and Kydland on the other, answered that the difference was in their view of the sources of the trend:

> Well, they [Kydland and Prescott] talk about business cycles in terms of deviations from trend as well. The difference is that Friedman, Tobin and I would think of the sources of the trend as being entirely from the supply side and the fluctuations about the trend as being induced by monetary shocks. Of course, we would think of very different kinds of theoretical models to deal with the long-run and the short-run issues. Kydland and Prescott took the sources that we think of as long-term to see how well they would do for these short-term movements. The surprising thing was how well it worked. I am still mostly on the side of Friedman and Tobin, but there is no question that our thinking has changed a lot on the basis of this work.

The gist behind the RBC position of explaining fluctuations on the basis of real factors lies in two "facts" reported by Kydland and Prescott (1990): first, that prices are countercyclical, rather than procyclical (suggesting that movements in prices are associated with shifts of the aggregate supply function along a given aggregate demand function), and, second, that monetary aggregates (such as monetary base or M1) do not lead the cycle, against the prevailing view (associated with the works of Milton Friedman and Anna Schwartz (1963) and Chris Sims (1972, 1989)) that they do lead it. Therefore, both of these facts went against "the prevalence in the 1970s of studies that use equilibrium models with monetary policy or price surprises as the main source of fluctuations" – that is, new classical models (Kydland and Prescott 1990: 7). Despite the fact that Kydland and Prescott (1991a: 176) affirmed that monetary shocks "are a leading candidate to account for a significant fraction of the unaccounted-for aggregate fluctuations" (that is, fluctuations not accounted for technology shocks), and that they foresaw the coming of an RBC model with money, the first RBC models did not have room for money and, thus, could in no way talk about monetary policy and inflation stabilization.[38] In contrast, new classical thinkers did have unsystematic monetary shocks in their equilibrium models of the business cycle and talked about "purely monetary cycles" and monetary policy (Lucas 1975).

The differences about the sources of economic fluctuations between new classical and RBC theoreticians come out crystal-clearly in two letters that Lucas and Prescott exchanged in 1990. In the early 1990s Lucas was working with Michael Woodford in a paper in which unanticipated changes in nominal spending flows imply a less-than-proportional adjustment in price levels (that is, these shocks have real effects).[39] After reading a draft sent to him by Kydland and Prescott, Lucas sent his comments to Prescott (copying Kydland as well) and wrote:

> I don't agree with your remark that "persistence" is a difficulty with monetary-shock business cycle theories. Monetary shocks must work because people react to them as if they were taste/technology shocks, because they can't tell the difference or because they are locked in to certain decisions. If so, then *any theory of the persistence of the consequences of actual taste/technology (like yours and Finn's) should be adaptable without change to monetary shocks.* If an investment project, say, is initiated in your model, this has consequences far into the future that should be independent of why the project was initiated. *In Frisch's language, I think the hard part of a monetary theory is getting a coherent picture of the impulses.*[40]

Prescott then replied (also copying Kydland) that he sticks to what he and Kydland have argued in the paper and that they originally had money in the model but decided to drop it because monetary shocks could not generate persistent real effects:

> I stick with my position that *a problem for monetary shock theories of business cycle fluctuations is the lack of a propagation mechanism.* So far, only relatively persistent changes in factors that affect steady state of the deterministic model have been shown to induce business cycle type fluctuations. Time-to-build, staggered contracts, and/or capital accumulation do not provide a mechanism that propagates nonpersistent shocks, (whether they be technology, monetary, preference or something else), in such a way that business cycle type fluctuations are induced. *Incidentally, we dropped the monetary example from the paper.*[41]

There is yet another letter from Lucas to Prescott earlier in this same year in which Lucas shows on the one hand his admiration for the RBC research agenda that he was then teaching to his graduate students, but on the other he stresses that money for him is an important element that is missing in RBC macro models:

> My first year macro course is now over half devoted to work by you and your students (here I count Kydland and Cooley, as well as your Minnesota protégés), and if you ever come around to taking money seriously again, I suppose that will go to 100 percent![42]

A third difference is the existence of imperfect information in the earlier new classical models and its non-existence in the first RBC models. Lucas's islands (following Phelps 1969, introductory chapter) work as a mechanism propagating the shocks and thus generating serially correlated movements in real output, for instance. In contrast, RBC macroeconomists initially developed equilibrium models under perfect competition and information. As a consequence, as Hartley, Hoover and Salyer (1997: 46) discuss (and as

Prescott explained in previous quote), these models "add relatively little to the pattern of fluctuations in real output beyond what is implicit in the technology shocks themselves."

3.2   The New Keynesians: Fighting the Opponents and Talking to them

The new Keynesians wanted to study monetary economies in which nominal rigidities and market failures make fluctuations costly and therefore open the door for stabilization policies. The typical environment to get all these elements in place is one of imperfect competition. Moreover, in contrast mostly to the RBC theorists, the new Keynesians identified monetary shocks as the major source of economic fluctuations, and against both the new classical and RBC economists they argued that economic (monetary) policy affects real output in the short run (these real effects originate not only from unanticipated monetary shocks, as in the new classical world). They brought back to macroeconomics unemployment and the non-neutrality of money in the short run. In terms of empirical research, the new Keynesians favored estimation (often equation-by-equation) techniques instead of calibration.

Mankiw (1989: 79) does summarize very well in the first paragraphs of his article the major differences between the "classical school" (especially the RBC theory, but with some elements in common with the new classical macroeconomics) and the "Keynesian school" (the new Keynesians):

> The debate over the source and propagation of economic fluctuations rages as fiercely today as it did 50 years ago in the aftermath of Keynes's *The General Theory* and in the midst of the Great Depression. Today, as then, there are two schools of thought. The classical school emphasizes the optimization of private economic actors, the adjustment of relative prices to equate supply and demand, and the efficiency of unfettered markets. The Keynesian school believes that understanding economic fluctuations requires not just studying the intricacies of general equilibrium, but also appreciating the possibility of market failure on a grand scale.
>
> Real business cycle theory is the latest incarnation of the classical view of economic fluctuations. It assumes that there are large random fluctuations in the rate of technological change. In response to these fluctuations, individuals rationally alter their levels of labor supply and consumption. The business cycle is, according to this theory, the natural and efficient response of the economy to changes in the available production technology.[43]

Mankiw then states that he does not believe that real business cycle theory offers an "empirically plausible explanation of economic fluctuations" (p. 79). Moreover, the "facts" that RBC macroeconomists brought to criticize the new Keynesians did not serve as conclusive evidence to refute these models. For instance, Ball and Mankiw (1994) examined the major criticisms raised against the new Keynesian agenda and refuted them on the basis of being unconvincing. As one example: for the authors, the counter-cyclicality of the price level is an artifact produced by the RBC practice of detrending data with the so-called Hodrick–Prescott filter.[44]

Yet another important illustration of the schism between new classical/RBC macroeconomists and the (new) Keynesians is given by Ball and Mankiw's 1994 article from the saltwater camp and, from the freshwater flank, Lucas's comments on it. Ball and Mankiw (1994: 127) stated that there are two kinds of macroeconomists, those who are "part of a long tradition in macroeconomics," including "John Maynard Keynes, Milton Friedman, Franco Modigliani, and James Tobin," who believe "that price stickiness plays a central role in short-run economic fluctuations," and those who do not, whom the authors label as "heretics." For the authors, "a macroeconomist faces no greater decision than whether to be a traditionalist or a heretic" (p. 128).

On the other hand, Lucas (1994: 154) reproached Ball and Mankiw's treatment of the "heretics" as "'silly' people, 'almost pathological'," on the grounds that "the cost of [this] ideological approach ... is that one loses contact with the progressive, cumulative science aspect of macroeconomics." He deplored that Ball and Mankiw followed "the tradition of argument by innuendo, of caricaturing one's unnamed opponents, of using them as foils to dramatize one's own position" and asked them to put all this behind "and return to the research contributions we know they are capable of making" (p. 155). What is interesting is not only Lucas's call for paying attention to the cumulative knowledge produced in macroeconomics in both the freshwater and saltwater camps, but also his criticism of Ball and Mankiw for not envisioning that a "synthesis of old and new ideas" might happen and, thus, "might leave us better off" (p. 155).

Therefore, despite the major points of disagreement among the new classical and RBC macroeconomists, on the one hand, and the new Keynesians on the other, these two camps share significant methodological and theoretical grounds: they all adopt the rational expectations hypothesis, favor general equilibrium models with microfoundations, and have in their benchmark models a representative agent in an environment of complete markets and complete information. It is true that, for instance, the new Keynesians George Akerlof and Janet Yellen (1985) introduced small deviations from rationality at the individual level that generated significant aggregate effects. Nonetheless, rational expectations were the benchmark from which to deviate.

With respect to the fact that both new classical/RBC and new Keynesian macroeconomists assume rational expectations, it is important to stress that there was a sort of domestication of this hypothesis by mainstream macroeconomists. Initially, in the 1970s, the new classical economists were known as "rational expectationists" (only later they were labeled "new classical") and rational expectations was understood to make economic policy ineffective (that is, only policy surprises could affect real variables like output). And this ineffectiveness result went against the Keynesian understanding that stabilization policies can be systematically used over the cycle.

The identification of rational expectations with policy ineffectiveness occurred not only in academia, but also appeared in magazines like *Business Week* and *Newsweek*. On November 8, 1976 (p. 74), *Business Week* published an article titled "How Expectations Defeat Economic Policy," which starts by announcing that "a controversial new theory called rational expectations is sweeping through the economics profession. It says that economic policy is impotent" because "the public ... takes actions that offset [systematic policy changes]." The magazine continues by stating that "the work of ivory-towered economists Robert E. Lucas Jr. of the University of Chicago and Neil Wallace and Thomas Sargent of the University of Minnesota is giving [Milton] Friedman's [critique of policy fine-tuning] something it lacked for two decades – a solid theoretical base." Moreover, the article explains that monetary policy is where "the rationalists are making major breakthroughs:" for it to generate real effects it "must come from out of the blue. ... Says Lucas: 'To affect real output, the monetary authorities must resort to trickery, and how long can you keep pulling that off?' And Wallace adds: 'For countercyclical policy to work, it must surprise people, and that's not a policy, that's throwing dice.' Throwing dice is a dangerous game. ... this increases uncertainty. Uncertainty damps economic activity." The article also features dissenting voices at the time, such as those of Benjamin M. Friedman (Harvard University), Robert E. Hall and Franco Modigliani (MIT), basically arguing that it takes time for people to adjust their expectations, which means that monetary policies have real effects in the short-run. They agree with "rationalists" on some issues, but do not accept that the monetary effects would be incorporated into prices fully and instantaneously. "Minnesota's Sargent and Wallace remain unconvinced. They maintain that time lags in the system are a thin reed on which to hang the success of stabilization policy." Finally, monetarist Allan H. Meltzer argues for the need of more empirical evidence before, according to his own words, "we can know that rational expectations cripple stabilization policy." It is important to notice that Lucas was pleased with this article.[45]

About two years later, *Newsweek* (June 26, 1978) featured an article titled "The New Economists", which started as: "Most of their names are still obscure, and their work is little known to the public. But in scholarly crannies across the country, a new breed of economists is emerging." It says that this new generation was then laying the intellectual foundations of a national political shift to the right: "All of them are basically conservative, though some bristle at the label," but "they are not necessarily conventional political conservatives. Instead they have been inspired by the seeming impotence of Keynesian economic theory." It then goes on to say that this group varies ideologically "from a variety of monetarism which spurns activist government intervention in the economy to a pragmatic 'neoclassicism' that accepts some government action but is profoundly critical of past policies." The article then goes to the association of rational expectations to policy ineffectiveness:

> Thomas Sargent represents a more radical branch of the new economists. He and University of Minnesota colleague Neil Wallace, 38, both advisers to the Federal Reserve Bank of Minneapolis, and Robert Lucas, 40, of the University of Chicago, are part of the "school of rational expectations" – a monetarist branch that, says one economist, "out-Friedmans Milton Friedman." In essence the rationalists maintain that the government is impotent in the economic sphere. (Sheils and Thomas 1978: 59)[46]

Another similar but shorter article was published in 1978 in the newspaper *The Minneapolis Star*, titled "Rational people may be economy's thorn," and collected by Lucas.[47] The article starts by asking: "Are you a rational person?" Then it goes on to explain the theory that "is almost embarrassingly simple:" the public anticipates the advent of a policy and acts in a way of eliminating its real effects; the final outcome is only changes in inflation. It adds:

> To call this conclusion radical is an understatement. It challenges views on how to run the economy that have held sway in this country since World War II. And adherence to those views is precisely why we have both high inflation and high unemployment, the rationalists hold. (Greenwald 1978)

Over time, the "sweeping implications" of the rational expectations hypothesis (Mankiw in Snowdon and Vane 1995: 52), as first believed, were dismissed.[48] New Keynesians could then embrace the rational expectations cause more freely. Alan Blinder (1989: 104, emphasis added) nicely summarizes this point:

> It took a while, and some help from Fischer (1977) and Phelps and Taylor (1977), for the profession to get clear that rational expectations (RE) is an assumption about behavior which may be right or wrong but which is logically disconnected from the hypothesis that prices move instantly to clear markets. It is more from

the latter than from the former that the new classical economics (NCE) derives its distinctive implications [as policy ineffectiveness].

Separating those two ideas helped spread the RE gospel, since formal econometric tests of the joint hypothesis of RE and market clearing almost always rejected it. Most economists had a strong suspicion that the market-clearing hypothesis was the weak link in the partnership.[49]

The hypothesis of rational expectations was one of a series of elements that were shared by new classical/RBC and new Keynesian theorists (others were: general equilibrium models, microfoundations, representative agent, complete markets and complete information). Microfoundations was the game that new Keynesians also wanted to play in order to resuscitate Keynesian macroeconomics by supposedly making it immune to the Lucas critique. In fact, Mankiw (1992b) wrote about "the reincarnation of Keynesian economics" after Lucas's announcement that Keynesian economics was dead:

> From our current perspective, it is clear that this obituary was premature. Today Keynesian theorizing does not inspire whispers and giggles from the audience. ... If Keynesian economics was dead in 1980, then today it has been reincarnated.
> ... Yet one can say that the new classical challenge has been met: *Keynesian economics has been reincarnated into a body with firm microeconomic muscle.* (Mankiw 1992b, 559–60, emphasis added)

Not all new Keynesians took the call for microfoundations as a justification for the use of a representative agent in their general equilibrium models. Although the new Keynesian work that became part of the new synthesis (as the RBC counterpart) was characterized by that conceptual tool, there were members of this group who subscribed to microfoundations but were against a model with a representative agent, in which "problems of coordinating prices and wages simply cannot be studied" (Greenwald and Stiglitz 1993: 42). These were new Keynesians, like Stiglitz, who were interested in studying asymmetric and costly information and market failures associated with this.[50]

Besides this, one might argue against the view that both groups (new classical/RBC and new Keynesians) shared important methodological elements by noting that Mankiw (1985) and other new Keynesians made a static partial equilibrium analysis instead of using the general equilibrium models for which new classical and RBC theorists were well known. However, Mankiw (1985: 536) explicitly mentioned that it was possible to construct simple general equilibrium models in which his results would not only hold but also be more pronounced. Moreover, the static analysis was just a first step to explaining how nominal rigidity works in their models; such work was understood to be "largely complete" in the early 1990s (Ball and Mankiw 1994: 137) and the challenge of the new Keynesians at the time was to construct *quantitative* general equilibrium models (in line with the RBC literature).[51]

Those central elements common to both the new classical/RBC and the new Keynesian camps (rational expectations, general equilibrium models, representative agent, complete markets and complete information, monetary policy) allowed them to trade and communicate, negotiate new empirical findings through which they resolved most of the previously listed points of disagreements, which they turned into core features of the new consensus macroeconomics.

4. TRADING IN THE TRIANGLE AND SYNTHESIZING MACROECONOMICS

In the early 1990s, the merge of the new Keynesian and RBC models into "some grand synthesis that incorporates the strengths of both approaches" was "just a hope."[52] By the end of that decade it was a reality. Goodfriend and King coined the term new neoclassical synthesis in 1997 when such synthesis was still on the way: "macroeconomics is moving toward a *New Neoclassical Synthesis*" (1997: 231).[53] According to them, the main features of this new consensus macroeconomics are methodological: "the systematic application of intertemporal optimization and rational expectations." But the synthesis also "embodies the insights of monetarists ... regarding the theory and practice of monetary policy" (p. 232).[54]

In that same year, Robert Solow, John Taylor, Martin Eichenbaum, Alan Blinder, and Olivier Blanchard all tried to answer the question "is there a core of usable macroeconomics we should all believe in?", which was the theme of a session at that year's AEA meeting – with a clear emphasis on how models come to practice. Solow (1997: 230) advocated that part of the common core of macroeconomics consists of: (a) "trend movement is predominantly driven by the supply side of the economy (the supply of factors of production and total factor productivity)" and that it is best analysed "in some sort of growth model, preferably mine"; (b) fluctuations around the trend "are predominantly driven by aggregate demand impulses" best studied with "some model of the various sources of expenditure". Solow recognizes that there is some dissent from proposition (b). He explicitly denies the RBC explanation of fluctuations, as supply-driven, and then commends the "flexible, observant members of the real-business-cycle school, like Martin Eichenbaum and his coworkers" for opening up "the fabric of their underlying model so that it will allow – or insist – that demand-side impulses play the dominant role in the short-run macro-economic fluctuations.[55] Then this proposition is indeed part of the usable core of macroeconomics" and economists can thus discuss what is the best way of modeling such demand-side forces (p. 230). Solow also voices his disapproval of assuming rational expectations in the modeling of short-run equilibrium: "I can see a role for rational expectations in the modeling of long-run equilibrium. In the short-run part of macroeconomics, the rational expectations hypothesis seems to have little to recommend" (p. 231). He then recognizes that his core of macroeconomics lacks "real coupling between the short-run picture and the long-run picture" (pp. 231–2).

Taylor (1997) defined macro as the study of both economic growth and fluctuations, and identified a practical core in this field that "is having beneficial effect on macroeconomic policy, especially monetary economics" (p. 233). He then listed five key principles of such a core: (1) long-run growth depends on movements along as well as shifts of a production function (which corresponds to Solow's proposition (a)); (2) there is no long-run trade-off between inflation and unemployment; (3) there is a short-run trade-off between inflation and unemployment (rationalized either by new Keynesian sticky prices or by asymmetric information *à la* Lucas); (4) expectations matter because they are highly responsive to economic policy (he then states that the rational expectations approach is "the most feasible empirical way to model this response" (p. 234)); and (5) evaluating monetary and fiscal policy requires thinking in terms of "a series of changes [in instruments] linked by a systematic process or a policy rule" (p. 234).

Blinder (1997) follows basically the line of Taylor and emphasizes how useful such a core is in terms of policy analysis, "where contact with reality is a necessity" (p. 240). Eichenbaum (1997) approaches the question of the existence of a core in macroeconomics from the perspective of stabilization policy. He then stresses that macroeconomists converge mostly in terms of method. However, they also agree on principles like the ones listed by Taylor: (1) "monetary policy is neutral in the long run"; (2) "*persistent* inflation is always a monetary phenomenon"; (3) "monetary policy is not neutral in the short run"; (4) "most aggregate economic fluctuations are not due to monetary policy shocks" (p. 236). All these points are at the core of the new synthesis, as discussed later. Finally, Blanchard (1997a) identifies two propositions only: (1) short-run movements in economic activity are driven by aggregate demand; (2) "over time, the economy tends to return to a steady-state growth path" (p. 244).

What I want to underline is that although many macroeconomists wanted to answer with an "unambiguous yes" the question of the AEA session (Blanchard 1997a: 244), there were still important differences in the key elements of the new consensus, as just discussed. Nevertheless, the majority of these economists agreed not only on the methodological elements implicitly or explicitly stated – dynamic general equilibrium models with rational expectations and a representative agent – but also with most of the central principles of such a core of usable macroeconomics. Among these, two are noteworthy: short-run fluctuations are demand driven, and real disturbances are often inefficient – with the degree of inefficiency being a function of the response of the monetary policy to such disturbances. Thus, monetary policy is non-neutral in the short run as a consequence of some sort of nominal rigidity. Clearly, the original RBC models could not join this discussion and give policy recommendations because they had no role for money and treated short-run fluctuations as optimal supply-side adjustments that occur in an environment of flexible prices in which all markets clear.

However, Solow was a dissonant voice in this group of people without considering himself an economist outside the mainstream.[56] The reason was his insistence on, first, using different models for analyzing short and long-run movements in economic activity and, second, on rejecting the rational expectations hypothesis for short-run analysis. Later, when he commented on Chari and Kehoe's 2006 article (Solow 2008) and repeated his longstanding criticism to the use of a representative agent in macro-economics, his comments were not well received by those authors:

> Solow eloquently voices the commonly heard complaint that too much of modern macroeconomics starts with a model with a single type of agent. In our response, we clarify that modern macroeconomics does not end there – and may not end too far from where Solow prefers. ... Solow seems to think that using that sort of model requires ignoring all the rich heterogeneity which he sees in the modern economy. While that may have been true many years ago, today it is not. (Chari and Kehoe 2008: 247)[57]

By the turn of the century the new synthesis was more clearly a reality. According to Stanley Fischer, one of the evolutions that characterized macroeconomics in the early 2000s, that makes him very happy, "is the beginning of the end of the great split between freshwater and saltwater economics. Although the split is still evident, convergence is also clearly under way. And I think that is very healthy for the profession" (interview to Blanchard 2005: 257).

It is important to have in mind that macroeconomists from both camps, RBC/new classical and new Keynesian, had to negotiate theoretical argu-ments on the face of growing empirical evidence. This negotiation led to a consensus view. Clearly, negotiations can happen only among those who speak the same language and share core theoretical elements. Roughly, the new Keynesian camp had the goal of building dynamic general equilibrium models, which were then typical of the real-business-cycle literature, with nominal rigidities and other market imperfections. As a result of using dynamic general equilibrium models, these economists became more concerned with discussions about commitment and credibility that they inherited from the RBC literature.

On the other hand, the RBC (and new classical) models were criticized empirically and economists in this camp had to handle growing evidence that monetary policy has real effects in the short-run – implying that they had to go beyond their general equilibrium models with flexible prices and technology shocks.[58] In fact, the evidence on price stickiness came also from international data, as Krugman (2000: 39) notes: in the 1980s advanced countries reduced their inflation rates while they experienced wild fluctuations in nominal exchange rate; the implied co-movement of nominal and real exchange rates had to be explained by price stickiness in those countries.[59] In the end, there was a significant change of attitude from some people in the new classical/RBC camp towards price stickiness: after all, they became more comfortable to be considering price rigidities as important to fluctuations because they could discuss this issue in a dynamic general equilibrium framework.[60] Therefore, we see that the interplay of opposing forces on both sides was important in the construction of the new synthesis, as well as the existence of "moderates on both sides of the fence," who "have done a little converging; stridency comes from the extremes" (Solow 2000: 154).[61]

Many mainstream macroeconomists believe that the main advantage of such synthesis is that it bridges "the methodological divide between microeconomics and macroeconomics, by using the tools of general equilibrium theory to model Keynesian insights," in Woodford's (2000: 29) words. The central point of convergence in the new synthesis was methodological: the use of dynamic stochastic general equilibrium (DSGE) models that explain not only the evolution of the potential output over time as mostly a supply-side phenomenon, but also short-run and inefficient deviations of the actual output from its "natural" level (the level achieved if prices were flexible) that arise as a consequence of wages and prices rigidity.

Another very important methodological point of convergence is the empirical approach macroeconomists now use. As previously argued, in the 1980s and early 1990s the real-business-cycle theorists and the new Keynesians were almost in opposite camps: the former defended calibration methods and were against econometric estimation while the latter favored estimation methods.[62] In the new synthesis no such divide exists. As Chari and Kehoe (2008: 248) aptly described, modern mainstream macro-economists have now a "big-tent approach to data analysis" through which they "confront both the micro aspects and the macro implications of general equilibrium models with data." Today not only is there no opposition between calibration and estimation (of a system of equations) but both strategies are used complementarily: it is a current practice to calibrate a subset of the parameters (those that economists feel they have more information about) and to estimate the remaining parameters via likelihood or Bayesian methods.[63]

The other points of disagreement between RBC and new Keynesian economists already mentioned were real versus nominal shocks as sources of fluctuations, the irrelevance or not of monetary policy, and the assumption of flexible or sticky prices and wages (perfect versus imperfect competition). Just to give a more vivid example of how divided macroeconomists were at the time about the sources of fluctuations, I take Lucas's insistence that money matters, contrary to what RBC economists would advocate. Lucas (1998: 125) classed himself an "old-fashioned monetarist," someone who assigns an important role to monetary forces in economic fluctuations. He then adds that, at the time, a consensus had already emerged: that econometrically money does not account for most of fluctuations in the postwar period:

> There is the real business cycle theory which assigns no importance to monetary forces. This work has been hugely influential, on me as well as on others, although I still think of myself as a monetarist. Then there are those whom Sargent calls 'fiscalists'... Then there are old-fashioned monetarists, which is where I would class myself, with people like Friedman and Allan Meltzer. ... I used to think that monetary shocks were 90 per cent of the story in real variability and I still think they are the central story in the 1930s. But there is no way to get monetary shocks to account for more than about a quarter of real variability in the post-war era. At least, no one has found a way of doing it.[64]

The current consensus view is indeed that real shocks account more for the variability of major macroeconomic variables than monetary shocks: for example, Altig et al. (2005) show that about 28 percent of each of the variances of output, inflation and average hours worked is explained by real shocks in their model, while only 14 percent can be attributed to monetary policy shocks. These numbers can vary from model to model as there are still issues about how to properly identify shocks but they give the general picture that real shocks are more important in this dimension.[65] Nonetheless, this result does not mean that monetary policy is irrelevant in explaining economic fluctuations, as stressed by Woodford (2009: 11): not only does the existence, uniqueness and stability of equilibrium depend on the policies designed, but also "the equilibrium effects of real disturbances depends substantially on the character of *systematic* monetary policy." Therefore, monetary policy design should be part of a stabilization program.

Monetary shocks have well-documented effects on real variables in the short run (Christiano, Eichenbaum, and Evans 1999). While they do not explain much of the variability of major real variables, they are still useful for discriminating between alternative models: nowadays it is common to have papers introducing all kinds of rigidities (as habit persistence on consumption, price and wage rigidities, adjustment costs on investment, capital utilization, etc.) that serve to smooth the dynamic responses of aggregate variables after a monetary shock. This is done in order for the models to be able to reproduce the effects of a monetary policy shock identified in the data – so it is not properly an empirical test of these models but rather a reverse engineering strategy to have the models accounting for features of the data that macroeconomists consider relevant.[66]

Therefore, we can see that the major issues that used to divide mainstream macroeconomists in the past are no longer valid. Nowadays a consensus view emerged among these economists also in terms of stabilization policies, as summarized by Eichenbaum (1997). The set of macroeconomic principles that characterize the new synthesis and the fact that these economists believe such principles make their models immune to the Lucas critique gave them confidence to apply their models to policy analysis, especially to monetary policy. The motivation of Woodford in his 2003 book is exactly to show how economists can now discuss monetary policy in practice by drawing from theoretical principles of the new consensus macroeconomics.[67] But Woodford (2003: 11–12) carefully states that "no attempt is made to set out a model that is sufficiently realistic to be used for actual policy analysis in a central bank. Nonetheless, the basic elements of an optimizing model ... are ones that I believe are representative of crucial elements of a realistic model" – and these crucial elements include being free of Lucas's 1976 curse, according to the author. As Hoover (2006: 146) argues, mainstream economists like Woodford present here an "eschatological justification" for constructing simple general equilibrium models (with a representative agent): they are used as guides for policymaking not because they provide adequate descriptions of the economy, but because they are seen as "the starting point for a series of fuller and richer models that eventually will provide the basis for" such adequate descriptions.

Going one step further than Woodford's (2003) simple model, Christiano, Eichenbaum, and Evans (2005) and Frank Smets and Raf Wouters (2003, 2007) enrich the basic model in several dimensions to make it replicate features of the data that mainstream macroeconomists consider important (as already mentioned, these features are usually summarized in impulse response functions to a monetary policy shock, but there are correlations among variables as well). Both the basic and the larger models are based on representative households and firms. Although there are two types of firm (one that produces an intermediate good and one that assembles the final good), and a continuum of intermediate firms (each producing one of the infinite number of intermediate goods), heterogeneity plays no substantive role in these models.[68] By enlarging the basic model and enriching its dynamics, those authors present the clearest incarnations of quantitative general equilibrium models oriented to policy application typical of the new synthesis.

As mentioned in the introduction of this chapter, advertising a consensus in macroeconomics – a field often seen as composed by rival schools – has the advantage of making the case for both academic cohesion and scientific progress, and for a unified body of knowledge from which to prescribe policies. In his comments to Goodfriend and King's 1997 article, Blanchard (1997b) questioned both the labels "new" and "synthesis" on the grounds that the principles behind such a synthesis were always a part of macroeconomics. (Later, he explicitly elaborated on his view that the history of macroeconomics in the twentieth century is not a "series of battles, revolutions and counterrevolutions," which suggests that the field start anew "every twenty years or so" and has "little or no common core," but it is rather a history of "a surprisingly steady accumulation of knowledge" (Blanchard 2000, 1375).[69]) According to the author, macroeconomists differ by the weights they attach to the different ingredients in their models (intertemporal optimization, nominal rigidities, and imperfect competition), but they live in the same world, which he characterizes by a triangle:

> Think of a triangle. At the top is the Ramsey–Prescott model, with its emphasis on intertemporal choice. At the bottom left is the Taylor model, with its emphasis on nominal rigidities. At the bottom right is the Akerlof–Yellen model, with its focus on imperfections in the goods and the labor markets. Most of us live somewhere in the triangle. So do Goodfriend and King. Seen in this light, "new" and "synthesis" may both be a bit of an overstatement. (Blanchard 1997b: 290)

Blanchard's triangle is indeed very useful for my point here: that the synthesis emerged from a trade among economists working in a narrowly defined area, one in which a representative agent was often assumed to answer the Lucas critique in their dynamic general equilibrium models based on optimizing agents, as in microeconomics. Questions about the non-neutrality of money (in the long run), the appropriate type of micro-foundations, non-market clearing models, and about the limitations of assuming a representative agent, for example, are simply not in that triangle and thus are not central to the new synthesis. In this sense it is not surprising that Leijonhufvud's concern with the ability of a market economy to coordinate economic activities of decentralized agents, and his "corridor hypothesis" – which states that the market mechanism generates coordination only within certain limits but not outside these limits (Leijon-hufvud 1973) – are both outside the triangle. As he later explained his opposition to Lucas's resolution of the tension between micro and macro:

> That cut the Gordian knot, all right. But why was this path not taken before? Let me give a personal answer: because macroeconomics (I thought) is about system co-ordination, and one should not adopt a method that threatens to define away the main problem. The New Classical economics has the priorities the other way around – and carrying through from individual optimizing behaviour, it all but eliminates the co-ordination problem. (Leijonhufvud 1992: 28–9)

And he adds that since his 1973 paper he became interested in behavior outside the corridor and in understanding agents' behavior as the search or computation of an equilibrium price vector (instead of knowing it, as in a Walrasian general equilibrium model). Because of his interests he became a macroeconomist outside Blanchard's triangle:

> Since that time, I have been particularly interested in "out-of bounds" behavior, i.e., in what happens in economics under extreme conditions: hyperinflations, great depressions, transformation from socialism. ...
> My disenchantment with this [Lucas's] brand of microfoundations ... was such that, to be frank, I drifted out of the professional mainstream from the mid-70s onwards, as intertemporal optimization became all the rage. (Leijonhuf-vud 1993: 8, 11)

Not surprisingly, Leijonhufvud (2004: 139) sees the new neoclassical synthesis as an enterprise that misses the crucial elements of how the economy works:

> Conceptually, the recent trend you mention, the so-called new neoclassical synthesis, reminds one of the discussions that took place in the 1920's and early 1930's. It's *classical economics with frictions*. Again we have come full circle. But few economists these days want to think or talk about the corridor problem.

It is curious that Blanchard (1997b) chose a triangle to summarize the core elements behind macroeconomics and the new synthesis because it parallels

a common way in which microeconomists geometrically represent preferences under uncertainty in the case of lotteries with three possible outcomes: the so-called simplex has at each vertex a lottery in which one
outcome is certain and the others have zero probability; macroeconomists
of the new consensus have theoretical preferences over a two dimensional
simplex – Blanchard's triangle.

However, the consensus state of mainstream macroeconomics does not
mean that even within such a triangle macroeconomists do not disagree, or
that they are not trying to reshape their space and transform the triangle
into a geometric figure with more vertexes. The dissent inside the triangle
relates to two major points. First, that the new consensus models are not yet
ready for policy analysis because they introduced many shocks that are not
invariant to policy (Chari, Kehoe, and McGrattan 2009).[70] Second, that the
development of macroeconomics since the 1970s has emphasized mostly
theoretical issues at the expense of practical ones – therefore, the recent
theoretical developments have had little effect on macroeconomists in
charge of conducting actual economic policies; in other words, macroeconomists prioritized the development of macroeconomics as a science
rather than as engineering (Mankiw 2006).[71]

In terms of expanding the triangle or transforming it into a polyhedron,
macroeconomists living in the triangle have their lists of improvements
ready.[72] Chari and Kehoe (2006: 21–6), in a more standard RBC vein, list:
(1) work more on labor market rigidities; (2) incorporate the idea that
differences in taxes are a key source of the differences in the labor markets
in Europe and the US; (3) introduce unemployment benefits to understand
cross-country differences in unemployment.

Mishkin (2007: 27–30) goes in the direction of improvements to make
monetary policymaking a science more than an art: (1) enrich estimated
DSGE models so as to make them more realistic to the eyes of central
bankers; (2) improve or extend the way nominal rigidities are usually
incorporated in such models; (3) move from models with representative
agent to ones with heterogeneity of agents; (4) incorporate (and better
understand the role of) financial frictions; (5) go beyond rational expectations and embed behavioral economics into macroeconomics; (6) introduce
learning in macro models; (7) keep a scent of art in monetary policymaking
because economists "can never be sure what is the right model of the
economy" (p. 30).

Galí and Gertler (2007: 41–3) echo the aim to make "the model more
realistic, by adding a variety of features that are likely to enhance its fit of
the data" (p. 41), and list as new directions of research: (1) replace Calvo's
time-dependent pricing scheme, in which the timing of adjustment of prices
is exogenous, for state-dependent pricing, which makes that timing depend

on the evolution of the economy (endogenous); (2) incorporate labor market frictions that help economists account for the observed fluctuations in employment and job flows; and (3) abandon the complete markets hypothesis and introduce financial market imperfections. To Galí and Gertler's points (2) and (3), Blanchard (2009: 216–22) argues that macro-economists should answer the questions of how markups move, in response to what, and why. He also repeats Chari, Kehoe, and McGrattan's criticism that several shocks in a DSGE model may not be invariant to the policy adopted – proposing the use of less structural approaches, in contrast to them – and he urges economists to pay more attention to the role of anticipations, suggesting departures from rational expectations.

Before concluding this section I would like to discuss in more detail the major criticisms that Solow raised against the new synthesis in general, and to the idea that modern macroeconomics has changed for better because it is now "firmly grounded on the principles of economic theory" (Chari and Kehoe 2006: 3). Solow (2008) comments on Chari and Kehoe's 2006 article, which they start, according to him with a self-congratulatory phrase and with the statement about macro having firm microfoundations. To Solow, the last sentence is "simply false" (p. 243). He then criticizes the consensus macroeconomics through Chari and Kehoe's positions:

> When Chari and Kehoe speak of macroeconomics as being firmly grounded in economic theory, we know what they mean. They are not being idiosyncratic; they are speaking as able representatives of a school of macroeconomic thought that dominates many of the leading university departments and some of the best journals, not to mention the Federal Reserve Bank of Minneapolis. They mean a macroeconomics that is deduced from a model in which a single immortal consumer–worker–owner maximizes a perfectly conventional time-additive util-ity function over an infinite horizon, under perfect foresight or rational expecta-tions, and in an institutional and technological environment that favors universal price-taking behavior. In effect, the industrial side of the economy carries out the representative consumer–worker–owner's wishes. It has been possible to incorporate some frictions and price rigidities with the usual conse-quences – and this is surely a good thing – but basically this is the Ramsey model transformed from a normative account of socially optimal growth into a positive story that is supposed to describe day-to-day behavior in a modern industrial capitalist economy. It is taken as an advantage that the same model applies in the short run, the long run, and every run with no awkward shifting of gears. And the whole thing is given the honorific label of "dynamic stochastic general equilibrium." (Solow 2008: 243)

Solow is explicit about not being against the idea that, as a first approxima-tion, "individual agents optimize as best as they can," which does not imply that the whole economy "acts like a single optimizer under the simplest possible constraints" (p. 244). He stresses that the Sonnenschein–Mantel–

Debreu theorems that "the only universal empirical aggregative implication of general equilibrium theory are that excess demand functions should be continuous and homogeneous of degree zero in prices, and should satisfy Walras' Law." Many macro models, Solow continues, can satisfy these requirements "without imposing anything as extreme and prejudicial as a representative agent in a favorable environment" (p. 244). In addition to retaking his preferred view on macroeconomics already sketched in his 1997 presentation at the AEA meetings (stressing his preference to small, tailored, partial equilibrium models), Solow (2008: 245) comes up with his irony:

> I suppose it could also be true that the bow to the Ramsey model is like wearing the school colors or singing the Notre Dame fight song: a harmless way of providing some apparent intellectual unity, and maybe even a minimal commonality of approach. That seems hardly worthy of grown-ups, especially because there is always a danger that some of the in-group come to believe the slogans, and it distorts their work.

As already mentioned, Chari and Kehoe responded to the criticisms by Solow that they considered of substance.[73] They recognize that the challenges facing modern macroeconomics are not small, but reject Solow's criticisms to the use of a representative agent and to their claim that macroeconomics is now firmly grounded in economic theory. With respect to the representative agent hypothesis, Chari and Kehoe (2008: 247) state that modern macroeconomics does not end with such hypothesis, and in fact it does not end "too far from where Solow prefers": "Most of macroeconomic research over the last 20 years has precisely been about incorporating the heterogeneity and the rich interactions that Solow seems to think it needs." They argue that macroeconomists just start with a representative agent and then enrich the model "with the detail necessary to answer the question at hand" (p. 248). They also criticize Solow for his use in his growth papers of a single production function with aggregate labor and stock of capital, with which he "sacrificed realism for an abstraction that has proven invaluable" (p. 247).

In relation to Solow's point about aggregation and the Sonnenschein–Mantel–Debreu implications, Chari and Kehoe (2008: 248) evade the aggregation problem:

> Solow's argument is based on an appeal to the Sonnenschein–Mantel–Debreu result, which implies that if we have only aggregate data, then theory imposes little discipline on how we model aggregates. Fortunately for macroeconomics, the Sonnenschein–Mantel–Debreu result notwithstanding, discipline is available elsewhere. If we have microeconomic data on how individual households and

firms behave, then theory imposes discipline on the behavior of aggregates over and above Walras' Law and zero-degree homogeneity.

The way macroeconomists use microeconomic data to discipline their models is still developing.

The debate between Solow and Chari and Kehoe illustrates that macroeconomists can disagree more widely when they distance themselves a bit from the narrow definition of macroeconomics aptly captured by Blanchard in his triangle, which is grounded on Lucas's call for microfoundations and the use of the representative agent apparatus, among other things.

5. SOME FINAL THOUGHTS

Nowadays, mainstream macroeconomists advertise that there is a methodological consensus in their field to the extent that "there are really no longer alternative approaches to the resolution of macroeconomic issues," as Woodford (2009: 274) argues for. The new consensus is perceived to have promoted a greater merging than the "old" neoclassical synthesis – an idea reinforced by De Vroey's (2004: 75–6) observation that the old one was not truly a synthesis but rather "a metaphorical compromise between two approaches that did not want to enter into an open intellectual fight."

One may suppose that defining a common area in which macroeconomists could trade and narrow disagreements, namely Blanchard's triangle, builds in a synthesis almost by definition, as it leaves outside the triangle those who disagree more widely; but there is something even stronger: the defining of macroeconomics (of fluctuations) by that area; meaning that, therefore, dissenters are either not macroeconomists or not scientists to begin with. That was the case of Leijonhufvud, just to give one such example, as I argued earlier: disenchanted with intertemporal optimization of rational agents, he drifted away from mainstream macroeconomics. But as I tried to argue, and what is interesting from a historical point of view, is that the definition of such an area is not immutable and that it left some room for disagreements.

It is tempting to consider the role of MIT in promoting the new synthesis. Paul Samuelson had announced in the second edition (1951) of his bestselling textbook *Economics* that economists had worked toward a synthesis. But it was in its third edition (1955) that he coined "one of the most famous phrases in the history of macroeconomics" (Pearce and Hoover 1995: 202): the neoclassical synthesis. The old synthesis vanished with the new classical conquest of macroeconomics in the 1970s and 1980s. And nowadays we are back to a synthesis, the new neoclassical one. Although the term was first used by Goodfriend and King (1997), the idea of a new synthesis was welcomed in print by economists like Blanchard, Woodford, Mishkin, Romer and Galí and Gertler (and Mankiw and Fischer in interviews). All these enthusiasts but Gertler obtained their PhDs at MIT: Blanchard, Mishkin, Romer and Mankiw were advised by Stanley Fischer, while Galí was advised by Olivier Blanchard, and Woodford by Robert Solow. On the other hand, the group of adherents to the new synthesis went beyond MIT graduates and included people like Goodfriend (Brown University), King (Brown University), and Gertler (Stanford University). It is indeed hard to strongly indentify the new synthesis with MIT, as it was the case of the old neoclassical synthesis. Nonetheless, the fact that Blanchard and Woodford (and later Galí) were the leading writers of narratives about the evolution of the new synthesis and that they both studied at MIT has nice connotations that suggest that they are perhaps the Samuelsons of the new synthesis, even if unintentionally.

But as I have tried to show in this chapter, the acceptance of the idea of a synthesis did not mean that mainstream macroeconomists all saw it the same way and all agreed about which policies to prescribe. The somewhat nuanced views that these economists have about such consensus reflect a deeper understanding about how their field evolves. Having a synthesis is so much valued by them because they see that, in contrast to microeconomists, they work in a battlefield, with alternative schools constantly debunking one another. A synthesis, understood by them as implying that fights are over – as it was Samuelson's view in 1955 that "90 per cent of American economists have stopped being 'Keynesian economists' or 'anti-Keynesian economists'" (Samuelson 1955: 260) – and that knowledge progresses at a faster rate, is a way of boosting credibility, both in academia and in the policymaking arena: if you tell a story that in a synthesis you merge the strengths of the competing schools that preceded it, how can one oppose the view that synthesis means progress?

With respect to the views these macroeconomists have about their field, while some favor the notion of revolutions and counter-revolutions, and others deny it, all seem to see macroeconomics progressing over time, with knowledge accumulating and improving.[74] Moreover, implicitly or explicitly, most accounts are centered on internal progress: new theories improving on older ones by fixing logical and empirical flaws. Empirical facts are central in the construction of a synthesis because they do not go away, as Blanchard said, and therefore they force economists to change their theories in order to account for them. Those mainstream macroeconomists see the merging of the new classical/RBC and new Keynesian theories as driven by facts: an effort to convince that prices are sticky and that monetary policy matters in the short run. This was possible because both camps shared important methodological and theoretical convictions: they both distinguished rational expectations from the policy ineffectiveness result, they took up Lucas's microfoundational program, and they both, over time, leaned towards quantitative general equilibrium models (usually with a representative agent).

However, Mankiw (2006) favors a rather broader understanding of the evolution of macroeconomics by stressing that the field has a dual role: macroeconomics as science, devoted to "understand how the world works" (pp. 29–30), and as a type of engineering, concerned with solving practical problems. Besides this, Goodfriend (2007) makes a clear attempt at going beyond purely internal histories of macroeconomics by relating theoretical developments to historical events (Mishkin 2007 goes in the same direction as well).

While Blanchard (2009) at once cast the new synthesis as a revolution with a mild Kuhnian flavor, Mankiw (2006: 39) preferred to see it as a truce:

> It is tempting to describe the emergence of this consensus as great progress. In some ways, it is. But there is also a less sanguine way to view the current state of play. Perhaps what has occurred is not so much a synthesis as a truce between intellectual combatants, followed by a face-saving retreat on both sides. Both new classicals and new Keynesians can look to this new synthesis and claim a degree of victory, while ignoring the more profound defeat that lies beneath the surface.

There is some truth in Mankiw's truce: while the new neoclassical synthesis can be identified with the new Keynesian macroeconomics to the extent that RBC models were simply silent about monetary policy, RBC followers make the case that the new consensus is just a convergence to "policy recommendations similar to those made by neoclassical economists like Lucas and Stokey 25 years ago" (Chari, Kehoe and McGrattan 2009: 265). Neither side is willing to accept that they had to concede and change their models which failed in some dimension.

All the different views mainstream macroeconomists have about the state of their field and about possible areas of improvement should not diminish the degree to which they converged methodologically in studying fluctuations. They all analyse such phenomena usually through a dynamic stochastic general equilibrium model with a representative agent, firmly grounded on microeconomic principles. Moreover, several of them agree with Chari (2010: 2) that "any interesting model must be a dynamic stochastic general equilibrium model. From this perspective, there is no other game in town." Therefore, he continues, "a useful aphorism in macroeconomics is: 'If you have an interesting and coherent story to tell, you can tell it in a DSGE model. If you cannot, your story is incoherent.'"[75]

To the historians of economics, not only is this consensus an interesting object of study but so are the histories about its evolution that have been already produced, mostly by economists:[76] such narratives illustrate that the history of macroeconomics can be intentionally used to organize the present developments in ways to reaffirm the solidness of the new consensus and its policy prescriptions (despite the recognition that further work is necessary to improve it even more). The challenge of a serious recession brings back the ghost of another period of disarray in macroeconomics.

NOTES

1. This chapter was presented at the First International Symposium on the History of Economics ("The Integration of Micro and Macroeconomics from a Historical Perspective"), University of São Paulo, São Paulo, Brazil, August 3–5, 2009, and at the American Economic Association Meeting in Atlanta, January 2010. I am very grateful for the helpful comments I received at both events, especially those from Kevin Hoover, Michel De Vroey, Perry Mehrling and Gilberto Tadeu Lima, and also for those made by Tiago Mata. In addition, I thank Edward Prescott, Michael Lovell, Martin Eichenbaum, Lawrence Christiano, Robert King, and Michael Woodford for kindly answering a few questions. None of them is in any way responsible for the final outcome. I gratefully acknowledge Robert Lucas's generosity in permitting me to quote from his archival material as well as financial support from Fapesp (Brazil) and CNPq (Brazil).

2. It is important to emphasize that I discuss the mainstream economists' perception of the evolution of their field without taking issues with some of their claims. I want to explore the diversity that still exists on their understandings about both the consensus and the history of macroeconomics despite the alleged convergence that currently characterizes the field.

3. Here I borrow William Nordhaus's (1983: 247) term used later by Karl Brunner (1989) and N. Gregory Mankiw (1992a) right on the title of their papers (the latter paper draws heavily on Mankiw 1990). This expression was used earlier during the stagflation of the 1970s: see for instance Saul Hymans and Harold Shapiro (1975), a paper presented at the 1975 American Economic Association meetings but published in 1978 in the *Review of Economics and Statistics* in a different version that did not use the term disarray.

4. Blaug (1975) argues that by the mid-1970s economists have abandoned Popper and embraced Kuhn. However, some doubts on the applicability of Kuhn's ideas to economics (and the Keynesian revolution) were already raised, which led Blaug to propose that Lakatos's framework may work better in economics. See Redman (1991: chap. 7) for further references on economists who were the first to apply Kuhn's concepts to understand the evolution of their field. De Vroey in this volume discusses the transition from IS-LM to new classical/RBC macroeconomics in Kuhnian terms. In contrast to this view of revolutions in macroeconomics, Lucas (2004: 21–2) has recently argued that economics is a field technically progressing in a common paradigm that was initiated and structured by Smith and Ricardo. He then denied the existence of either paradigm changes or scientific revolutions. A few years earlier, in an interview with Snowdon and Vane, Lucas (1998: 127) observed that economists have used the concept of scientific revolutions loosely and disagreed that the new classical approach resulted in a revolution in macroeconomics: "Sargent once wrote that you can interpret any scientific development as continuous evolution or discontinuous revolution, at your pleasure. For myself, I do not have any romantic association with the term 'revolution'. To me, it connotes lying, theft and murder, so I would prefer not to be known as a revolutionary."

5. See Weintraub (2002: chap. 9) for a sharp discussion on how the kind of historical analysis produced by economists and historians of economics is tied to the methodological conceptions they have. In fact, the notion of a scientific revolution in economics predates Kuhn and was put forward by Keynes's followers in the late 1940s (Pearce and Hoover 1995: 183) – see also Laidler (1999), who argues that although Keynes himself understood that his work would revolutionize economics, "an element of myth-making is involved whenever the phrase 'Keynesian revolution' is deployed" because "the re-arrangement of ideas to which it refers was neither revolutionary in the usual sense of the word nor [was] by any means uniquely Keynesian in origin" (p. 3). Besides this, as Roger Backhouse (2010: chap 9) correctly pointed out, Kuhn's ideas were appealing to dissenting economists: through a scientific revolution, a new paradigm emerges, with the old and new paradigms being incommensurable. In the 1970s the talk of crisis in economics was widespread, which led those heterodox economists to seek "consciously to create a new paradigm" (p. 159). Although this certainly is important for understanding the popularity of Kuhnian ideas among economists, I want to explore here how mainstream economists, those defending the status quo, loosely used Kuhn ([1962] 1970) and even combined him with a notion that he was opposing, that science developed in a cumulative progress.

6. Snowdon and Vane (1996) write a history of macroeconomics since the 1970s, when it was in a state of "disarray," as a succession of revolutions and counter-revolutions among "conflicting and competing approaches" (p. 382). They then talk about "the new classical *research programme*" that "replaced monetarism as the main rival to Keynesianism." A few lines later they talk about "the new classical and new Keynesian *schools*" (p. 382, emphasis added). This is just one example of economists using a school of thought as a synonym for Lakatos's concept of a research program.

7. Kevin Hoover (1988: chap. 1) places the new classical economists "among the principal schools of macroeconomic thought" (p. 6). Howard Vane and John Thompson (1992) kept it simple: just three "mainstream schools of thought" (Keynesian economics, monetarism, and new classical economics). There are too many articles by macroeconomists in which several schools of thought are appraised. Among the most recent that I shall discuss, follow this tradition: Goodfriend and King (1997), Taylor (1997), Woodford (2000), Mankiw (2006), and Akerlof (2007). See also Greenwald and Stiglitz (1988: 207) and Romer (1993: 5-6) for a brief overview of recent macroeconomics along these lines.

8. Would either the Marxist or the institutionalist theories be included as schools of macroeconomic thought? Sheila Dow (1996: chap. 4) did include them (and others).

9. Michael Woodford received his A.B. from the University of Chicago in 1977 and then went to Yale Law School, obtaining his J.D. in 1980. He then went to MIT for his PhD in economics, finished in 1983. According to the MIT catalogue, there he was supervised by Timothy J. Kehoe (PhD in economics in 1979 from Yale, who was at MIT from 1980 to 1984) and wrote a thesis on intertemporal economics. However, in the preface of his 2003 book, Woodford writes that his supervisor was Robert Solow. In fact, due to the technical nature of his work, Solow was his official supervisor while Kehoe was his de facto supervisor. Mankiw also obtained his PhD from MIT, in 1984 under Stanley Fischer. Fischer is another PhD from MIT, graduated in 1969 under Franklin Fischer.

10. Historians of economics have produced narratives that show how complex the history of microeconomics is, denying that this area progressed smoothly and steadily within an unchanged explanatory framework. For a few examples, see Weintraub (1992), Mirowski and Hands (1998), and Mirowski and Hands (2006).

11. For instance, Mankiw (1992b: 564–5) denies that macroeconomics is a pendulum that "is destined to oscillate between two irreconcilable extremes," the classical and the Keynesian views, and argues that it does make progress. Bill Gerrard (1996: 54) reviewed the book by Snowdon, Vane and Wynarczyk (1994) and argued that "macroeconomics can be seen as an evolving classical-Keynesian debate from which a developing consensus is ever-emerging as current disagreements are resolved, but new disagreements continually appear requiring the consensus to re-emerge." He then adds: "Within mainstream

macroeconomics a clear case can be made that the competing schools of thought have generated cumulative progress" (p. 65), and concludes that "macroeconomics is, and will remain, controversial as classical and Keynesian schools provide contending views on the self-adjusting nature of the macro economy and the necessity or otherwise of stabilization policy. This classical-Keynesian debate has been progressive and an ever-emerging, albeit partial, consensus has resulted. ... All schools of thought need to recognize more fully the inherent limitations of their own perspectives. Progress in macroeconomics requires competition and co-operation" (p. 66).

12. Different from this view that the neoclassical synthesis of the 1950s represented economic knowledge in progress, Wade Hands, this volume, challenges the view of a synthesis between micro and macroeconomics (as does De Vroey 2004). In his narrative, he proposes that a co-evolution, rather than a synthesis, captures much better the main point of his analysis: "that although Walrasian economics had certain core conceptions that were identifiable over time, it also evolved and changed in response to, and because of, its contact with Keynesian economics," while in the end "microeconomics and macroeconomics remained identifiable and distinct fields" (p. 122, fn. 8). Additionally, Philip Mirowski (Chapter 4 in this volume) challenges the view that the synthesis was "Keynesian" because there was, according to him, an anti-Keynesian hostility by the major neoclassical schools in the US in the postwar period. In my narrative, notice that I usually refer to the neoclassical (instead of Keynesian) synthesis and I present it according to the views held by practicing economists.

13. Goodfriend and King both obtained their PhD in economics from Brown University in 1980. King joined the University of Rochester faculty in 1978 without completing his PhD. He finished his thesis by spring of 1979 but missed the graduation deadlines and, thus, was awarded his degree in 1980.

14. Lucas (1998: 133) denied the view that there is more consensus among microeconomists compared to macroeconomists, as defended by Woodford (2000). But Lucas agrees that there is now a consensus in macroeconomics: "What is the microeconomic consensus you are referring to? Does it just mean that microeconomists agree on the Slutsky equation, or other purely mathematical propositions? Macroeconomists all take derivatives in the same way, too. On the matters of application and policy, microeconomists disagree as vehemently as macroeconomists – neither side in an antitrust action has any difficulty in finding expert witnesses. I think there is a tremendous amount of consensus on macroeconomic issues today. But there is much that we don't know, and so – necessarily – a lot to argue about." Lucas also makes the point that consensus refers to specific issues, not to a whole area, which needs certain disagreement among its members to progress: "Consensus can be reached on specific issues, but consensus for a research area as a whole is equivalent to stagnation, irrelevance and death" (p. 133).

15. This is particularly clear in the defense that V. V. Chari made of DSGE models in a testimony before the Subcommittee on Investigations and Oversight of the Committee on Science and Technology, US House of Representatives (Chari 2010): "I will argue that macroeconomics has made huge progress, especially in the last 25 years or so" (p. 1). This hearing intended to "examine the promise and limits of modern macroeconomic theory in light of the current economic crisis" (Committee on Science and Technology 2010: 1).

16. As Robert Solow (1983: 279) wrote: "Why ... is macroeconomics in disarray? 'Disarray' is an understatement. Thoughtful people in other university departments look on with wonder. Professional disagreements exist in their field too – at the frontier there is always disagreement – but as outsiders they are shocked at the way alternative schools of thought in macroeconomics describe each other as wrong from the ground up. They wonder what kind of subject economics is. (Some of them are not above a little *Schadenfreude* either.)" Solow (2000: 151) starts his article with similar lines: "These days macroeconomics has become more respectable that it used to be. I can remember when many economists liked to say: Microeconomics is not problematic, but I just can't *understand* macroeconomics." On page 155 he explicitly identifies the current consensus with Kuhn's concept of normal science. Snowdon and Vane (1995) chose as the epigraph

of the article they wrote based on an interview with Gregory Mankiw the words of Knut Wicksell (1851–1926), in a lecture in 1904 to an audience interested in science: "in other fields of science these conflicts come to an end ... It is only in the field of economics that the state of war seems to persist and remain permanent."

17. Blinder (1989: viii) argued that the state of macroeconomics in the late 1980s was very different from the early 1970s, after he obtained his PhD from MIT (in 1971 under Robert Solow) and became an assistant professor at Princeton: "The academic world I entered in 1971 was quite different from the one I have inhabited ever since. ... The monetarist controversy was simmering, but the Keynesian paradigm reigned supreme." Later, he also referred to the new classical economics as a revolution ("Lucasian revolution") that was largely destructive compared to "the period of normal science that had preceded it" (interview to Snowdon 2001: 112)

18. The participants of this session included Robert Solow, John Taylor, Martin Eichenbaum, Alan Blinder, and Olivier Blanchard, whose essays were published in the Papers and Proceedings issue of the *American Economic Review* of 1997 (vol. 87, no. 2).

19. Mishkin is another of the economists being discussed in this paper who obtained his PhD in economics from MIT, in 1976 under Stanley Fischer. His first position after graduating was as an economist in the Board of Governors of the Federal Reserve System, in the summer of 1977. After this he held several academic and policy-oriented positions.

20. Continuing to pay attention to the academic training of the economists under study, Galí received his PhD in economics also from MIT, in 1989 under Olivier Blanchard who has also a PhD in economics from MIT (1977, under Stanley Fischer). Chari, Kehoe, and Gertler are all non-MIT graduates: they received their PhD in economics from Carnegie-Mellon (1980), Harvard (1986), and Stanford (1978), respectively.

21. See also Blanchard (2008). Mankiw (2006: 38) states that accompanying the emergence of the new consensus there was the retirement of an older generation of vitriolic macroeconomists and its replacement by "a younger generation of macroeconomists who have adopted a culture of greater civility." One may question Mankiw's view and have trouble identifying this new generation of civilized men after reading for example the response that Chari and Kehoe gave to Solow's comments on their 2006 article (Chari and Kehoe 2008).

22. Blanchard (2009: 212) once again exemplifies this understanding among present-day macroeconomists: "Facts have a way of eventually forcing irrelevant theory out (one wishes it happened faster). And good theory also has a way of eventually forcing bad theory out."

23. Zouache (2004: 98) calls this ground a "common methodological reference to the microeconomic foundations of macroeconomics." As it will become clear later, while I agree with this point, I disagree with the author's view that the new neoclassical synthesis is "more an extension of the Real Business Cycle research programme than a synthesis between two research traditions [RBC and new Keynesian]" (p. 108).

24. Goodfriend (2004: 21) and Galí and Gertler (2007: 25) share with Chari and Kehoe their enthusiasm about the state of macroeconomics.

25. See for example Mankiw (1989: 79), Goodfriend and King (1997: 232) and Woodford (2000: 29).

26. Blanchard (2009: 210) referred to the crisis in macroeconomics in the 1970s in more histrionic terms, as the "explosion (in both the positive and negative meaning of the word) of the field in the 1970s."

27. On the importance of the high inflation of the 1970s to the defeat of Keynesianism and the development of the new classical economics, Lucas (1998: 122) argued that: "The main ideas that are associated with rational expectations were developed by the early 1970s so the importance of the inflation that occurred was that it confirmed some of these theoretical ideas. In a way the timing couldn't have been better."

28. The point here is not to draw a complete scenario of the evolution of macroeconomics in the postwar period, which should include the general disequilibrium theory of the 1960s

and 1970s (which, in contrast to Mankiw 2006: 35, I do not consider to be the first wave of the new Keynesian work – for me this wave was initiated in the 1980s with the work on static (usually partial equilibrium) models done by Mankiw, Romer, Akerlof and others), and many other issues. I want just to give a rough sense of how practitioners see the major changes in their field.

29. This was how Lucas described to Otto Eckstein (Harvard University) his intentions in the article he eventually published in 1973, in a letter of January 20, 1970, in which he accepted to present a seminar at Harvard (Folder "1970 Correspondence R. E. Lucas", Box 32; Robert E. Lucas, Jr. Papers, David M. Rubenstein Rare Book and Manuscript Library, Duke University).

30. The call for microfoundations is not simply a result of the Lucas critique. Hoover (in Chapter 1 of this volume) provides a detailed analysis of the different microfoundational programs that marked the history of macroeconomics since the 1930s and argues that they even have a pre-history. His discussion historicizes the notion of microfoundations. De Vroey (in Chapter 5 of this volume) explores in detail the microfoundations requirement as expressed by Lucas and the justification he presented to his enterprise.

31. Spear and Wright (1998: 547).

32. José-Víctor Ríos-Rull obtained his PhD in 1990 at the University of Minnesota, under Edward Prescott.

33. In several rational expectation models the Phillips curve is also vertical in the short run. Hoover (1988: 28–31) explains that these models have an "ephemeral Phillips curve."

34. In fact, RBC macroeconomists can be seen as following up the research agenda set up by new classical economists like Lucas. This was what Prescott wrote to Lucas in 1991: "much of what we are doing [at Minnesota] is working out the research program that you defined. I wish there were a noun for calibrate or a noun that captured the idea of being rigorous" (letter from Prescott to Lucas, Feb. 19, 1991, folder "1991 Correspondence", Box 25; Robert E. Lucas, Jr. Papers, David M. Rubenstein Rare Book and Manuscript Library, Duke University).

35. See Lucas (1973) and several articles in the volume Lucas and Sargent edited in 1981.

36. This does not mean that there were no estimated RBC models, but rather that calibration was the preferred method used by RBC theorists. Nonetheless, there is a saying that people attribute to Prescott that incarnates the RBC distaste for estimation and support of calibration: "don't regress; progress." Some of Prescott's students tell the story that he had this phrase on his office door in Minnesota in the 1970s to tease his then colleague and econometrician Christopher Sims. Confronted with this story, Prescott (email message June 11, 2010) wrote: "My mentor Michael C. Lovell in an interesting paper attributed the quote to me. He told me that I had said it I think in the early 1970s. I like the statement. Measurement without theory has delivered little. As the result of inter-action between theory and measurement, great progress has been made and is being made in our science." In fact, this phrase was the epigraph attributed to Prescott in Lovell and Selover's 1994 article, published in the software reviews section of the *Economic Journal* (I could not locate any other reference to this phrase in economic articles). Lovell (email message June 11, 2010) explained further: "I don't remember the precise source of 'Progress, Don't Regress.' I don't think it was when we overlapped at Carnegie-Mellon in the 1960s. ... Perhaps I picked the quote off of his home page. I looked up his home page just now, and it is not there. I had not heard the office door and Chris Sims story, but it could be true." He then pointed out to me a magazine article published in 2003 by the Minneapolis Fed, in which it is written: "[some authors] employ a technique Prescott generally scorns: statistical regression. 'Progress, don't regress,' he says with a smile, quoting the slogan featured prominently on his Internet home page" (Clement 2003). Even if this phrase was not on Prescott's office door, it seems nonetheless to have teased Chris Sims (2004), who wrote a critical article on "econometrics for policy analysis" in which he discussed calibration and estimation and used the words progress and regress on its title.

37. See, for example, Thomas Cooley and Edward Prescott's chapter in Cooley (1995). For a thorough discussion on the idealized nature of RBC models, on how they fit the data and how they can be tested, see Hartley, Hoover, and Salyer (1997). For more on calibration, see also Boumans (2002) and Prescott and Candler (2008).

38. Nonetheless, in the early 1990s these economists expanded their agenda to include things like money, heterogeneous agents, and imperfect competition, for instance (see Cooley 1995).

39. Lucas wrote the first draft alone in 1989 (see draft "The Effects of Monetary Shocks When Prices are Set in Advance", November 1989, in folder "FIXP / BANK", Box 1; Robert E. Lucas, Jr. Papers, David M. Rubenstein Rare Book and Manuscript Library, Duke University). In the introduction he wrote not only that this model, resembling Lucas (1972), was designed to be "consistent with the centuries old observation, documented most recently and comprehensively by Kormendi and Meguire (1984), that increased monetary instability is associated with increased real instability" (p. 1), but also that "in its reliance on nominal prices that are set in advance, the model in this paper is similar to those of Fischer, Phelps and Taylor" (p. 2). These three papers are part of the new Keynesian literature that advocated the non-neutrality of money in the short run. Woodford came in in the second semester of 1990, but their paper has not been published to this date (there is a version available as the NBER working paper 4250, of January of 1993, and a revised version from Woodford's webpage). There is a curious letter from Lucas to Lars Svensson, on March 20, 1990. Svensson made comments on this paper by Lucas ("The Effects of Monetary Shocks When Prices are Set in Advance") and he sent reprints of his papers with sticky-price models, including one that he presented in the same session that Lucas presented a paper of his at the "Econometric Society World Meeting in Cambridge around 1985." Lucas then replied (emphasis added): "My apologies for not relating this work to yours on sticky prices, which you had sent me long ago in working paper form. At that time [mid 1980s], *I was so hostile to the idea of pre-set prices* that I simply filed your paper unread and forgot about it!" However, in 1979 Lucas had drafted a paper whose introduction shows he believed that there was clear evidence that prices do not adjust instantaneously (Folder "Price Fixing", Box 1). This did not mean that Lucas favored the way price stickiness was treated in the so-called disequilibrium macroeconomics. In a report to Henri Theil in 1978, Lucas was uneasy with Negishi's book proposal, in which, as in the works of Barro and Grossman and Malinvaud, he attempted "to obtain 'Keynesian' results from a general equilibrium model by arbitrarily fixing some prices". Lucas concluded: "I am not very sympathetic to this line – I think it assumes away the difficult and most crucial issues – and have not followed it very closely. Because of this I cannot judge its contribution to this literature very fairly." (Letter from Lucas to Theil, Feb. 24, 1978, folder "Correspondence – 1978-1", Box 30).

40. Emphasis added. Letter from Lucas to Prescott, October 22, 1990, folder "1990 Correspondence", Box 26; Robert E. Lucas, Jr. Papers, David M. Rubenstein Rare Book and Manuscript Library, Duke University.

41. Emphasis added. Letter from Prescott to Lucas, November 1, 1990, folder "1990 Correspondence", Box 26; Robert E. Lucas, Jr. Papers, David M. Rubenstein Rare Book and Manuscript Library, Duke University.

42. Letter from Lucas to Prescott, May 18, 1990, folder "1990 Correspondence", Box 26; Robert E. Lucas, Jr. Papers, David M. Rubenstein Rare Book and Manuscript Library, Duke University.

43. Greenwald and Stiglitz (1993: 24) also stress the differences between the two groups despite their agreement upon two methodological premises (founding macroeconomics on microeconomic principles and the use of simple general equilibrium models). The authors argue that RBC and new classical economists "base their theories on simple (we would say simplistic) models of markets that employ perfect information, perfect competition, the absence of transactions costs, and the presence of a complete set of

markets. ... In contrast, modern Keynesians have identified these real world 'imperfections' as the source of the problem: leaving them out of the model is like leaving Hamlet out of the play."

44. Hartley, Hoover, and Salyer (1997: 46–8) provide a broader discussion on the problems associated with the way RBC macroeconomists detrend the data.

45. Lucas wrote a letter to Seymour Zucker of *Business Week* showing his satisfaction with the article published, based on "our long and (I thought) confusing conversations, I was dubious that anything coherent would emerge. The article was thus a pleasant surprise." Letter from Lucas to Seymour, November 11, 1976, folder "Correspondence-1976", Box 31; Robert E. Lucas, Jr. Papers, David M. Rubenstein Rare Book and Manuscript Library, Duke University.

46. Sargent and Lucas seemed to embrace fully this missionary activity of advocating rational expectations as the policy ineffectiveness result. It is interesting that this article in *Newsweek* was translated into Spanish and published in a newspaper (not identifiable), which Sargent sent to Lucas with the following undated note: "Dear Bob, I thought you might be interested in learning of Kareken and Wallace's missionary activities. Tom" (folder "1978-2", Box 30; Robert E. Lucas, Jr. Papers, David M. Rubenstein Rare Book and Manuscript Library, Duke University).

47. Folder "Correspondence-1978-1", Box 30; Robert E. Lucas, Jr. Papers, David M. Rubenstein Rare Book and Manuscript Library, Duke University.

48. As Blanchard (1992: 123) puts this, in terms of his preferred understanding of fights and scientific progress: "Initial fights were about the appropriateness of the assumption of rational expectations, as the assumption seemed so damaging to mainstream macroeconomics. But, by the late 1970s, regrouping had occurred, and progress happened in two phases:" the integration of supply shocks and rational expectations, and an analysis of the structure of markets.

49. Blinder would later repeat similar words in an interview to Snowdon (2001: 113). Greenwald and Stiglitz (1993: 41) also observe that the policy ineffectiveness result depends on instantaneous market clearing rather than on rational expectations.

50. See also Stiglitz (1992) for a careful discussion about his view of microfoundations and asymmetric information.

51. This was the opinion voiced by Greenwald and Stiglitz (1993: 35) and Mankiw (in Snowdon and Vane 1995: 56). For Lucas (1998: 130–31) this challenge had still not been settled by the end of the 1990s.

52. These are Mankiw's words in an interview he gave to Snowdon and Vane in 1993, published two years later (Snowdon and Vane 1995: 60–61).

53. Lucas (1998: 130) also saw the synthesis coming. Clarida, Galí, and Gertler (1999) observed that the resurgence of interest in monetary policy was based both on consensus that empirically monetary policy affects the real economy and on an improvement in the theoretical framework used for policy analysis: one that "incorporated the techniques of dynamic general equilibrium theory pioneered in real business cycle analysis" together with "the explicit incorporation of frictions such as nominal price rigidities" (pp. 1661–2).

54. According to these authors, the new synthesis "inherits the spirit of the old, in that it combines Keynesian and classical elements" (p. 232). The old was characterized by three principles, they argue: (i) give practical macro policy advice; (ii) short-run price stickiness is the major source of economic fluctuations; (iii) macro models need microfoundations.

55. Eichenbaum received his PhD from the University of Minnesota in 1981, under Thomas Sargent (who is a Harvard PhD, 1968).

56. Before he raised once again his criticisms to modern macroeconomics for offering no guidance or insight about the recent crisis and the deep and prolonged recession that many developed countries experienced, Solow (2010: 1) explicitly warned: "Before I go on, there is something preliminary that I want to make clear. I am generally a quite traditional mainstream economist. I think that the body of economic analysis that we have piled up and teach to our students is pretty good; there is no need to overturn it in any wholesale way, and no acceptable suggestion for doing so."

57. In a recent survey, Heathcote, Storesletten, and Violante (2009: 320) advertised a similar point: due to improvements in numerical methods and faster computers, macroeconomists are now able "to study rich heterogeneous-agent models." They "reached several conclusions about the importance of including household heterogeneity in their models" (p. 320). They identified that "macroeconomics is expanding from the study of how average values for inputs ... and outputs ... of production are determined in equilibrium to the study of how the entire distribution of these variables across households is determined" (p. 321). While this broad trend is observable (but leaving it open to question how much this route will be explored by many economists), Solow's point is still valid because the consensus macroeconomics is one in which the representative agent reigns to this day, despite Chari's (2010: 3) opinion that "any claim that modern macro is dominated by representative agent models is wrong."

58. See for instance Greenwald and Stiglitz (1993: 39–41) and Hartley, Hoover, and Salyer (1997), and references therein, for the major empirical criticisms to the real business cycle theories. Sims (1992) challenges RBC modelers to reproduce the multivariate time series facts that he presents in the article and claims that data is imposing theoretical changes (p. 996).

59. See Obstfeld and Rogoff (1996: chap. 9) for further discussion of price stickiness in international data and open economy models.

60. As Hoover (2006: 144) notes, "even the founders of the new classical macroeconomics, such as Lucas and Sargent, have to come to see that the assumption of sticky prices is essential if models have any hope of capturing observed economic behavior." However, in the 1970s and 1980s the attitude from most new classical/RBC macroeconomists was against price stickiness. As the Keynesian Alan Blinder (interview to Snowdon 2001: 124) points out: "The parts of macroeconomics that took off in the 1970s and 1980s were those based on denying sticky prices. The attitude of new classical and real business cycle theorists seemed to be ... 'if you don't have a coherent theoretical explanation of sticky prices then it cannot be true that prices are sticky'. Personally I found that approach unscientific." Nowadays the often-used Calvo price setting would be hardly qualified as a "coherent explanation of sticky prices." Even if we take into account that it is justified for simplifying the model (because it reduces the number of state variables) and for delivering results similar to better models of price stickiness, the currency in the consensus macroeconomics of Calvo pricing is a sign that the opposition to which Blinder referred really weakened over time.

61. Solow (2000: 155) classifies Christiano and Eichenbaum as moderate RBC macroeconomists: "My reading is that the work of Christiano, Eichenbaum and others has moved in the direction of incorporating frictions and imperfections into the real business cycle framework. The result sounds a little more like the observed economy."

62. With hindsight, Woodford (2000: 27) commented that "the rejection of traditional econometric methods by the early RBC literature has surely been overdone."

63. See Christiano, Eichenbaum, and Evans (2005: 15–17), who followed Rotemberg and Woodford (1997), for a description of the econometric methodology of calibrating a subset of parameters and estimating the others by minimizing the distance between the impulse response functions from the data and the model. Even though Bayesian methods in principle can be used to estimate all parameters of a model, in macroeconomics it has been common still to calibrate a few parameters that are either hard to estimate or, more importantly, are not identified (see for instance Smets and Wouters 2007).

64. In fact, this association of new classical economics with monetarism was part of an intense debate in the early 1980s. Hoover (1988: chap. 9), largely reproducing his 1984 article on the *Journal of Economic Literature* (vol. 22, no. 1), clarifies the relationship between monetarism and the new classical school and provides references to that earlier literature.

65. See Dupor, Han, and Tsai (2009), Canova and Sala (2009), and references therein.

66. Blanchard (2009: 224) considers the strategy of uncritically introducing such features to reconcile the theory with the data as "clearly wrongheaded."

67. For a discussion on whether or not Woodford has succeeded see Hoover (2006), Laidler (2006), Mehrling (2006) and Woodford's (2006) own comments on these papers.
68. Hoover (2006: 145) states that although these models have "a measure of stylized heterogeneity… there is no agent-by-agent modeling of the sort that would really qualify as microeconomics." But the central point is that the focus of the consensus model is on symmetric equilibrium in which intermediate firms only differ because they do not charge the same price, and in which the dispersion of relative price does not affect the dynamics of the variables because these models are usually solved with first-order approximation methods (and price dispersion has an effect which is of second order, thus ignored in these methods).
69. But the same author went back to Kuhn's notion of revolution in his 2009 essay, in order to argue that the macroeconomics of the 1970s has exploded and converged to the new synthesis, as previously mentioned. He then writes: "Not everything is fine. Like all revolutions, this one has come with the destruction of some knowledge, and suffers from extremism, herding, and fashion. But none of this is deadly. The state of macro is good" (p. 2).
70. These authors strengthen their criticisms by questioning the view of a broad consensus in macroeconomics right in the opening paragraph: "Viewed from a distance, modern macroeconomics, whether New Keynesian or neoclassical, are all alike. … Viewed up close, however, we disagree considerably" (p. 242).
71. Mankiw (2006) retakes and updates here a concern already present in his 1990 article (repeated in his 1992a essay). See Woodford (2009: 275–7) for a criticism of Mankiw's view.
72. For critical assessments of the new consensus and the role of monetary policy in it, see Arestis (2007) and Arestis and Sawyer (2008). The literature critical on the use of a representative agent in macroeconomics is extensive. See Kirman (1992), Caballero (1992) (who is someone not exactly living outside the triangle), Janssen (1993), Hartley (1997), Hoover (2001), van den Bergh and Gowdy (2003), and references therein.
73. Chari and Kehoe (2008: 248) wrote: "Analogies about school colors and carrots aside, there does not seem to be much of substance here to argue about." On a side note, it is interesting to note that they published their response as an NBER Working Paper (13655, Nov. 2007), which had as its title, "the heterogeneous state of modern macroeconomics: a reply to Solow". The reply was later published in the *Journal of Economic Perspectives* without a title.
74. Transposing Weintraub's (1979: 6) words to this context, mainstream economists need to guarantee that progress and synthesis are logically possible in order to look to the past and tell stories of progress and synthesis in their field: "Writing doctrinal history with an eye to progress and synthesis becomes difficult if progress was absent and synthesis is logically impossible."
75. Nevertheless, nowadays there are voices in favor of more pragmatism, of exploring ideas with partial equilibrium models, and of facing the pretense-of-knowledge syndrome of DSGE macroeconomists: see for instance Krugman (2000), Colander (2006), Colander et al. (2008), and Caballero (2010). Even Blanchard (1992) was once more skeptical of the microfoundations of macreoconomics as dictated by Lucas.
76. It is curious to observe that some of the articles written by economists and constructing such histories are published in major economics journals under the classification of either "general economics and teaching" or "macroeconomics and monetary economics" (as Woodford 2009), but not as "history of economics" (or history of economic thought).

REFERENCES

Akerlof, George A. (2007). The Missing Motivation in Macroeconomics. *American Economic Review,* 97 (1):5–36.

Akerlof, George A., and Janet L. Yellen (1985). A Near-Rational Model of the Business Cycle, with Wage and Price Inertia. *Quarterly Journal of Economics,* 100 (Supplement):823–38.

Altig, David, Lawrence J. Christiano, Martin Eichenbaum, and Jesper Linde (2005). Firm-Specific Capital, Nominal Rigidities and the Business Cycle. *NBER Working Paper,* no. 11034.

Arestis, Philip (ed.) (2007). *Is There a New Consensus in Macroeconomics?* New York: Palgrave Macmillan.

Arestis, Philip, and Malcolm Sawyer (2008). A Critical Reconsideration of the Foundations of Monetary Policy in the New Consensus Macroeconomics Framework. *Cambridge Journal of Economics,* 32 (5):761–79.

Backhouse, Roger E. (2010). *The Puzzle of Modern Economics.* Cambridge: Cambridge University Press.

Ball, Laurence, and N. Gregory Mankiw (1994). A Sticky-Price Manifesto. *Carnegie-Rochester Conference Series on Public Policy,* 41:127–51.

Blanchard, Olivier J. (1992). For a Return to Pragmatism. In *The Business Cycle: Theories and Evidence.* Edited by Michael T. Belongia, and Michelle R. Garfinkel. Boston: Kluwer Academic Publishers.

Blanchard, Olivier J. (1997a). Is There a Core of Usable Macroeconomics? *American Economic Review,* 87 (2, Papers and Proceedings):244–6.

Blanchard, Olivier J. (1997b). Comment on Goodfriend and King: "The New Neoclassical Synthesis and the Role of Monetary Policy". *NBER Macroeconomics Annual,* pp. 289–93.

Blanchard, Olivier J. (2000). What Do We Know About Macroeconomics that Fisher and Wicksell Did Not? *Quarterly Journal of Economics,* 115 (4):1375–409.

Blanchard, Olivier J. (2005). An Interview with Stanley Fischer. *Macroeconomic Dynamics,* 9 (2):244–62.

Blanchard, Olivier J. (2008). Neoclassical Synthesis. In *The New Palgrave Dictionary of Economics.* 2nd edn. Edited by Steven N. Durlauf, and Lawrence E. Blume. Palgrave Macmillan (*The New Palgrave Dictionary of Economics Online,* available at http://www.dictionaryofeconomics.com/article?id=pde2008_N000041, doi:10.1057/9780230226203.1172, accessed 12 March 2012).

Blanchard, Olivier J. (2009). The State of Macro. *Annual Review of Economics,* 1:209–28.

Blaug, Mark (1975). Kuhn versus Lakatos, or Paradigms versus Research Programmes in the History of Economics. *History of Political Economy,* 7 (4):399–433.

Blinder, Alan S. (1989). *Macroeconomics Under Debate.* New York: Harvester Wheatsheaf.

Blinder, Alan S. (1997). Is There a Core of Practical Macroeconomics That We Should All Believe? *American Economic Review,* 87 (2, Papers and Proceedings):240–3.

Boumans, Marcel (2002). Calibration. In *An Encyclopedia of Macroeconomics.* Edited by Brian Snowdon, and Howard R. Vane. Cheltenham: Edward Elgar.

Brunner, Karl (1989). The Disarray in Macroeconomics. In *Monetary Economics in the 1980s.* Edited by Forrest Capie, and Geoffrey Wood. London: Macmillan.

Business Week (1976). How Expectations Defeat Economic Policy. November 8:74–5.

Caballero, Ricardo J. (1992). A Fallacy of Composition. *American Economic Review,* 82 (5):1279–92.

Caballero, Ricardo J. (2010). Macroeconomics After the Crisis: Time to Deal with the Pretense-of-knowledge Syndrome. *NBER working paper*, no. 16429.

Canova, Fabio, and Luca Sala (2009). Back to Square One: Identification Issues in DSGE Models. *Journal of Monetary Economics*, 56 (4):431–49.

Chari, V. V. (2010). *Testimony before the Committee on Science and Technology*. Subcommittee on Investigations and Oversight, U.S. House of Representatives, July 20. Washington, DC (available at: http://science.house.gov/publications/ hearings_markups_details.aspx?NewsID=2916, accessed on Oct. 13, 2010).

Chari, V. V., and Patrick J. Kehoe (2006). Modern Macroeconomics in Practice: How Theory Is Shaping Policy. *Journal of Economic Perspectives*, 20 (4):3–28.

Chari, V. V., and Patrick J. Kehoe (2008). Response from V. V. Chari and Patrick J. Kehoe. *Journal of Economic Perspectives*, 22 (1):247–9.

Chari, V. V., Patrick J. Kehoe, and Ellen R. McGrattan (2009). New Keynesian Models: Not Yet Useful for Policy Analysis. *American Economic Journal: Macroeconomics*, 1 (1):242–66.

Christiano, Lawrence J., Martin Eichenbaum, and Charles L. Evans (1999). Monetary Policy Shocks: What Have We Learned and to What End? In *Handbook of Macroeconomics*. Edited by John B. Taylor, and Michael Woodford. Amsterdam: North-Holland.

Christiano, Lawrence J., Martin Eichenbaum, and Charles L. Evans (2005). Nominal Rigidities and the Dynamic Effects of a Shock to Monetary Policy. *Journal of Political Economy*, 113 (1):1–45.

Clarida, Richard, Jordi Galí, and Mark Gertler (1999). The Science of Monetary Policy: A New Keynesian Perspective. *Journal of Economic Literature*, 37(4):1661–707.

Clement, Douglas (2003). European Vacation: Why Americans Work More Than Europeans. *The Region – Banking and Policy Issues Magazine*. December.

Colander, David (ed.) (2006). *Post Walrasian Macroeconomics*. Cambridge: Cambridge University Press.

Colander, David, Peter Howitt, Alan Kirman, Axel Leijonhufvud, and Perry Mehrling (2008). Beyond DSGE Models: Toward an Empirically Based Macroeconomics. *American Economic Review*, 98 (2, Papers and Proceedings):236–40.

Committee on Science and Technology (2010). *Hearing Charter: Building a Science of Economics for the Real World*. US House of Representatives. July 20. Washington, DC (available at: http://science.house.gov/publications/hearings_markups_ details.aspx?NewsID=2916, accessed on Oct. 13, 2010).

Cooley, Thomas F. (ed.) (1995). *Frontiers of Business Cycle Research*. Princeton: Princeton University Press.

De Vroey, Michel (2004). The History of Macroeconomics Viewed Against the Background of the Marshall–Walras Divide. In *The IS-LM Model: Its Rise, Fall, and Strange Persistence*. *History of Political Economy* 36 supplement. Edited by Michel De Vroey, and Kevin D. Hoover. Durham, NC: Duke University Press.

De Vroey, Michel, and Kevin D. Hoover (2004). Introduction: Seven Decades of the IS-LM Model. In *The IS-LM Model: Its Rise, Fall, and Strange Persistence*. *History of Political Economy* 36 supplement. Edited by Michel De Vroey, and Kevin D. Hoover. Durham, NC: Duke University Press.

Dow, Sheila C. (1996). *The Methodology of Macroeconomic Thought – A Conceptual Analysis of Schools of Thought in Economics*. Cheltenham: Edward Elgar.

Dupor, Bill, Jing Han, and Yi-Chan Tsai (2009). What Do Technology Shocks Tell Us About the New Keynesian Paradigm? *Journal of Monetary Economics,* 56 (4):560–69.

Eichenbaum, Martin (1997). Some Thoughts on Practical Stabilization Policy. *American Economic Review,* 87 (2, Papers and Proceedings):236–9.

Fischer, Stanley (1977). Long Term Contracts, Rational Expectations, and the Optimal Money Supply Rule. *Journal of Political Economy,* 85 (1):191–205.

Fischer, Stanley (1983). Comment on Nordhaus's "Macroconfusion: The Dilemmas of Economic Policy". In *Macroeconomics, Prices, and Quantities – Essays in Memory of Arthur M. Okun.* Edited by James Tobin. Washington, DC: The Brookings Institution.

Friedman, Milton (1968). The Role of Monetary Policy. *American Economic Review,* 58 (1):1–17.

Friedman, Milton, and Anna J. Schwartz (1963). *A Monetary History of the United States, 1867–1960.* Princeton: Princeton University Press.

Galí, Jordi, and Mark Gertler (2007). Macroeconomic Modeling for Monetary Policy Evaluation. *Journal of Economic Perspectives,* 21 (4):25–45.

Gerrard, Bill (1996). Competing Schools of Thought in Macroeconomics – an Ever Emerging Consensus? (Review Article). *Journal of Economic Studies,* 23 (1):53–69.

Goodfriend, Marvin (2004). Monetary Policy in the New Neoclassical Synthesis: A Primer. *Federal Reserve Bank of Richmond Economic Quarterly,* 90 (3):21–45.

Goodfriend, Marvin (2007). How the World Achieved Consensus on Monetary Policy. *Journal of Economic Perspectives,* 21 (4):47–68.

Goodfriend, Marvin, and Robert G. King (1997). The New Neoclassical Synthesis and the Role of Monetary Policy. *NBER Macroeconomics Annual,* 12:231–83.

Gordon, Robert J. (1989). Fresh Water, Salt Water, and Other Macroeconomic Elixirs. *Economic Record,* 65 (2):177–84.

Greenwald, Bruce C., and Joseph E. Stiglitz (1988). Examining Alternative Macroeconomic Theories. *Brookings Papers on Economic Activity,* 1988 (1):207–60.

Greenwald, Bruce C., and Joseph E. Stiglitz (1993). New and Old Keynesians. *Journal of Economic Perspectives,* 7 (1):23–44.

Greenwald, John (1978). Rational People may be Economy's Thorn. *The Minneapolis Star.* May 18.

Hall, Robert E. (1976). *Notes on the Current State of Empirical Macroeconomics* (available at: http://www.stanford.edu/~rehall/Notes%20Current%20State%20 Empirical%201976.pdf, accessed on Dec. 18, 2009).

Hartley, James E. (1997). *The Representative Agent in Macroeconomics.* London: Routledge.

Hartley, James E., Kevin D. Hoover, and Kevin D. Salyer (1997). The Limits of Business Cycle Research: Assessing the Real Business Cycle Model. *Oxford Review of Economic Policy,* 13 (3):34–54.

Heathcote, Jonathan, Kjetil Storesletten, and Giovanni L. Violante (2009). Quantitative Macroeconomics with Heterogeneous Households. *Annual Review of Economics,* 1:319–54.

Hoover, Kevin D. (1988). *The New Classical Macroeconomics: A Sceptical Inquiry.* Oxford: Basil Blackwell.

Hoover, Kevin D. (2001). *The Methodology of Empirical Macroeconomics.* Cambridge: Cambridge University Press.

Hoover, Kevin D. (2006). A Neowicksellian in a New Classical World: The Methodology of Michael Woodford's Interest and Prices. *Journal of the History of Economic Thought*, 28 (2):143–9.

Hymans, Saul H., and Harold T. Shapiro (1975). Econometric Review of Alternative Fiscal and Monetary Policies, 1966–75: Part II. *Franco Modigliani Papers*. David M. Rubenstein Rare Book and Manuscript Library, Duke University, Draft, box RW27, folder "'Models of the Economy… ,' -Russian Paper, Notes, 1976."

Janssen, Maarten (1993). *Microfoundations: A Critical Inquiry*. London: Routledge.

Kirman, Alan P. (1992). Whom or What Does the Representative Individual Represent? *Journal of Economic Perspectives*, 6 (2):117–36.

Kormendi, Roger C., and Philip G. Meguire (1984). Cross-Regime Evidence of Macroeconomic Rationality. *Journal of Political Economy*, 92 (5):875–908.

Krugman, Paul (2000). How Complicated Does the Model Have to Be? *Oxford Review of Economic Policy*, 16 (4):33–42.

Kuhn, Thomas ([1962] 1970). *The Structure of Scientific Revolutions*. 2nd edn. Chicago: University of Chicago Press.

Kydland, Finn E. (1992). On the Econometrics of World Business Cycles. *European Economic Review*, 36 (2–3):476–82.

Kydland, Finn E., and Edward C. Prescott (1982). Time to Build and Aggregate Fluctuations. *Econometrica*, 50 (6):1345–70.

Kydland, Finn E., and Edward C. Prescott (1990). Business Cycles: Real Facts and a Monetary Myth. *Federal Reserve Bank of Minneapolis Quarterly Review*, 14 (2):3–18.

Kydland, Finn E., and Edward C. Prescott (1991a). The Econometrics of the General Equilibrium Approach to Business Cycles. *Scandinavian Journal of Economics*, 93 (2):161–78.

Kydland, Finn E., and Edward C. Prescott (1991b). Hours and Employment Variation in Business Cycle Theory. *Economic Theory*, 1 (1):63–81.

Laidler, David (1999). *Fabricating the Keynesian Revolution – Studies of the Interwar Literature on Money, the Cycle, and Unemployment*. Cambridge: Cambridge University Press.

Laidler, David (2006). Woodford and Wicksell on Interest and Prices: The Place of the Pure Credit Economy in the Theory of Monetary Policy. *Journal of the History of Economic Thought*, 28 (2):151–9.

Lakatos, Imre (1970). Falsification and the Methodology of Scientific Research Programmes. In *Criticism and the Growth of Knowledge*. Edited by Imre Lakatos, and Alan Musgrave. London: Cambridge University Press.

Leijonhufvud, Axel (1973). Effective Demand Failures. *Swedish Journal of Economics*, 75 (1): 27–48.

Leijonhufvud, Axel (1976). Schools, "Revolutions", and Research Programmes in Economic Theory. In *Method and Appraisal in Economics*. Edited by Spiro Latsis. Cambridge: Cambridge University Press.

Leijonhufvud, Axel (1992). Keynesian Economics: Past Confusions, Future Prospects. In *Macroeconomics – a Survey of Research Strategies*. Edited by Alessandro Vercelli, and Nicola Dimitri. Oxford: Oxford University Press.

Leijonhufvud, Axel (1993). Towards a Not-Too-Rational Macroeconomics. *Southern Economic Journal*, 60 (1):1–13.

Leijonhufvud, Axel (2004). Outside the Mainstream: An Interview with Axel Leijonhufvud. *Macroeconomic Dynamics*, 8 (1):117–45.

Lovell, Michael C., and David D. Selover (1994). Econometric Software Accidents. *Economic Journal,* 104 (424):713–25.

Lucas, Robert E., Jr. (1972). Expectations and the Neutrality of Money. *Journal of Economic Theory,* 4 (2):103–24.

Lucas, Robert E., Jr. (1973). Some International Evidence on Output-Inflation Tradeoffs. *American Economic Review,* 63 (3):326–34.

Lucas, Robert E., Jr. (1975). An Equilibrium Model of the Business Cycle. *Journal of Political Economy,* 83 (6):1113–44.

Lucas, Robert E., Jr. (1976). Econometric Policy Evaluation: A Critique. *Carnegie-Rochester Conference Series on Public Policy,* 11:19–46.

Lucas, Robert E., Jr. (1994). Comments on Ball and Mankiw. *Carnegie-Rochester Conference Series on Public Policy,* 41:153–5.

Lucas, Robert E., Jr. (1998). Transforming Macroeconomics: An Interview with Robert E. Lucas Jr. *Journal of Economic Methodology,* 5 (1):115–46.

Lucas, Robert E., Jr. (2004). My Keynesian Education. In *The IS-LM Model. Its Rise, Fall and Strange Persistence. History of Political Economy* 36 supplement. Edited by Michel De Vroey, and Kevin D. Hoover. Durham, NC: Duke University Press.

Lucas, Robert E., Jr., and Thomas. J. Sargent (1979). After Keynesian Macroeconomics. *The Federal Reserve Bank of Minneapolis Quarterly Review,* 3 (2).

Lucas, Robert E., Jr., and Thomas. J. Sargent (eds) (1981). *Rational Expectations and Econometric Practice.* London: George Allen & Unwin.

Mankiw, N. Gregory (1985). Small Menu Costs and Large Business Cycles: A Macroeconomic Model of Monopoly. *Quarterly Journal of Economics,* 100 (2):529–37.

Mankiw, N. Gregory (1989). Real Business Cycle: A New Keynesian Perspective. *Journal of Economic Perspectives,* 3 (3):79–90.

Mankiw, N. Gregory (1990). A Quick Refresher Course in Macroeconomics. *Journal of Economic Literature,* 28 (4):1645–60.

Mankiw, N. Gregory (1992a). Macroeconomics in Disarray. *Society,* 29 (4):19–24.

Mankiw, N. Gregory (1992b). The Reincarnation of Keynesian Economics. *European Economic Review,* 36 (2–3):559–65.

Mankiw, N. Gregory (2006). The Macroeconomist as Scientist and Engineer. *Journal of Economic Perspectives,* 20 (4):29–46.

Mehrling, Perry (2006). Mr. Woodford and the Challenge of Finance. *Journal of the History of Economic Thought,* 28 (2):161–70.

Mirowski, Philip, and D. Wade Hands (1998). A Paradox of Budgets: The Postwar Stabilization of American Neoclassical Demand Theory. In *From Interwar Pluralism to Postwar Neoclassicism. History of Political Economy* 30 supplement. Edited by Mary S. Morgan, and Malcolm Rutherford. Durham, NC: Duke University Press.

Mirowski, Philip, and D. Wade Hands (eds) (2006). *Agreement on Demand: Consumer Theory in the Twentieth Century. History of Political Economy,* 38 supplement. Durham, NC: Duke University Press.

Mishkin, Frederic S. (2007). Will Monetary Policy Become More of a Science? *NBER Working Paper,* no. 13566.

Nordhaus, William D. (1983). Macroconfusion: The Dilemmas of Economic Policy. In *Macroeconomics, Prices, and Quantities – Essays in Memory of Arthur M. Okun.* Edited by James Tobin. Washington, DC: The Brookings Institution.

Obstfeld, Maurice, and Kenneth Rogoff (1996). *Foundations of International Macroeconomics.* Cambridge: The MIT Press.

Pearce, Kerry A., and Kevin D. Hoover (1995). After the Revolution: Paul Samuelson and the Textbook Keynesian Model. In *New Perspectives on Keynes. History of Political Economy* 27 supplement. Edited by Allin R. Cottrell, and Michael S. Lawlor. Durham, NC: Duke University Press.

Phelps, Edmund S. (1967). Phillips Curves, Expectations of Inflation, and Optimal Unemployment over Time. *Economica,* 34 (3):254–81.

Phelps, Edmund S. (ed.) (1969). *Microeconomic Foundations of Employment and Inflation Theory.* New York: Norton W. W.

Phelps, Edmund S. (1990). *Seven Schools of Macroeconomic Thought.* Oxford: Oxford University Press.

Phelps, Edmund S., and John B. Taylor (1977). Stabilizing Powers of Monetary Policy Under Rational Expectations. *Journal of Political Economy,* 85 (1):163–90.

Prescott, Edward C., and Graham V. Candler (2008). Calibration. In *The New Palgrave Dictionary of Economics.* 2nd edn. Edited by Steven N. Durlauf, and Lawrence E. Blume. Palgrave Macmillan (*The New Palgrave Dictionary of Economics Online,* available at http://www.dictionaryofeconomics.com/article?id=pde2008_C000571, doi:10.1057/9780230226203.0184, accessed 12 March 2012.

Redman, Deborah A. (1991). *Economics and the Philosophy of Science.* Oxford: Oxford University Press.

Romer, David (1993). The New Keynesian Synthesis. *Journal of Economic Perspectives,* 7 (1):5–22.

Rotemberg, Julio, and Michael Woodford (1997). An Optimization-Based Econometric Framework for the Evaluation of Monetary Policy. *NBER Macroeconomics Annual,* pp. 297–346.

Samuelson, Paul A. (1955). *Economics.* 3rd edn. New York: McGraw-Hill.

Sheils, Merrill, and Rich Thomas (1978). The New Economists. *Newsweek.* June 26, pp. 59–60.

Sims, Christopher (1972). Money, Income, and Causality. *American Economic Review,* 62 (4):540–52.

Sims, Christopher (1989). Models and Their Uses. *American Journal of Agricultural Economics,* 71 (2):489–94.

Sims, Christopher (1992). Interpreting the Macroeconomic Time Series Facts – the Effects of Monetary Policy. *European Economic Review,* 36 (5):975–1000.

Sims, Christopher (2004). Econometrics for Policy Analysis: Progress and Regress. *De Economist,* 152 (2):167–75.

Smets, Frank, and Raf Wouters (2003). An Estimated Dynamic Stochastic General Equilibrium Model of the Euro Area. *Journal of the European Economic Association,* 1 (5):1123–75.

Smets, Frank, and Raf Wouters (2007). Shocks and Frictions in US Business Cycles: A Bayesian DSGE Approach. *American Economic Review,* 97 (3):586–606.

Snowdon, Brian (2001). Keeping the Keynesian Faith – Alan Blinder on the Evolution of Macroeconomics. *World Economics,* 2 (2):105–40.

Snowdon, Brian, and Howard Vane (1995). New-Keynesian Economics Today: The Empire Strikes back. *American Economist,* 39 (1):48–65.

Snowdon, Brian, and Howard Vane (1996). The Development of Modern Macroeconomics: Reflections in the Light of Johnson's Analysis after Twenty-five Years. *Journal of Macroeconomics,* 18 (3):381–401.

Snowdon, Brian, Howard Vane, and Peter Wynarczyk (1994). *A Modern Guide to Macroeconomics: An Introduction to Competing Schools of Thought.* Cheltenham: Edward Elgar.

Solow, Robert M. (1979). Alternative Approaches to Macroeconomic Theory: A Partial View. *Canadian Journal of Economics,* 12 (3):339–54.

Solow, Robert M. (1983). Comment on Nordhaus's "Macroconfusion: The Dilemmas of Economic Policy". In *Macroeconomics, Prices, and Quantities – Essays in Memory of Arthur M. Okun.* Edited by James Tobin. Washington, DC: The Brookings Institution.

Solow, Robert M. (1997). Is There a Core of Usable Macroeconomics We Should All Believe In? *American Economic Review,* 87 (2, Papers and Proceedings):230–32.

Solow, Robert M. (2000). Toward a Macroeconomics of the Medium Run. *Journal of Economic Perspectives,* 14 (1):151–8.

Solow, Robert M. (2008). The State of Macroeconomics. *Journal of Economic Perspectives,* 22 (1):243–6.

Solow, Robert M. (2010). *Building a Science of Economics for the Real World.* House Committee on Science and Technology, US House of Representatives – Subcommittee on Investigations and Oversight. July 20. Washington, DC (available at: http://science.house.gov/publications/hearings_markups_details.aspx?NewsID= 2916, accessed on Oct. 13, 2010).

Spear, Stephen E., and Randall Wright (1998). Interview with David Cass. *Macroeconomic Dynamics,* 2 (4):533–58.

Stiglitz, Joseph E. (1992). Methodological Issues and the New Keynesian Economics. In *Macroeconomics – a Survey of Research Strategies.* Edited by Alessandro Vercelli, and Nicola Dimitri. Oxford: Oxford University Press.

Taylor, John B. (1997). A Core of Practical Macroeconomics. *American Economic Review,* 87 (2, Papers and Proceedings):233–5.

van den Bergh, Jeroen C., and John M. Gowdy (2003). The Microfoundations of Macroeconomics: An Evolutionary Perspective. *Cambridge Journal of Economics,* 27 (1):65–84.

Vane, Howard, and John L. Thompson (1992). *Current Controversies in Macroeconomics.* Cheltenham: Edward Elgar.

Weintraub, E. Roy (1979). *Microfoundations – the Compatibility of Microeconomics and Macroeconomics.* Cambridge: Cambridge University Press.

Weintraub, E. Roy (ed.) (1992). *Toward a History of Game Theory. History of Political Economy,* 24 supplement. Durham, NC: Duke University Press.

Weintraub, E. Roy (2002). *How Economics Became a Mathematical Science.* Durham, NC: Duke University Press.

Woodford, Michael (2000). Revolution and Evolution in Twentieth-Century Macroeconomics. (Available at: http://www.columbia.edu/~mw2230/macro20C.pdf, accessed on Dec. 18, 2009.)

Woodford, Michael (2003). *Interest and Prices: Foundations of a Theory of Monetary Policy.* Princeton: Princeton University Press.

Woodford, Michael (2006). Comments on the Symposium on Interest and Prices. *Journal of the History of Economic Thought,* 28 (2):187–98.

Woodford, Michael (2009). Convergence in Macroeconomics: Elements of the New Synthesis. *American Economic Journal: Macroeconomics,* 1 (1):267–79.

Zouache, Abdallah (2004). Towards a "New Neoclassical Synthesis"? An Analysis of the Methodological Convergence Between New Keynesian Economics and Real Business Cycle Theory. *History of Economic Ideas,* 12 (1):95–117.

Index

stickiness 38, 131, 203, 208, 210,
211–12, 219, 226–8
pure exchange economy 74, 104, 123

quantity theory of money 49, 142

Ramsey
Frank P. 34
model 213, 216–17
RAND corporation 149, 157
Rapping, Leonard 2, 5, 20, 46–7, 49,
168, 186
rational 3, 37, 80, 83, 87, 93, 100–101,
150, 202, 218
behavior 150–51
choice theory *see* choice theory
expectationists 169, 204
expectations 2–4, 8–9, 14, 20, 27,
48–9, 54, 89, 150, 164, 168, 184,
186, 197–8, 203–209, 215–16,
220, 224, 227
rationalists 204–205
real
business cycle (RBC)
macroeconomics 3–4, 9, 12–13,
57, 185, 191–2, 195–8, 202,
210–11, 224, 227–8
disturbances *see* shocks
shocks *see* shocks
representative agent 5, 7–10, 14–15, 27,
38, 46, 50–52, 55, 111, 123, 135,
196, 203, 206–207, 209, 212–15,
217–18, 220, 228–9
program *see* microfoundational
programs
research program 222, 224–5, 93–6, 98,
108, 115, 117, 121–2, 140, 143, 163,
169, 191, 196
Robbins, Lionel C. 1, 14, 70
Rockefeller Foundation 70, 142, 144,
156

saltwater and freshwater views *see*
macroeconomics
Samuelson, Paul A. 12, 70, 83, 96–7, 99,
103–108, 114, 118, 135–9, 158–9,
161–2, 169, 218–19
Sargent, Thomas 1–2, 14, 20, 49–50,
170–71, 173, 176–7, 196, 204–205,
211, 221, 225, 227–8

schools of thought 122, 135, 191, 202,
222–3
Austrian school 19, 63, 72–3, 79,
88–9
Keynesian school 12, 202, 223
new classical school 8, 192, 222, 228
new Keynesian school 2, 4, 8–9, 20,
46, 50, 55, 131, 185, 192, 195–8,
202–203, 205–208, 211, 219–20,
222, 224–6, 229
Schultz, Henry 97, 99–100, 102
Schumpeter, Joseph A. 55, 150, 163–4
scientific revolution 168, 185, 221–2
Shiller, Robert 131, 161
shocks
demand shocks 47–8, 197, 207–208
monetary shocks 200–202, 211–12,
226
nominal shocks 211
real shocks 197, 199, 211
technology shocks 197, 200–202, 210
see also Solow residual
short-run fluctuations *see*
macroeconomics
signal-extraction errors 48
Sims, Christopher A. 199–200, 225, 228
simultaneous equations estimation *see*
econometrics
Slutsky, Evgeny ("Eugen") E. 97, 99,
112–14, 117–18, 120
Slutsky
equation 112–14, 223
matrix 119
Smith, Adam 21, 31, 55, 71, 171, 173,
178, 221
Solow
growth model 137, 170
residual 199
Robert M. 10, 15, 137–8, 141–2, 152,
158, 174, 177, 190, 195–6,
207–10, 216–19, 222–4, 227–9
Sonnenschein–Mantel–Debreu
theorems 8–9, 37, 40, 51, 56, 93,
101, 216–17
Spann, Othmar 62, 65–6, 69, 89
stability *see* general equilibrium
stagflation 151, 168, 196, 221
Stiglitz, Joseph E. 193, 206, 222, 226–8
Stone, J. Richard N. 30
structural 2, 141, 172, 216